OCCUPATION
CIRCUMNAVIGATOR

OCCUPATION CIRCUMNAVIGATOR

LARS HÄSSLER

SAILING AROUND THE WORLD

Translated by Katarina Smith

ADLARD COLES NAUTICAL
LONDON

Published by Adlard Coles Nautical
an imprint of A & C Black Publishers Ltd
36 Soho Square, London W1D 3QY
www.adlardcoles.com

First edition published 2009

ISBN 978-1-4081-1201-4

A CIP catalogue record for this book is available from the British Library.

This book is produced using paper that is made from wood grown in managed, sustainable forests. It is natural, renewable and recyclable. The logging and manufacturing processes conform to the environmental regulations of the country of origin.

Typeset in 10 pt Sabon by Palimpsest Book Production Limited,
Grangemouth, Stirlingshire

Printed and bound by Caligraving Ltd, Thetford, UK

DEDICATION

I wish to thank my parents, who not only taught me to sail and take good care of boats, but also, together with my brother and sister-in-law, helped me out when my finances were low. Thank you also to my sister, who took care of all the boring bills at home.

'Sailing is a lifestyle of freedom, exploring and touring the world while being at home.'
Vasco da Gama Yacht Rally

'Those sailing days were the freest and happiest of my life.'
Harry Pidgeon
World's second single-handed circumnavigator, 1921–25 (after Joshua Slocum)

CONTENTS

FOREWORD BY JIMMY CORNELL

On a balmy summer evening, a yacht sailed slowly into the crowded port of Fiskardo in the Ionian Sea, its decks crowded with a motley crew displaying the 'lightly clothed' dress code of a charter boat. Passing within inches of the bows of my yacht *Aventura*, a deeply tanned male of uncertain age called over from the wheel 'Hi Jimmy, long time no see!' Judging by his nubile companions it took only a nano-second for the euro to drop; this could only be only Lars, the modern day Odysseus. Indeed, he wasted no time in reminding me of my promise to write an introduction to his book. Then, with a flick of the wheel, he pointed the bows towards the neighbouring island and, like his famous predecessor, continued his quest towards Ithaca for new adventures.

Lars, or Lasse to his friends, is in every respect an extraordinary person; a man who had the guts to chuck it all in and opt for a lifestyle that others spend their entire life dreaming about. A trained lawyer with excellent career prospects, Lasse gave up his well-paid job as an international trader, turned his back on the stress and hassle of the corporate world, and set off on a ten year 100,000nm voyage on his 15m (50ft) yacht *Jennifer*. In between a surfeit of adventures, Lasse describes how he managed to finance such a long voyage, mostly by taking on paying guests. However, the true essence of this book is a vivid description of a life that is never dull – his adventures are full of incident and the occasional mishap. The voyage took him and his faithful if occasionally capricious *Jennifer* on a roundabout route, by doing everything he could to avoid sailing the shortest route between two places. This is how they ended up with lengthy detours to the Marshall Islands, the site of the US atomic tests and to some rarely visited atolls in Micronesia. It is how he became the first yachtsman to sail up the Saigon River to Ho Chi Minh after the Vietnam War, dropped in on the rarely visited Andaman Islands, and, for good measure, made a long and arduous trip up the Amazon River.

Any reader planning to follow the author's example will find many useful tips on how to earn a living while cruising. But this is not a 'how-to' book and most of us will probably turn the last page with a deep sense of gratitude to its author for having gone to all that trouble so that we can relive those adventures in the comfort and safety of our own homes. We can be thankful not to have to put up with freak waves, corrupt officials, cranky passengers, 30,000-volt strikes from overhead cables and bloodthirsty hammerhead sharks. Thank you, Lasse!

Jimmy Cornell

PREFACE

I was 42 years old when I decided to wager everything I had in order to fulfill my dream of sailing round the world – not knowing how it would turn out or if I could carry it through.

I chose to do it in an unusual way – to have 'paying crew' on board; people I didn't know and who didn't know me but who, through their trust and adventurous spirits, helped to finance my project. I use the word 'project' intentionally. On top of the challenge of sailing around the world, I was also running a small business, with the same problems and worries that all small business men face – how should I organize the business of chartering a yacht and how should I manage the finances? My occupation was: Circumnavigator.

I spent the first four years of my project in the Caribbean, using my newly-built sailboat *Jennifer* to take paying customers out on charter trips. Those early years were a great deal of fun, and I also gained a lot of experience. I met many interesting people and the web of contacts I built up among guests and agents in those years helped me to reach the next step in my project – sailing around the world. The time in the Caribbean also gave me the chance to really get to know my boat and get her equipped in the way that I felt she needed to be.

In the beginning I had an unrealistic view of the size of the world and planned to circumnavigate in three years. But the concept worked so well – a combination of the right timing, a good product, and the fact that I really enjoyed the lifestyle that went with it, that I ended up spending ten years at sea; five years in the West Indies and another five years circumnavigating. This enabled me to see more of the world than I had ever dared hope.

A life at sea is, naturally, quite different from a life on land. The biggest difference is time. Never before had I had so much free time – this was one of the trip's greatest luxuries. There was plenty of time to read during the day and, during the countless night watches, there was ample time to think about life, relationships, humanity and what we are doing to our world.

I am glad I decided not to make my trip around the world alone; being single-handed is not my idea of sailing. Of course, sailing with strangers on board has its advantages and disadvantages. The disadvantages include losing your privacy, always having guests in your home, sticking to a schedule that has been planned for everyone in advance and socializing with people you don't always like. However, financially, the advantage of paying guests makes it all worthwhile. The vast majority of my guests were very dedicated to fulfilling their own dreams – sailing in the South Pacific for a month or two,

for example. They came from different countries, were different ages and genders and had different backgrounds. This made for a constantly shifting and interesting combination of crewmembers. Having a crew also creates a large web of contacts when the boat arrives in a harbour; the crew is quickly able to get to know people on other boats.

Whilst sailing around the world with *Jennifer*, I became closest to two women, Ylva and Johanna. Ylva stayed with me from Stockholm in 1991 until she decided to disembark in New Zealand in 1993. Johanna joined in New Zealand in 1994 and we stayed together for the rest of the trip. During the periods when we didn't have paying crew on board we enjoyed being together and exploring different parts of the world.

This book is not just a story about sailing around the world. It is also a handbook for aspiring long-distance sailors. It is for people who want to start a career in the charter boat business (perhaps going around the world with a paying crew), for people who want to go hitchhiking on various yachts and for people who, for various reasons, never made it on their dream trip.

My voyage only included stops in the so-called Third World – with the exception of New Zealand, Australia and Singapore, the South Pacific (despite all its wonderful islands, atolls and lagoons) is still considered part of the Third World. I have tried to include some background information on each region I visited to help readers understand what is behind the beautiful façade – including the relevant historical, social and political realities. They have not always been pleasant discoveries; sometimes just the opposite. This book reflects how I spent those ten years sailing – the adventures, the crews, the mishaps, the many different places we visited. Welcome aboard!

Lars Hässler

PART I

PLANNING

WHY A LIFE AT SEA?

I chose a sailing lifestyle after seeing a film about a square-rigger at the age of 12, sailing with a group of friends and living on what might have been the last hippy ship, the three-masted schooner *Sofia*, in the South Pacific in 1979–80. This was a boat where there weren't any normal rules, where most people went nude and where power and financial struggles existed between its crewmembers. Unfortunately *Sofia* eventually sank in the Pacific Ocean.

EARLY INFLUENCES

WINDJAMMER – THE FILM ABOUT *CHRISTIAN RADICH*

Certainly at one time or another many people have dreamed about sailing around the world, and I was no exception. Ever since I went to the old Winter Palace in Stockholm at the age of 12, and saw the 1958 film *Windjammer* about the Norwegian square-rigger *Christian Radich* sailing to the Caribbean, I longed to head out and see the world.

The film was about young cadets in the Norwegian navy that spent a year sailing the three-masted ship to the Caribbean and back. I remember that one of the parents had demanded that their son take his piano along with him on the voyage. He practised every day and upon his arrival back home he was not only a sailor, but also a piano player. The film was technically very advanced for its time and it was shown on one of the first big screens. It made a lasting impression on me.

THE 12M INTERNATIONAL RULE YACHT *GOLUM*

When I was older my brother, two friends and I bought an old 12m International Rule yacht that we christened *Golum*. She was built in Scotland at the famous Fife Shipyard in 1932, was 65ft (20m) long and weighed about 30 tons. We had often sailed together on small sailboats but we decided that we should get our own boat. We had no idea what we were getting into. We started by making repairs and equipping her properly, a gigantic job that used up all of our free time and money. But for three summers in the mid-1970s we were able to enjoy our beautiful boat as we sailed around Sweden, Finland, Norway and Denmark. I was able to get time off work to be on board for 7–8 weeks every summer. I was very happy with sailing life – planning routes and organizing crews. We could accommodate up to 12 people on *Golum*, but it could get a little crowded. But we had a lot of fun, and we were the obvious centre of attention in every harbour we visited. In the 1970s there weren't very many large sailboats around.

THE SCHOONER *SOFIA* – THE LAST HIPPY SHIP

A COOPERATIVE

After taking my law degree at Stockholm University in 1972 and a Master's degree in Comparative Law in the USA in 1973, I spent a year at the Graduate Institute of International Studies in Geneva in 1974 and worked as a clerk for a judge in Stockholm from 1975–77. We sold *Golum* in 1977, and I worked as a ski-guide in the French Alps during the winter season of 1977–78 and then in the autumn set off to sail around the world. My plan was to work as a deckhand on sailboats. After stints on a number of different boats I wound up in the Caribbean. From there I made my way to South America, where I travelled around for six months on land, and eventually reached Panama, looking for a boat to take me across the South Pacific. It was there that I found the three-masted schooner *Sofia* and signed on as a crewmember. I had seen her in the Caribbean a year before and asked a friend if he knew anything about her: 'It's a hippy ship, they have a Harley-Davidson motorbike on board and live on one dollar a day', was the answer.

Sofia is difficult to describe. She was neither a cruise ship nor a charter boat; not a private yacht, research vessel, school ship or common leisure craft. *Sofia* was her own kind of boat. She had no set course – she was a lifestyle. And she was, most probably, the last of the hippy ships.

Sofia operated as a floating cooperative in which all decisions were taken in general meetings in a truly democratic way, which is to say that each member of the cooperative had one vote. For example, if a member wanted *Sofia* to sail to Tasmania, all he or she had to do was try to put together a majority in favour of Tasmania before the next meeting.

It may sound impossible to run a boat in this way, but *Sofia* had been sailing like this since 1969. A group of American college students had travelled to Scandinavia to search for a suitable sailboat. They found the Baltic trader *Sofia* in Sweden, where she had been built in 1921, and bought her for $4,500. They then sailed her to Spain and added three masts, two yardarms,

a diving compressor, surfboards, a library and a large saloon. At that point *Sofia*'s career as a floating cooperative on the seven seas began in earnest.

MOST WENT NUDE

When I saw *Sofia* in Panama she was on her second tour around the world. The first time I boarded her things seemed a bit primitive and most of the people on board were nude. They worked as cooperative and they didn't eat meat (there was no refrigerator or freezer on board to store food). I was unsure how I felt about the idea of the cooperative, but I liked *Sofia* immediately. She was unique and she had charm, sailing through the South Pacific in the style of the old seafarers. The fact that there were eight tanned, attractive women among the 16-person crew did not lessen my inclination to sign on.

My main doubt was about the food – was it really possible to live without meat? I had to admit all the crew looked strong and healthy. After an agreed two-day tryout, I was accepted as a crewmember. The South Pacific lay ahead of us and it was exhilarating. Before we set sail there were a thousand things to be repaired, sorted out and bought. Rice, beans and wholewheat flour were our staples and we bought large quantities of these, storing them in barrels to protect them from cockroaches.

NO PRIVATE LIFE

How do 16 people live together on a 92m (28m) sailboat? Four of the crewmembers had their own cabins, four lived in double-cabins and the rest lived in the forepeak. The division of the berths was made according to a seniority system: when somebody left *Sofia* the one who had been on board longest got to choose if he or she wanted to take over the empty bunk. I managed to get a cabin to myself after six months.

The cramped living conditions added an interesting problem to the crewmembers' love lives. To not have a sex life at all was not considered an option. If a crewmember wanted to have sex (which of course all of us did) and didn't have a private cabin, the couple would simply close the curtain around their bunk in the forepeak to be alone together. At night the net under the bowsprit was a popular place for lovers to go.

THE ECONOMICS OF *SOFIA*

FIRST PAYING – THEN A PART OWNER

The economics of *Sofia* were based on each person on board paying $10 per day (this was the 1970s), which covered all their expenses. After ten months on board a crewmember had paid $3,000 and became a part owner of *Sofia*. After that the person didn't have to pay for anything at all, not even food. The system was built on a presumed continuous turnover of the crew – a constant stream of new people coming aboard and supporting the system, paying the running costs with their $10 per day.

Yet many of the crewmembers had been on board for three to five years without paying more than their original investment during their first ten months. Evan, a tall, slender 30-year-old from California, had been on board for five years, and was chosen as captain. He could, however, be removed from that position at any time by a majority at a general meeting. Just like each of the others, he had one vote at meetings, even though his vote had quite a lot of weight. When we were at sea, on the other hand, he was a traditional captain – his orders were followed. There was no compromise when it came to *Sofia*'s safety at sea.

NO PENALTIES FOR NOT WORKING

Everyone (or nearly everyone) helped with the chores on board. There were no penalties for not helping, except that everyone had to take turns on night-watch duty. Nobody could force anyone else to work, not even the captain.

It took me a long time to figure out how *Sofia* really worked. The first month in Panama was difficult. I worked all day every day getting the boat equipped and ready for the sail to Tahiti, so I was very tired in the evenings. However, I received no thanks for my efforts. No one took any notice of me or explained the rules. As a new crewmember I realized I had to manage on my own before being accepted. I remember when Rick spoke to me for the first time. He was an American stonemason with a black belt in Tai Chi who had been on board for two years, and we had worked together for a number of days scraping the outer planking. One day he suddenly said, 'Are you really a lawyer?' Rick could not comprehend that a highly paid lawyer would put his career on hold to sail and cruise around. From that day forward we were best friends and spent days hiking and climbing together on the islands. He later wound up sailing with me aboard *Jennifer*.

Normally when you come to a new environment you bring a past with you – an education, social status, etc. You are somebody. That was unimportant on *Sofia*. Here you were accepted based on who you showed yourself to be on the ship. For those who had been used to exerting power, getting respect or having status in their earlier lives, the adjustment could be too much. You couldn't prop yourself up with your background – everyone on *Sofia* had to start from the beginning. A few people left *Sofia* for just this reason, perhaps with a feeling of failure.

NO RULES

It took a few months before I realized why no one had explained the rules on board. The answer was simple – there were no rules. It was the absence of rules that made *Sofia* so unique. This was the hippy/flower power era; the idea was to get away from conventional society and build a new, freer and simpler community. How did such a community work? Well, we had a lot of stormy meetings on this point. It was fascinating the way the crew was constantly creating new norms. Unlike conventional life, there was no hierarchy here – no judiciary or ownership structure. On *Sofia* everyone made their own decisions. With this background, it is easier to understand the lack of assigned chores.

However, it was certainly necessary to have a certain harmonization and organization to make this small (but, at the same time, complicated) society work. This was ironed out at various general meetings. Lists of chores were put up in the saloon and each person was to sign up for different jobs. Eventually all of the chores were completed.

I WAS CHOSEN AS 'BANKER'

Most crewmembers had their own special responsibilities – for the engine, sail repair, electricity, rigging, or supplies, for example. After complaining about *Sofia*'s sloppy accounts, I was chosen to be 'banker'. It turned out to be one of the most difficult positions on board. For the first few days in Panama everyone was coming up to me and asking for $50 for this, $100 for that, and so on. I quickly realized that if we continued in this manner our money would soon run out. I then initiated a rule that no money would be paid out unless the expenditure was approved at a general meeting.

At this point all hell broke loose. Never in my life have I been the recipient of so much abuse. The money-seekers argued that I had no right to tell them what they could or could not buy and they demanded money for their pet projects. But I stood my ground and at the next general meeting a heated discussion took place. I won in the end. Everyone realized that even a hippy ship needed money to survive and we were forced to hang on to the little of it that we had.

NO HEADS

All sailors know that the heads (toilets) often go on strike. Knowing this, *Sofia* had long since got rid of hers. Bodily waste was disposed over the side of the boat at the stern. Each morning there could be as many as four naked people sitting together on the railing having their morning bowel movements, happily chatting about the night's sailing with the person who had been on watch. Of course this was awkward for newcomers. I should point out an important exception to all of *Sofia*'s cooperative ideals: Each person on board was responsible for providing his or her own toilet paper. Experience had shown that the crew tended to use far too much otherwise.

SOFIA GOES UNDER

In spite of the conflicts and the often-stormy general meetings we had a fantastic time on board *Sofia*. We used to joke that *Sofia* survived not thanks to, but in spite of, her crew. I stayed aboard *Sofia* for a year in the South Seas and then returned home to Sweden. One night back in Stockholm, I was woken by a phone call from Australia. *Sofia* had gone down in a bad storm on the Pacific Ocean. Two giant waves had capsized her, one female crewmember had followed her down to the deep; the other 15 people on board survived on two rafts for five days in poor conditions before a Russian trading vessel picked them up.

The news of the accident made me feel like a part of my life had been torn away. But my thoughts went quickly to my surviving comrades on *Sofia*. They had lost everything, not just their home and all their earthly belongings, but worst of all, their way of life.

SOFIA RESURRECTED AS *ALVEI*

The crew scattered around the world, but the captain, Evan, couldn't let go of the idea of sailing the seven seas again in his own boat. In 1986 he travelled to Scandinavia to search for a new boat. In Norway he bought a steel ship called *Alvei* and sailed her down to Portugal where he began a major refit. Due to a lack of funds it took a full nine years before *Alvei* was ready to set sail. Today, she is still in the South Pacific and sails with a paying crew – a beautiful sailboat with three raked-back masts, and yardarms on the foremost mast, almost like *Sofia*.

CASTING OFF – A FEELING OF FREEDOM

In the 1980s the decision to quit my job and order a yacht gradually became a reality. What followed were the decisions about how I would finance the boat and how she was to be built and equipped. I eventually chose a Beneteau, and her name was to be *Jennifer*.

MAKING PLANS

DARING TO MAKE UP YOUR MIND

That October day in 1988 when we left the UK aboard *Jennifer* to sail towards the West Indies, and eventually around the world, was fantastic. The road there had been long – I was only 12 years old when I watched the movie *Windjammer* – now I was 42. Somewhere in the back of my mind I had known that someday I would live my dream, but not how or when.

After returning from *Sofia* in the early 1980s I landed a job at a law firm in Stockholm but after three days I resigned. After three years in the freedom of the South Seas, I felt trapped in an office environment. After a few months I took a job as a commodity trader for a Swedish mining group in Stockholm. Eventually, in the mid-1980s, I was transferred to Switzerland, where I was based for several years. During this time the world economy was strong, the belief in the future steadfast and the financial crises of the 1990s were unthinkable. My job was both stable and financially lucrative.

My dream to sail around the world in my own boat was, however, still in my mind. Was it wise to quit a challenging and exciting job? When was the right time to do it – at 45, 50 or 65? Later in life, when my finances would be better? If I stopped earlier, would I have money to buy a boat but no money to sail with? Or could I 'work' during the circumnavigation with charter guests and 'paying crew'? Ultimately, I decided I would have to work anyway – either on land as a trader, or on a boat as a charter skipper.

Circumstances arose at work that finally helped me make a decision. I was supposed to be transferred to San Francisco, to a job covering both North and South America. After everything was arranged, the American-affiliated company bosses changed their minds. My boss didn't want to take up the fight immediately, but promised that in a few years I would have a position there. I was already prepared for a new and exciting challenge in the States so was very disappointed. My plan had been to work in the USA for a couple of years and then to fulfill my dream. The setback forced me to make up my mind more quickly. I flew to Beneteau's shipbuilding yard in France and ordered a new boat! It sounds easy, but I now had many serious concerns in my mind. What if the charter business was a flop? What if no paying crew signed up? What did I know about the charter business anyway? I was aware of the big risk I was taking, the biggest in my life so far. However, once the final decision was made, it was relatively easy to carry through – the next steps were essentially a series of practical tasks.

SELL EVERYTHING – PAY CASH

One of the many practical details was to quit my job. One day I arranged a lunch with my boss. He didn't suspect anything, but was familiar with my future plans. Unexpectedly, he said: 'If you decide to leave the company, I hope you will let us know in good time'. I asked what he meant by 'good time'. 'A year or at least six months' was the answer. I was already going to tell them in two days, when the big boss was arriving from Stockholm, and answered, 'I'd better give notice now, then'. He was aghast. But we parted ways as friends, and the company chartered with me for two summers when I was back in Sweden with *Jennifer*.

To finance the boat I had to sell everything: My apartment (which I had previously rented out) was just enough to pay the boatyard fee of $260,000. Almost immediately I got my first 'charter'. Beneteau asked if they could exhibit the boat at the Southampton Boat Show for a week in September. They offered to pay $7,000. The answer was of course yes.

Another problem arose. A new boat that comes directly from a boatyard is not actually ready to sail. *Jennifer* needed to be fitted out as a first class charter boat, which was an expensive undertaking. During my years chartering in the Caribbean I discovered that many charter boats went bankrupt. The main reason was that their owners were unable to pay the interest on the big loans they had taken out. The bank doesn't care about your problems out in the Caribbean: their money has to be returned. On many occasions I saw charter boat crews that didn't get paid, especially in the 1990s. When this happened the crew asked for the boat to be seized as

collateral, and salaries were paid before other expenses were paid off. The message for me was clear: debt was a bad start for a business. Still, I had no choice when *Jennifer* was delivered in 1988. I borrowed $45,000 to buy the necessary equipment, which I gradually managed to pay back.

I visited the boatyard six times during the construction, almost every third Saturday during the spring and summer of 1988. The Beneteau boatyard is situated on the Atlantic coast of France, between Nantes and La Rochelle. It is a family business run by managing director Madame Roux, an energetic woman born into the Beneteau family. At the time of purchase, I was the buyer of Beneteau's biggest boat, the Oceanis 500, a 50ft (15m) sailboat.

Many people have asked me why I choose a Beneteau. I had a fairly clear view of what I wanted in a boat: a sloop (a boat with one mast), with a comfortable aft cockpit rather than a centre cockpit and at least four cabins. Furthermore, it needed to be attractive and not too expensive. When I investigated the market, my conclusion was that the Beneteau Oceanis 500, with four guest cabins, all with bathrooms (plus a crew cabin with a bathroom) was the best-priced and most appropriate boat for my purposes.

FINALLY – *JENNIFER'S* LAUNCH

It was rewarding and exciting to watch the boat come together over the five months it took to build her. I took a lot of photos, so even today I can remember the building process. One day in August, with a big crane lorry, she was launched without any special ceremony. I was there alone. It was an unreal feeling – I was watching but could hardly believe it was for real. I named her *Jennifer*, after my brother's youngest daughter, to whom I am godfather.

After the Southampton Boat Show, when the yacht finally became mine, I sailed over to Cowes on the Isle of Wight to equip her. Over three long, hard weeks everything was installed and some parts rebuilt. Beneteau had been very inventive with the design, both above and below deck. The cabins, on the other hand, had limited storage space. Amongst other things I had new shelves built in all the cabins, and bookshelves in the saloon. I had sheets, towels, crockery and kitchen equipment sent from Sweden.

I made some practical changes to suit a large crew. The original boat had a fixed table in the cockpit, which is the main area, where the crew spends much of the day. However, the built-in table was not big enough for everyone on board, and could only seat six people. Instead I had two tabletops made that together could seat up to ten people and could be stored during sailing.

I worked every day to get the equipment installed: the watermaker (desalinator), generator, diving compressor, heater, instruments, satellite navigator, Decca navigator (landbased radio navigator), liferaft, transformer, battery charger, SSB-radio, VHF-radio and CD-player. I also needed to buy two anchors, tools, charts, sextant, brass lamps, life harnesses and life jackets, a dinghy and an outboard motor. The mainsail and genoa were included in the price of the boat. I ordered an extra foresail, storm foresail and jib and got hold of an old spinnaker. At the Beneteau boatyard I had ordered double jib equipment, double halyards, spinnaker booms, up- and downhauls, sheets and spinnaker guys. The reason for this was to be able to run (ie with the wind behind) in the Trade winds with two foresails, so called 'wing-on-wing' or goose-wing sailing. The three weeks were a race against time and money and fraught with stress and nervousness. In the end I had to cancel the autopilot.

THE FIRST VOYAGE – ACROSS THE BAY OF BISCAY

My crew started to show up in the middle of October. First to arrive was Christine, who was going to work as a chef during our first season in the Caribbean. She had heard that I was looking for someone who could cook on the boat and had contacted me herself. Christine had worked at the deli counter in a large department store in Stockholm and taught gourmet cookery courses in the evening. Her CV seemed good, so I hired her.

The rest of the crew were friends; some from a Stockholm aerobics company where I had been an instructor, and skiers from Verbier where I had spent many weekends during my time in Switzerland. There was Kjelle, ski instructor and troubadour, Sissi, a flight attendant and Kjelle's girlfriend, Håkan, a friend of Kjelle, a fellow troubadour and ski instructor and Bosse, owner of a ski rental business in Verbier. There was also Pimse, a department store manager at IKEA in Germany who had also spent many weekends in Verbier, and 18-year-old Filip, who was the son of one of my friends.

Finally we were on our way. We were supposed to reach Falmouth on the first day, and we hadn't got far out to sea before I started to feel nauseous and vomited – the result of the last few weeks of stress and the race to be ready in time. Once we arrived at Falmouth we were stuck there for a few days due to a strong gale, and the crew started to become restless. According to the meteorologists there was a window of good weather coming that could give us the chance to continue sailing. After a vote we decided to set off across the notorious Bay of Biscay.

For the first few days we had fine sailing with good winds and this gave us the time and opportunity to get to know the boat. Then the storm came,

from the south. We had to reef the mainsail and the genoa, and push through gigantic waves that were about 23ft (7m) high. I looked at the wild scene around us and thought it looked rather beautiful. The wind took the water, lifted it up and dropped it straight towards us. It was tough for the crew, but everybody managed to make it through. Most of all I remembered Pimse. He was incredibly helpful and always happy. He even offered to cook the food when the person responsible was too seasick to go down below.

It took a while to learn how the boat performed at sea. Once, when I was laying in my bunk on a break, I looked up through the hatch. I thought for a moment that the movements were calmer and that there was less water coming on board. But when I went up to the cockpit on my watch I realized that the wind was even stronger than ever. After two days of abuse we decided, along with many other sailors, to take refuge in the Spanish harbour of La Coruña. When we went into the bar, tired but relieved, and met some other sailors, Håkan said, 'It was so windy that the anemometer went off the scale'. It was actually only a statement of fact, but it sounded like bragging. *Jennifer* and her first crew had managed the shakedown cruise perfectly.

CHARTER SKIPPER IN THE CARIBBEAN – A NEW CAREER

The yachting industry provides many different types of sailing experiences – crewed charters, bareboat charters and paying crew. Here you will find out about the charter fairs, the agents, the salaries and what's included in the job. You will also find out how to run a boat as a business and the main charter areas.

THE TRAVEL INDUSTRY – THE BIGGEST BUSINESS IN THE WORLD

Global tourism expands by about 4 per cent a year, and is today the biggest industry and employer in the world. After the oil industry it is also the biggest source of income of foreign currency for developing countries. Tourism accounts for up to 25–50 per cent of the gross national product in the Caribbean, for example, while it represents less than 3 per cent in the Western world. For most households in the developed world, tourism is the third biggest expense after living and food costs. The charter business is a part of this growing world tourism, even if it is a relatively small part of it. There has been a rapid expansion, with specially designed boats and marinas designed for chartering. The charter business in divided into two types: crewed charters and bareboat charters; the first can be compared with a limousine service and the second with Hertz or Avis.

TYPES OF CHARTER

CREWED CHARTER – THE LIMOUSINE SERVICE

Crewed charters are boats that are rented out with crew on board, almost like a small cruise ship. Apart from the skipper, there is always a chef who cooks all the food. The bigger charter boats can have as many as 8–15 people in the crew: captain, mate, purser, engineer, deckhands and hostesses. All wear uniforms with the boat's logo. The guests don't need to help – it is full service all day, and the only things they are expected to do are eat, drink, swim, tan and sleep.

The sizes of the boats range from 50–300ft (15–91m), and include the biggest private sailing boats and power yachts in the world. The cost to charter a boat like this varies from $6,000 per week for a boat the size of *Jennifer*, to $200,000 or more per week for a large motor yacht. The crewed boats are typically owned privately, or by companies and run by a professional crew. The owners, who might live in New York, London or Stockholm, may sometimes visit, but also put out their boats for charter by agents.

Some of the smaller boats are run by a single owner, or by a couple working together. Chartering too is their profession. The boats usually work on their own, unlike the fleets of bareboat charters. They are marketed by agents who inspect them at charter fairs in different parts of the world. The crewed boats often have a central agent, a clearing house, who takes the bookings and does the billing.

Most of the crewed boats spend the winter in the Caribbean, and the summer on the east coast of the US or in the Mediterranean. Due to the long passage across the Atlantic, which can take 4–6 weeks in each direction, few crewed boats work more than 25 weeks of charter per year, in fact 10–20 weeks is more normal. Many crewed boats have only a couple of charters per year.

BAREBOAT CHARTER – HERTZ AND AVIS

This type of charter boat is rented out, similar to car hire. As the name suggests, you just hire the boat, without crew or food. The boats are significantly smaller than crewed charter, with yachts from 30–50ft (9–15m). For an extra fee most companies will provide a boat-provisioning service, as well as a chef and/or a captain as needed. The cost for these boats is between $2,000–6,000 per week. The bareboat industry is more sophisticated than the business for crewed boats, in terms of organization, size and infrastructure. The two biggest bareboat companies, Sunsail and The Moorings, have around 600 sailing boats each in several fleets all over the world: the Caribbean, Mediterranean, South Pacific, USA, Australia and Mexico. They have their own marinas, staff to look after the boats, and modern computer systems for booking, maintenance and spare parts.

Agents around the world book the boats, which are supplied by the bareboat companies. The boats are mostly not owned by the bareboat companies, but by private individuals, or sometimes by independent companies. The boats are purchased by the owners, and after that put into the charter companies' fleets under a management deal. The bareboat company takes care of chartering the boat, insurance, maintenance, briefing the guests on the boat, and so on. For this, they retain up to 50 per cent of the cost of the charter. Some companies guarantee a certain number of weeks of chartering per year. Many boats are chartered 20 weeks per year and some up to 25 weeks. As part of the deal, it is guaranteed that the owner can use either his or her own boat, or a similar boat somewhere else in the world, for a certain number of weeks every year at no charge.

PAYING CREW

Sailing as paying crew is the third type of chartering. Guests can sail as crewmembers for a much lower price than a crewed charter. In return, the paying crew helps out with the sailing and cleaning of the boat, and the cooking. The prices vary from $30–100 a day. In the USA, my American agent charged guests $600 a week, while my Swedish agent charged around $400 (during the 1990s).

Another difference is that the paying crew can come aboard alone – organizing a group is not necessary, as it usually is on an ordinary charter. For crewed charters and bareboat charters, the whole boat is rented out to a group, for example a family or friends that know each other. A paying crew is often on board for a longer time, maybe one or two months, and an ocean crossing can be included; a typical crewed or bareboat charter is one or two weeks long. A charter vessel with paying crew is usually maintained by its owner, who lives on the boat and sails the vessel as a way of life. It helps his finances to take on paying crew, often to the Caribbean, in the Mediterranean or even around the world.

The boat owners either use agents, or put up advertisements at sailing clubs or advertise in yachting magazines. The number of boats that have paying crew is small, as is the number of agents that work with them. Ocean Voyages in San Francisco specializes in paying crew, and many Americans that have sailed aboard *Jennifer* have been introduced through them. Sometimes even regular charter boats take on paying crew for ocean crossings between the West Indies and Europe. Long-distance sailors sometimes take a crew that pays a little less, perhaps only food expenses, while on long ocean crossings.

CHARTER FAIRS AND AGENTS

In 1949, the British Commodore Desmond V Nicholson sailed from England with his family on board *Mollihawk*, a 70ft (21m) schooner. Their original plan was to sail around the world. However, when they arrived in English

Harbour on Antigua, they were so charmed by the beautiful little harbour (which also is one of the most protected in the Caribbean) that they stayed there. English Harbour was also the site of Lord Nelson's old navy base. When Nicholson arrived it consisted of a number of old ramshackle buildings. Desmond and his brother Rodney began to rebuild the Nelson Dockyard. At the same time, guests at the only hotel in Antigua began to ask about going on day sailing excursions. This turned into a business (today known as VEB Nicholson & Sons) and the sailing charter was born.

After a couple of years, more long-distance sailors came to Antigua, and became engaged in a charter business that, during the 1950s, consisted of perhaps 7–8 sailing boats. Nicholson's two sons eventually became skippers and agents for the other boats. Later, a booking office opened in Boston. Today, Nicholson Yacht Charters is the oldest charter agency and one of the biggest clearing houses in the world, with offices in Boston, Newport and Antigua. VEB Nicholson & Sons is also responsible for arranging the Antigua Sailing Week in April and the Antigua Charter Yacht Show held at the beginning of December every year. The last year we took part, 1997, everybody was there – from the biggest sailing yachts in the world to the smaller yachts in *Jennifer*'s class; some 200 boats in total.

The other charter shows are in the Virgin Islands in November – St Thomas in the US Virgin Islands, and Tortola in the British Virgin Islands. Both of the fairs have 40–50 boats and are mostly for the yachts that sail in the Virgin Islands. Lately, there is also a charter show in the Dutch-French island of St Martin, which tries to compete with Antigua for the biggest yachts. The largest charter show in the Mediterranean is in Genoa, Italy in May. Smaller local shows can also be found in Marmaris in Turkey and Newport on the East Coast of the USA.

In 1997, some 200 agents from all over the world came to the Antigua Charter Yacht Show, most of them from the USA and the rest from Europe. A few also came from South America and Asia. Agents get to know the boats and their crews at the shows and advertise them in different ways to their home markets; through boat shows, magazines, direct mail and over the internet. In the USA, the agents typically have a free-phone number for prospective guests to contact them.

I usually ask my charter guests how they found out about *Jennifer*. The most frequent answer is that they saw an advertisement in a sailing magazine. But one guest from New York had used an agent in Texas, another one from Chicago had used an agent in California, and a guest from Los Angeles had gone through the agent in Boston. In other words, there was no particular geographical distribution. For their services, including marketing, travel to fairs, phone/fax and office overheads, the booking agents take a 15 per cent commission and the main agent takes 5 per cent. With modern satellite communication some boats now handle the clearing house themselves. If there is a 'regular' travel agent involved who normally doesn't deal with sailboat charters, the commission can be as high as 25 per cent.

The agents can work with any of the boats, and the boats can have multiple agents. Only the main agent and clearing house (if one is used) remains the same. This means that more than one agent can offer a customer, who phones around the agents, the same boat. To keep track of the boats, the agents use the Charter Databank International or CDI-guide. There they can find all kinds of information, both geographical (for example which boats are in the Pacific Ocean or in the Mediterranean) and the type and size of boats available. The guide also shows how many cabins, bunks, bathrooms and types of equipment each boat has. About 250 boats and agents are organized in this way in alphabetical order. So, if a customer calls an agent and tells him that he or she wants to sail for a week with a group of six persons for $1,000 per person, the agent can use the CDI-guide to see which of the boats is available.

The Antigua Charter Yacht Show (or Agent's Week) lasts about a week. Before the show, the crews clean the boats so that they are immaculate. During the week, the agents visit the boats and inspect the toilets, varnish, brass, sheets, towels, crockery, the material in the main cabin and the cushions in the cockpit and the overall standard of the boat. They ask a lot of questions about your background, your sailing experience and whether you take children on board. They also ask about general equipment (such as televisions, videos, water skis, surf boards and diving equipment). The chef is asked about his or her experience, and is normally asked to provide a sample of the menu.

Most of the agents are not very interested in technical details. Few go up on deck to inspect the rigging and the sails or ask any questions about them. The agents ask about the price so that they can be sure that the CDI-guide and the main agent have given them the correct information and that the booking status is in order. Some even ask if one can be flexible about the price, to which I always answer 'yes'. It is often at these fairs that it is decided if a charter boat is going to be successful or not. The agent's impression of the boat, and more importantly the crew, is all-important. If they find the boat sound and the crew experienced and confident, they will be inspired to sell charters on that boat. A good crew can even balance out problems with a poor boat, but a good boat never balances out a bad crew.

A charter boat should have a good, well-designed brochure. Cheaply printed

material may indicate a cheap product. My first brochure had four good-sized pages in full-colour and looked very expensive and appealing. The agents told me that my brochures were quickly picked up at the boat shows and many of the guests told me that they booked *Jennifer* based only on the look of the brochure. New boats and crews often have a hard time during the first year so this was very encouraging.

Too many fortune-seekers try the charter industry thinking that it is an easy way to earn money. Nothing can be further from the truth. Agents want to see that you can handle a full season and not give up after just a couple of months. Good interpersonal relationships between the crew and the agents are paramount. Some owners serve lunch on board to the agents who have booked a special appointment. It is a great opportunity for them to try out the food, facilities, atmosphere and the service of the crew. I look at it the same way; the longer I can keep the agents on board my boat, the better. During my very first charter show in Antigua 1988, *Jennifer* was brand new and luckily she was an instant success.

So, as the agents are one of the main connections to the market, it is important to be on good terms with them. I regularly send them information about bookings and plans for the season. If nothing else, at least they will remember me. After each charter the agents give the guests a call to see how successful the charter has been. It is one of the most important moments in a trip. Satisfied guests are what count, and good reports will encourage agents to send more guests to the boat.

Success in chartering doesn't have much to do with driving a boat or sailing; it is mainly about establishing good relationships. In principle you could drive around in a bus – the bus and the boat are only the platform – it is your primary aim to take care of your guests and give them an unforgettable experience in one of the most beautiful places of the world.

COMPETITORS AND COLLEAGUES

The charter boats compete with each other within the same size and prize range. For example, it is clear that *Jennifer* and the beautifully rebuilt J-yacht *Endeavor*, which is 140ft (43m) in length and costs $10,000 a day, don't compete with each other. They don't associate with each other much either. Just as in everyday life, there is a type of hierarchy, where the employees on the biggest boats are most prestigious.

In your own class of boat there is some competition over price. When I was new to the charter business I kept my price fairly low because I was concerned that I would not get any bookings. The owners of boats in the same size range soon let me know what they thought of such a tactic.

When I didn't have any charters on *Jennifer* I spent time in Antigua in the main harbour. I often sat in Nicholson's office during the day. If an inquiry about a charter came in, I was already there and took it. Some other boats anchored far away from the office and didn't monitor the VHF at all (the most important way of communicating in Antigua). Those who missed the radio calls or only visited the office once a week may well have lost out on charter business. Remember that the salary and additional money you pay to your crew are important. An owner should encourage the crew to recruit guests by giving them more money per charter, or a bonus if they get their own guests.

Many of the Swedish boats were colleagues, not competitors. Every season during the early 1990s there were approximately ten Swedish boats in the Caribbean, many of them Swan boats, from 53–65ft (16–20m) and often more expensive. *Sway*, an enlarged Swan 65 that was rebuilt to 72ft (22m), is owned by an educational facility in Sweden and has been sailing charters for ten years, often with Harald as the captain. He is a professional, the agents like him and *Sway* was always well-booked. The owners made the decision, a couple of years ago, to replace Harald with a lower-paid captain. But the owners had not understood the main principle in the business; that you don't book the boat, but the crew. The result was that there were fewer bookings. It wasn't that there was anything wrong with the new captain, he just didn't have the same relationship with the agents as Harald. Later Harald was asked to return as captain for *Sway*. *Kirsti* was another Swan 65, where Per was the captain. When I returned home in 1998, Per was captain on the old Whitbread boat *Europolitan* in Stockholm. During the 1980s, a friend of mine, Roger Nilsson, who is one of Sweden's best-known Whitbread sailors, was the captain on a Swan in the Caribbean. He visited after a Whitbread race – with the boat *The Card* – and sailed with *Jennifer* during a well-earned vacation. During that week we found out that he had never sailed just for the fun of it. 'It should be criminal not to race', became his expression.

THE CHARTER CAREER

Most people think that you don't earn very much money as crew on a charter boat. This is true in one sense. But if you consider that the money you earn is often tax free, that you don't have to pay for a house, car, food or work clothes, the picture is rather different. The tropical lifestyle doesn't demand much – just a little food and clothing, and the nightlife is far cheaper than

at home. On some boats you receive tips, sometimes as much as your salary. Some crew are able to save their whole salary and use only tips for pocket money expenses.

There is a wide range of salaries. A deckhand or a hostess earns a minimum of $1,500 a month, often $2,000 and sometimes $3,000. One of the world's biggest and newest sailing boats pays $3,000 a month as the lowest salary. A chef earns from $1,500 up to $4,000 a month. Of course the bigger boats pay a lot more, but if you start on the smaller boats you can work your way up. A captain on a 65ft (20m) boat earns between $2,500–3,000 a month, while a captain on the biggest boats can earn more than $10,000 a month. And most of the time tips can be added on top of a salary.

A young person who wants to spend ten years of their life working on charter boats and seeing exciting new places can easily come home with some decent savings. A chef that earns $3,000 a month, and lives on the tips, will have more than $300,000 after ten years. A captain that earns about $6,000 a month will have more than $700,000. And if you are a captain on a really big boat you can become a millionaire in dollars. And on top of the salary and tip, the bigger boats often also pay the airfare home, insurance and further education.

'A HARD JOB FOR THE DRIVER AND THE CONDUCTOR'

However, a charter life is not an easy life. During a charter you work from 6am to midnight, but you always have to be ready to work outside these hours, you have no private life and you can face unpleasant, ungrateful guests. A typical day begins with an early start to bake bread, wash the boat and put out the cushions in the cockpit. While the guests wake up to the smell of fresh bread, the crew prepares a big breakfast. After breakfast, perhaps some of the guests want to swim or snorkel, and after that you sail for a couple of hours to an island or reef.

It is rare that any of the guests help out with sailing the vessel. Perhaps someone wants to steer for an hour or so, but after that they return to sunning themselves, reading on the deck cushions or sitting in the shade under the cockpit bimini (sunshade). During the morning, the hostess cleans all the cabins and bathrooms so the whole boat is kept clean and tidy.

The crew makes sure that the guests get plenty of cold beverages during the day, and maybe a cocktail before lunch or in the afternoon. You almost always anchor at lunch time, so that the guests can sit down in the cockpit and eat, which means that the table is put up and laid and the food prepared. There might be time for diving after lunch, if the guests have a diving certificate, or snorkelling among the reefs. We might stay all day, swimming and reading, or I might teach aerobics on the beach.

If the guests want to they can take the dinghy to an island to do some shopping, sightseeing or go to a bar. The alternative is to get a drink with some snacks on board, with the sunset in the background. Some guests may want to take a siesta before dinner. At around 7.30pm dinner is served; always a three course meal with wine, normally seated in the cockpit, and coffee with dessert if the guests so wish. If it is a lively group they might down a lot of drinks, laugh and talk until late into the night. When the guests have gone to bed, you can finally start to clean up and prepare for the next day. You're lucky if it's before midnight. There is never any night sailing on a charter, so you are at anchor every night. This means that you only sail a short distance during a week. In contrast, if you sail with a paying crew the tempo is a little faster and you tend to cover more distance.

The three most popular areas for chartering in the West Indies are the Virgin Islands, the St Martin/St Bart's area, and The Grenadines – a little archipelago between St Vincent and Grenada. *Jennifer* has had most of her charters in the Grenadines, which is one of the best sailing areas.

Aboard smaller boats like *Jennifer*, the guests and the crew always eat together. This is unthinkable aboard the bigger boats. On the smaller boats the guests often even treat the crew to a much-appreciated dinner once a week. If the crew follows along to a happy hour ashore, the guests always pay for any drinks. You should be sensitive to the situation between the crew and guests. Sometimes the guests prefer to be by themselves, and then you stay on the boat or go with them a little discretely. Most of the time, however, the guests insist on doing everything together with the crew. Sometimes you have to activate the guests, for example to take a walk along the beach, hike up a nearby hill or mountain, visit a picturesque village or look for the best snorkelling areas. Again it is important to have a sensitive ear; some guests lead a stressful life at home and just want to take it easy on their vacation – nothing except tanning, reading and resting.

Most of the time *Jennifer* had four to six guests at a time, sometimes eight. With eight guests aboard, it meant that the crew had to sleep in the forepeak. The total number aboard has been ten – a small hotel and restaurant business. Most charters were a week long, some 10–14 days, and a few were even three weeks long. Towards the end of each period we asked the guests to write in the guest book. If they were satisfied we often got tips. This was sometimes 10 per cent of the cost of the charter, but much of the time it was around 5 per cent, or a few hundred dollars. Once we had eight European passengers on board for three weeks. They were nice and polite, but a little loud. They didn't eat ashore once during three weeks, they almost never left the boat and they didn't give any tips. Christine, our chef, was totally exhausted and very disappointed. Since I own the boat, I don't get any extra money, but the chef should almost always receive tips.

During our charter years half our guests were American and half were European (mostly Swedes). They were usually relatively well off, interesting people: lawyers, accountants, doctors, managers and teachers. Charter vacations are relatively expensive, approximately $1,000 per person per week, plus airfare.

CHARTER SEASONS

You might think that the main charter business is in the Caribbean, but this is not the case. The Mediterranean is the most important market. It is here that you find the biggest and most expensive yachts and the most interesting and prestigious harbours on the French Riviera: Saint Tropez, Cannes, Nice and Antibes. Other popular sailing areas are Mallorca, Sardinia, Portofino and Marbella, and Malta, Greece and Turkey. The season in the Mediterranean is almost six months long, but it is only four months long in the Caribbean. The prices are also higher in the Mediterranean. Food is always included in the price in the Caribbean, as well as beverages in the Virgin Islands. In the Mediterranean, food and beverages are an extra cost, on top of the charter price.

Normally the boats alternate between the Caribbean and the Mediterranean, as the seasons go perfectly together, but when it is hard to fill the boats in the Caribbean it may not be profitable for their owners to sail the long distance there. Many American boats spend the summers on the East Coast of the US, where there is a strong charter market. In the rest of the world, besides Thailand, Mexico, Tahiti, Seychelles and Tonga, the charter business is almost non-existent, with only a few boats stationed in New Zealand, Australia, Singapore, Hong Kong, and Japan.

PROFILES OF CIRCUMNAVIGATORS

Here you will find out how many people sail around the world or across an ocean, and what countries they come from. I will also look at who owns and sails the boats, and the best places to sail.

HOW MANY VOYAGES?

'Who are we, where do we come from, where are we going?' Paul Gauguin wrote on one of his paintings in Tahiti. These are difficult philosophical questions that few people can ever fully answer. But when it comes to circumnavigators and cruisers – where they come from and where they are going is different problem entirely. Jimmy Cornell (who we met in Fiji) has been researching this very question. He counted the number of boats in different harbours during a 20-year period between 1974–93. He researched the Panama and Suez canals, Tahiti, New Zealand, Thailand and Cape Town.

Every year 300 sailing boats start their voyages around the world, and this number is increasing all the time. These circumnavigations usually travel from east to west, following the Trade winds, and take an average of three years to complete their voyage. It means that you can find almost 1,000 circumnavigators at any one time on the ocean. There are also a number of boats that sail around an ocean, mostly for a year: Europeans and East Coast Americans sail around the Atlantic (1,000–1,500 boats) and for these the Caribbean is the favourite destination; West Coast Americans, Kiwis and Aussies sail around parts of the South Pacific (500–1,000 boats) with Tahiti, Tonga and Fiji as favourite locations; and Aussies and South Africans sail around the Indian Ocean (100–200 boats) where Indonesia, the Maldives, Chagos and Madagascar are the favourite destinations.

Many of the circumnavigators (around 24%) come from the USA, but the Europeans are the biggest group with 57% (England 18%, France 16%, Germany 8%, Sweden and the Netherlands 3% each and the remaining

countries 1–2% each). Australia and New Zealand represent 4%, Canada represents 3% and the rest of the world contributes the remaining 12% of circumnavigators. From this you can conclude that the wealthy English-speaking countries are the biggest group – almost half of all circumnavigators. There are a few boats from Japan and Brazil, but practically speaking, most boats come from Western countries.

Jimmy Cornell found that the number of circumnavigators doubled, from 86 to 163 boats between 1974 and 1992 and became 200 boats by 1993. By 1999 there were, by my estimation, around 300–500 boats. The biggest increase in numbers occurred in the group of boats that sailed within the regions. Most of the boats are between 30 and 45ft (9 and 13m) in length. Around 80% of the boats are sailed by couples, 10% are sailed by single-handed sailors and the rest are families with children, paying-crew boats like *Jennifer*, and big, luxurious, private sailing boats.

Circumnavigators are not normally very wealthy people. Most have worked for much or all of their lives. Some are retired, whilst others have sold their house, car or company to sail for a couple of years and then make a brand new start. Some stop along the way to return to work (and replenish the travel budget) while others take on paying crew to finance their lifestyle as sailors. But almost all live fairly economically; the longer the money lasts, the longer the period of time they can be out there sailing.

The majority of long distance sailors choose the tropics. However, during the 1990s some boats started to sail towards the poles: Antarctica and Greenland. Today you can read about sailing among the icebergs in many of the boating magazines.

HOW TO HITCHHIKE THE WORLD

Many people have been backpacking around the world. But there is another way to see the world and the exotic atolls and islands that are hard to reach – namely 'hitchhiking', or working as a deckhand on board a sailing boat. Here you will find tips on how to become a crewmember, the costs you may need to cover and the best places to pick up a small boat.

A HITCHHIKER'S GUIDE

WHO SAILS?

With at least 300 sailing boats starting a three-year-long circumnavigation every year, there are more than 1,000 circumnavigators sailing the oceans at any given time. Added to the several hundred other boats sailing around an ocean for a year, there are a good number of opportunities for crew.

Normally crewmembers all have to pay a part of the food costs, but sometimes you can be lucky and pay nothing at all. As crew you are expected to help out with sailing, cooking and keeping the boat clean and tidy. If you get a position on a charter boat you can also get paid for an ocean crossing, but be prepared to work the whole way.

HOW CAN YOU BE ACCEPTED AS CREW?

Write your CV on a single letter-sized page, describe who you are and what sailing you have done. Then make at least 100 copies for distribution, along with a photo of yourself. Grades from schools and higher education are not necessary or relevant – it will be too much for the captain to read. Instead, include any certification pertaining to sailing: navigation courses, letters of recommendation from sailing clubs and/or boats that you have been sailing with. If you are good with generators, outboard motors, electronics or computers (most boats nowadays have laptops with a number of navigation/weather programs), if you are a chef or educated in medical care, you have a better chance of success. It is not always necessary to have had sailing experience. If you are a positive person who wants to learn this is sometimes considered more important than experience.

If you are handy you can make a deal: fix something aboard and sail for free. Put up your CV at yacht clubs, marinas, bars, showers and laundrettes or other places where sailing people will see it. It is most important to distribute it, in person, to all boats and captains you meet. You should go back every day, even if they have said they don't need help. The captains talk to each other and your details might be passed around to someone that needs crew. A lot of changes occur day to day on the boats too; crew can quit or get fired, someone's parent can become sick and he or she has to fly home, or someone can fall in love and want to stay on shore. As always, you have to be in the right place at the right time.

When a captain interviews you, you should interview the captain too. Has he had a paying crew before and how did that work out? If it seems positive, ask if you can come back the next day and continue the interview. It is just as important that both of you feel that it is right. You are about to spend several weeks in the same boat and there are many opportunities for friction. Both of you should take the chance to explore what the market has to offer.

You should try to get accurate information about what the captain is expecting from the crew. Is it only sailing and cooking, or is it boat maintenance as well; scraping, varnishing, working with the engine and washing the hull? How does the watch system work and how many hours of the night will you be on watch? Once I took on a paying crewmember in Panama who was going to sail with us to Tahiti. After one day at sea he refused to do his night watches. We went back to Panama and put him ashore.

Other questions to ask: are there life harnesses and life jackets for everyone? Is there a liferaft? Are there emergency flares? Is there an EPIRB (rescue beacon) for emergencies? If any of the emergency equipment is missing, you should choose another boat. What condition is the boat in? If it looks like a workshop above and below deck, maybe it won't be ready in time. Is the saloon full of beer, liquor bottles and cigarette ash? If the answer is 'yes' and this does not appeal to you, maybe it is not the right boat for you to sail on. Ask about the food. Some captains try to save money on the food and if you pay a part of the food cost it is good to know what you will get for your money. At breakfast, for example, is it corn flakes and muesli or a full cooked breakfast? Will there be plenty of fruit and vegetables to eat? Is it possible to bake on board? Will you be doing some fishing? Are snacks and soft drinks or beer included? If not, can you buy your own? How much fresh water is available? Are you allowed to take a fresh water shower? If it is dead calm will the captain use the motor? Is there a stereo system aboard and are you allowed to use it? How many rolls of toilet paper are available? I met a boat in Tahiti where the captain and the crew were at war. The captain complained that the crew had used too much toilet paper. Of course, that was not the real reason for the friction and it was more likely to be the last straw in a difficult voyage.

HOW MUCH DOES IT COST?

Most captains want you to pay about $10–25 a day to help cover the cost of the food. On some boats like *Jennifer*, who financed herself by having paying crew, this cost may be up to $50 per day or more. Remember that some boats are bigger, faster and more comfortable, the food is better and they may have more specialized facilities such as diving equipment.

Sometimes there can be a package price to a destination. It is wise to ask for an estimated timeframe so you can compare alternatives. Most of the time, you have to pay in advance. Always ask for a receipt that clearly shows your name, the boat's name, the captain's name, how much you have paid, what the destination is and the approximate timescale. If the captain refuses to give you a receipt, you should be very careful. Sometimes the boat never leaves the marina and the money simply disappears.

If you are going to be a deckhand during a long voyage, ask about the costs to the first stop (where you can leave the boat if you want) and then plan to pay one stop at a time. Most captains require you to have either an airline ticket home, or ask for a deposit that will cover the ticket home. According to the law, the captain is responsible for the crew and can end up having to pay the airfare home if you are not allowed to stay in the country; no country wants to have tourists or sailors that can't leave.

In the Maldives we met a boat with four paying crewmembers. They didn't get along at all, and there were conflicts aboard. The captain had originally made a deal with them to sail from Phuket to the Mediterranean, but changed his mind and wanted to sail to Indonesia instead. The crew went to the police and the captain had to pay their airfare home.

WHERE DO YOU FIND A BOAT?

The best places to find long-distance sailors and charter boats are: Mallorca, Gibraltar, the Canaries, Marmaris (Turkey), Antibes (France), Antigua, St Martin and St Lucia (Caribbean), Panama, Mexico, Tahiti, Fiji, Auckland, Cairns, Darwin, Bali, Phuket, Sri Lanka, Cape Town and Salvador.

CROSSING THE OCEANS

THE ATLANTIC

For people who want to sail to the West Indies, boats typically depart from northern Europe in September/October, and depart the Mediterranean in October/November. Southampton is one of the main departure ports for northern Europe. In the Mediterranean try Gibraltar, the French Riviera (Antibes) or Mallorca. The most popular departure point of all is the Canary Islands. On Gran Canaria there are three different marinas: Las Palmas, Puerto Rico and Puerto Mogan. You can travel by bus between the marinas, and you should do this every day if you are looking for a boat. The boats leave the Canaries in November or December to reach the Caribbean by Christmas. In late November, there is a popular rally called Atlantic Rally for Cruisers (ARC), where up to 150 boats sail together to St Lucia. Few boats sail earlier than November, because the Trade winds are not yet strong enough, and you don't want to get to the Caribbean before the end of November when the hurricane season ends (July–November). Some boats also sail to West Africa and Brazil from the Canaries.

You can find boats departing the Caribbean for the voyage back to Europe in April and May. The best place to go is Antigua, where the event of the year (Antigua Sailing Week) signifies the end of the season. Many boats, both private and charter, are then looking for crew for the trans-Atlantic crossing to northern Europe and the Mediterranean from the American East Coast. St Martin is also a good place to look for yachts going to the Mediterranean.

In the southern Atlantic, Cape Town is the perfect place to find a boat. Typically, these boats are departing for the Caribbean via Brazil, although some head directly to Europe.

THE SOUTH PACIFIC

The best way to find a boat en route to the South Pacific is in Panama, where almost all boats from Europe and the American East Coast pass from the Caribbean Sea to the Pacific Ocean. One way to get to know the boats is to help out along the Panama Canal, which usually takes a day or two. Every boat needs a captain and at least four crewmembers to handle the lines, so most of the boats need extra crew for the canal passage. This can be a fun trip to do, even if you are not looking for a boat. In Panama, you can also find boats that sail north to the American West Coast via Hawaii, or east to the Caribbean. Cabo San Lucas or Puerto Vallarta in Mexico and San Diego in the USA are also good places to find a boat to the South Pacific.

Once in the South Pacific, Tahiti is the best place to find a boat, although it is expensive to fly there. The boats that arrive in Tahiti come from many different places, including Mexico, Panama, Cape Town, Hawaii, New Zealand and Australia. The boats continue sailing in different directions, but the majority sail west-bound, through Tonga and Fiji, to New Zealand, where some 400–500 boats a year wait out the South Pacific hurricane season (December–April). Fiji, and to a lesser extent Tonga, are excellent places to find boats going not only to New Zealand, but also to the northern Pacific and Micronesia, or directly onwards to the Indian Ocean. In April and May it is time for the circumnavigators to continue from New Zealand on to Australia and the Indian Ocean, and for the New Zealanders to sail to Fiji and Tonga during the southern hemisphere's winter.

THE INDIAN OCEAN

The best place to find a boat to sail to the northern Indian Ocean is Phuket in Thailand. Most circumnavigators celebrate Christmas and New Year's Day in Phuket, and sail west in January and February when the north-east monsoon (December–April) has started. Most sail towards the Suez Canal, but some choose to sail to South Africa. Almost all stop in Sri Lanka, which is another good place to find a boat. For those who want to sail across the southern Indian Ocean, via Cocos Keeling, Reunion and Mauritius, then Bali and Darwin are the best harbours to go to. Here the boats have to cross the Indian Ocean by October at the latest, before the cyclone season (November–March) begins.

FOOD, MEDICINE AND COCKROACHES ON BOARD

One of the long-distance sailor's biggest problems – cockroaches! It is important to think about what type of food to take on board and how to store it properly. With good planning you can defeat the bugs and eat tasty, nutritious food during your circumnavigation for as little as $10 per person per day. We also look at what kind of medications you may need or wish to bring.

COCKROACHES

The Black Death came to Europe during the 14th century, carried by the rats that had boarded the European sailing ships while they were docked in Asia. Fortunately, modern sailors rarely have problems with rats. If a rat were to sneak aboard without permission, it would certainly be discovered quickly, as there are few places to hide.

But there is another pest that likes to live aboard – the cockroach. I have seen a specimen that was 6cm long, but most cockroaches are between 0.5–2.5cm in length. They can get into the boat across the docking lines, or when the boat is lying alongside a harbour wall. However, the most usual way for them to arrive is with the food, particularly inside the cardboard boxes often brought on board a boat.

Some skippers are extremely careful when they bring food on board. No cardboard boxes are allowed, and fruit and vegetables are all rinsed in water. All the labels are removed from the jars and cans, and a permanent marker is used to record the contents directly on the container's surface. This is because cockroaches love to lay their eggs underneath the labels. It is all very time consuming, but on the other hand the most careful boats are clear of cockroaches. I don't take the labels off jars, but I do empty the cardboard boxes and put the food into the dinghy as quickly as possible.

It is vital to keep the boat clean, most importantly the galley, so the cockroaches can't find anything to live on. It is just as important to store the food properly. Flour, pasta, bread and rice normally come from the store packed in paper or plastic packages. These won't last long, and cockroaches can easily get inside. Good plastic containers with sealable lids are the best solution for food storage, and an excellent investment.

Cockroaches usually hide during the day, but at night they come out to scavenge. If you suddenly switch on a lamp, you might see a whole army of cockroaches scuttling away. *Jennifer* has had cockroaches every now and then, but we have always managed to get rid of them. Extermination takes quite a lot of work, but fortunately you can buy cockroach spray bombs at many of the supermarkets in the Tropics. To use them you have to open all the cupboards and shelves, and lift up all the beds and floorboards. All food not stored in a sealed airtight container is removed from the boat. After that you trigger the spray bombs, one for each cabin. Then you close the boat and leave it for three hours. When you get back you will find dead cockroaches, especially by the companionway, but most of them will have died hidden away in the background. You will have to repeat the whole procedure in a couple of weeks – eggs can survive the initial extermination and a new generation has to be prevented from developing.

FOOD

STORAGE

Having good food on board is important as everybody wants to eat well. It is therefore critical to plan well in advance for long ocean crossings. So, what foods will last for a long time and how should they be stored? Rice, pasta and flour can last for a long voyage if stored well. But you have to be careful; small insects can infect them even before you bring them aboard. It is unfortunate if you have bought a lot of rice or flour and discover, when already at sea, that the containers are infested, so if you buy a large amount, it is worth examining it very carefully for infestation before you stow it away.

There are many kinds of vegetables that will stay fresh for a long time. Potatoes and onions will keep well if stored in a dry, dark place. It can be humid in a boat, but even so they will last for at least a month. Carrots and cabbages will last for a month if kept in the refrigerator. Root vegetables and pumpkins will also last for at least a month if you keep them cool. Eggs will keep fresh for a long time and do not need to be put in the refrigerator. Of all the different kinds of fruit you can buy, bananas are the cheapest and you can find them almost everywhere. A bunch of green bananas costs approximately

$10. A really big bunch costs double that, and the bananas will last a week to ten days before ripening. After that you have to eat the bananas quickly, or they will rot. Overripe bananas that don't look too tasty can still be used to bake banana bread. Many sailors buy bananas in harbour and dry them, which means they can last indefinitely.

For fresh food, it is an excellent idea to fish. Have a lot of bait and lures and a very strong line aboard – to be on the safe side, one that can take up to 200kg! There is nothing that tastes better on the open ocean than freshly caught tuna or barracuda.

COSTS

You can spend a lot of money on provisioning. On the other hand, it is quite easy to live very cheaply if you are careful. A typical circumnavigation often goes through developing countries, where you buy the same food that the local people eat, so it's reasonably cheap.

If you want to eat as you do at home, it doesn't have to be too costly either. During my ten years out sailing I kept a record of all the food expenses for the boat. During charter periods, food cost between $30–40 per person per day. This included a good breakfast, a two-course lunch and a three-course dinner with soft drinks and bottled water. With a paying crew, the average cost was only about $10 per person and day. This includes more ordinary plain food – muesli, with long life (UHT) milk or yoghurt, sandwiches for lunch and a cooked dinner. Beer and wine is not included in either of the alternatives. The total cost for paying crew today, including harbour fees, diesel and butane/propane – adds up to about $25 per person a day.

MEDICATION

Few long-distance sailors have a medical background, but despite this you can still learn and practice first aid. Organizations such as the Red Cross often provide free education in cardiopulmonary resuscitation (CPR). Their course takes a day and you receive a certificate if you pass the examination. It is also a good idea to take the course again to refresh your knowledge.

If you have a relative or friend who is a doctor, you can ask him/her to demonstrate how to do surgical stitches, although Steri Strips are far easier and safer to use. I practised stitches on a towel with a friend of mine who is a doctor. It is not easy to choose the right needle, or get the stitches exactly right, and it is even harder in a real life situation. But with practice you might be able to do a reasonable job in an emergency. See if you can also get hold of local anaesthetics – they will be very useful if stitches are needed. Disposable syringes should be bought and someone in the crew should be instructed in how to give an injection. Analgesics such as morphine can be trickier to source because it is a controlled narcotic. If you are planning on having medical drugs aboard, you have to label them clearly in English. A proper certificate, in English, that clearly describes all the articles, including all identifying marks, has to be kept aboard and shown to customs officials upon request.

Of course, the boat should have a first aid kit from a pharmacy, as well as pills for treatment of seasickness, diarrhoea, constipation and colds. Considering that you are likely to be swimming and snorkelling, it is a good idea to buy swimmers' ear fluid (an alcohol mix that makes the salt water evaporate, which you can find in diving stores). After each swim or snorkelling session you put a few drops in your ear, and this should help prevent swimmers' ear. Some sailors go as far as having their appendix removed before they cast off to avoid a surgical crisis at sea. I had my wisdom teeth removed to avoid toothache.

You should be aware that medicines are one of the few products that you can find all over developing countries. Their lack of regulation makes most medicines, including ones that require prescriptions in the western world, relatively easy to buy. We only had to show the WHO's health card once in Kenya. Even so, it is important to bring that card with you whenever you renew your vaccinations. Otherwise it is almost impossible to keep track of which immunizations you have had and when you've had them.

EMERGENCIES – *JENNIFER* IN DANGER

We had some close calls in *Jennifer* – in this chapter we go aground on a reef in the Caribbean, lose the wing from the keel and then spend many months sailing without it. We also narrowly miss a hurricane in Antigua and have a strange incident with our dinghy and a sea turtle.

JENNIFER AGROUND – ON THE REEF

One of the worst groundings I have ever experienced took place in the Caribbean and could have ended in disaster. It was 1991; the charter show in Antigua had just finished and we were sailing south. Our next stop was to be the island of Guadeloupe. To save time, I planned to go through the channel in the reef on the side to the north of the main city, Pointe-à-Pitre. The reef is treacherous but is properly marked and visible both day and night. We had left Antigua later than anticipated so we had to cross the reef in darkness. This shouldn't have given us any problems as I had passed through the reef many times before.

A properly marked channel in daylight is easy to follow. In darkness it can turn into a confusion of green and red lights, especially when the channel is changing direction many times. We passed through the two first sets of buoys and kept on going, motoring at a slow speed. Then I started to hesitate. It was impossible to decide which channel marker lights came next – which light should I aim for? I didn't have radar, which would have made it easy to determine the distance to the buoys, and all of a sudden it became shallow very quickly.

We were almost stationary, edging our way through at half a knot. The question was: were we too far to starboard or too far to port? I decided to reverse and abandon the attempt to cross the reef in the darkness. The current must have drifted us out of our channel because at that moment we ran aground. I immediately asked the crew to empty the water tanks and sit in the dinghy. For half an hour I tried to get the boat off the reef with the engine, but *Jennifer* was stuck hard. The tide was also going out, which made the whole effort look hopeless.

When a sailboat runs aground you can try to heave her off by putting out an anchor with the dinghy and hoisting the boat off from the side. This is impossible if you have a wing keel (where a substantial horizontal foil or 'wing' sits at the bottom of the keel) as the wing prevents the boat from leaning. The only thing we could do was to wait for high tide to return. We spent the night at an angle of 35°, while the surge made the side of the hull hit the bottom over and over. It felt terrible. In the darkness, I dived into the water with a snorkel and checked out the keel with a diving lamp. The wing was nearly broken, (the reason for our angled position) but a few bolts still held it in place. The night seemed to last forever, and it was impossible to sleep. Even if the hull survived the night, how would we get off the reef? At dawn a fishing boat passed by. It seemed to have a powerful engine so we asked them if they could pull us loose. After a few attempts, the fishing boat eventually succeeded in dragging us into deeper water. It felt unbelievably good to be floating again. I dived into the water again to check out the keel. The wing was gone, but at least the keel itself was still intact.

CROSSING THE ATLANTIC WITHOUT THE WING

On paper, *Jennifer*'s displacement is 13 tons. Fully equipped, she weighs nearer 17 tons. The weight of the keel including the wing is 4.5 tons, while the wing itself is 1.3 tons. I estimated that we had lost about 25 per cent of the weight of the total keel. I had neither the time nor the money, however, to salvage the wing; a charter was booked for the following week.

We sailed for the whole winter without the wing. During the following summer, we crossed the Atlantic to the Mediterranean, and in the autumn we sailed back to the Caribbean. A year after the grounding, we returned to the place where it had happened. I took the dinghy out and dived into the water to look for it. After only half an hour I found the wing, tied it to a rope and buoy as a temporary precaution and then returned to Pointe-à-Pitre. I found a boat with a crane that was strong enough to pick up the wing, and after some negotiation, everything was set up. I had *Jennifer* hauled out of the water, and the wing was re-attached. *Jennifer* was finally a complete boat again.

How did it feel to sail across the Atlantic without a wing? The boat was a little less steady than before, but we could compensate by taking the sails down and reefing earlier, and not sailing her too hard. Another Beneteau

with a wing keel ran aground in the Caribbean and managed to get off by itself. When they hauled the boat out to polish the hull back in Sweden, they discovered that the wing was missing – the owners hadn't even noticed that it was gone!

HURRICANES

Every year a number of tropical storms build up over the Atlantic and move in a north-westerly direction. Most of them burn out over the sea and do no harm. A few pass over the Caribbean, some causing considerable destruction, and then keep on moving towards the USA and Mexico, where they cause even more damage. If a tropical storm becomes very powerful it is upgraded to a hurricane. Teams of meteorologists observe any hurricane very closely, and regular reports on its developments are made, every hour if it approaches a populated place.

During 1990 I stayed in the Caribbean for the whole season. I was in Antigua during the autumn when we heard a hurricane was approaching. Four days before it arrived, we received the first warning. We either had to seek shelter in a 'hurricane hole', or sail away. In the Caribbean sailing away means going down to Trinidad or Venezuela, which are both outside the usual hurricane belt. The other option was the hurricane hole. In Antigua, one popular hurricane hole is English Harbour. It is a very safe harbour, and when a hurricane is approaching all the boats in the area head there to seek shelter. Most hurricane holes have mangrove trees along the shoreline, and the boats are secured to the mangrove trees stern-to, with the bows pointing out into the bay. With two or three anchors deployed, and four or five ropes tied to the mangrove trees, *Jennifer* lay relatively safely. I took down the wind generator and solar panels and secured all the loose things on deck. And then we waited.

The hurricane approached Antigua, but stopped just before making landfall. The message came on the radio: 'The hurricane has stopped. We do not know what direction it will take, but we do know that it is getting even stronger'. It hit the next day. Luckily for those of us who were in English Harbour on the island's southern side, the hurricane passed along the northern side of Antigua, where it destroyed everything in its way. Fortunately we experienced only small storm winds and did not suffer any great damage.

AN UNLIKELY EPISODE

One day in the Grenadines, with friends from Stockholm on board, we anchored *Jennifer* in a bay and took the dinghy out to a place where we were planning to dive on an old World War I wreck. We anchored the dinghy and started the dive. When I returned to the surface, I noticed that the dinghy had started to move away from us at a rapid pace. My first thought was that someone was trying to steal the dinghy by swimming away with it – or that a shark had grabbed hold of it and started to drag it away. It didn't seem possible.

There were eight of us in the water, and none of us could understand what was going on. Some of my friends started to get scared and thought that we were going to drown without the dinghy to take us back to *Jennifer*. Five of us had been scuba diving and were pretty heavy with all the gear, while three of the others had been snorkelling. Two of my friends went after the dinghy and finally managed to get aboard. Next, a wild struggle began. Eventually the pair came back with the dinghy and the truth was revealed. A giant sea turtle had become stuck in the anchor rope, had panicked and had tried to swim away as fast as it could. The wild struggle that we had witnessed from a distance had been to get the rope loose from one of the turtle's fins. In the evening we laughed about our adventure. Our only problem was – would anyone believe our story?

THE BUDGET – $650,000 PLUS OR MINUS A ZERO

Jennifer was a business – here is an overview of the income from the chartering and paying crews, against the costs of maintenance and marketing. Boat maintenance was one of the highest costs, at $1,500 per month, but there were some good results too, mostly from tips, totalling $15,000.

INCOME AND EXPENSES

TOTAL INCOME

The total income over the ten years came to $650,000, and our best year of chartering was in 1993 with an income of $90,000. Additional income came mostly from tips, but also from diving and sales of T-shirts, which yielded $15,000.

OPERATING COSTS

Food was the biggest single expense and amounted to $80,000 over the ten years. The agent's commission amounted to almost as much. Since the agents actually charged about a 20 per cent commission, I can conclude that I booked about half of the charters myself and the agents booked the other half. Fuel and various expenses amounted to $15,000 each. The total operating costs amounted to almost 30 per cent of the income.

FIXED AND UNEXPECTED COSTS

The biggest surprise for me was the maintenance cost. I would never have guessed that it was going to be so expensive to maintain *Jennifer*. Maintenance cost $185,000 over the ten years, giving an average of $1,500 per month. The salaries of the hired chef, and my close friends Ylva and Johanna during charters, amounted to almost $30,000. Of the remaining costs, insurance was $28,000, marketing cost $26,000 and represented the cost of the production of brochures in four different editions, plus postage, newsletters and so on. Communications cost $28,000, which covered the mobile phone in the Caribbean and satellite telex/fax/e-mail. Unexpected costs of $78,000 included $20,000 for a diving accident in Tahiti, $6,000 for a power line accident in Kenya, $10,000 for rudder damage in the Atlantic, and a stolen dinghy, which cost $5,000 to replace. Altogether, the fixed costs were almost $375,000, and including the unexpected costs amounted to almost 58 per cent of the total income.

THE BOTTOM LINE

After ten years, the bottom line was a profit of $85,000 or a profit margin of about 13 per cent. Out of that money, I paid the interest and mortgage payments on the $45,000 loan for the initial extra equipment, as well as my own living costs and pocket money of almost $3,000 per year. No write-offs were made. The boat had been paid for in cash, $260,000 up front. The rest of the money had been reinvested into the boat. When I finally came back to Stockholm after ten years of sailing, some $650,000 had passed through my hands. Financially, it was dead even – no money in my pocket and no debt either. But I had a sailing boat that was completely paid for and thousands of great memories.

PLANNING – THE ROUTE, THE DISTANCES AND THE HURRICANES

These are the various factors you need to take into account when planning a circumnavigation – how long it takes, the distances involved, the various hurricane seasons you need to be aware of and the rules for visas and passports.

THE TIME INVOLVED

Until recently the journey in Jules Verne's novel *Around the World in 80 Days* was impossible to duplicate with a sailboat. But in 2006 giant catamarans succeeded in doing it non-stop in 50 days. The Whitbread/Volvo Ocean Race boats do it in nine months, with several stops along the way. These times are of course not possible for the typical long-distance sailor. Organized circumnavigations, started by Jimmy Cornell's sailing rallies, normally last 17 months.

Assuming that you will want to see and experience things around at least some of the places that you pass, realistically 17 months is the shortest time scale to plan for. The shortest distance around the world, going through both the Panama and Suez canals, is still 28,000nm. With a 30ft (9m) boat, you can count on an average distance of 100nm per day. This translates into 280 days, or ten months, if you sail non-stop. Normally though, the purpose of circumnavigating is to experience the Tropics and see different parts of the world, so a voyage without stopping at all does not appeal to many people.

A 'normal' circumnavigation takes three years. You might start in Northern Europe in the summer or autumn, reach the Canary Islands in November, undertake the Atlantic crossing in November and/or December and celebrate your first Christmas in the Caribbean. Alternatively, you can start from the

East Coast of the US in the autumn and get to the Caribbean before Christmas. You then go through the Panama Canal in February or March and reach New Zealand by December, where you celebrate your second Christmas. You stay in New Zealand during the hurricane season (from December to April) in the South Pacific. You celebrate your third Christmas either in Phuket in Thailand, or Cape Town in South Africa, depending on whether you choose the Suez Canal or the Cape of Good Hope. During the summer of the third year, you can be back in northern Europe or on the US East Coast again.

DISTANCES

World Cruising Routes by Jimmy Cornell (6th edition, 2008), Imray's Cruising Guides, and *Landfalls of Paradise* by Earl R Hinz (5th edition, 2006) are excellent books to help you plan your circumnavigation. Here are some of the most important distances to consider:

- A trans-Atlantic crossing from the Canary Islands to the Caribbean is 2,700nm and takes 3–4 weeks depending on the size of the boat.
- The Caribbean to Panama is 1,100nm and takes approximately 2 weeks.
- The Pacific crossing, from Panama to Tahiti, is 5,500nm and can take 2–3 months including several pleasant stops along the way.
- Tahiti to Fiji is 1,900nm, and takes about 2–3 weeks, with stops in the Cook Islands and Nuie.
- Fiji to New Zealand is 900nm and takes a good week.
- New Zealand to Australia is 1,300nm and takes nearly 2 weeks.
- The southern route across the Indian Ocean, from Darwin to Durban, is 5,800nm with stops on the islands of Christmas, Cocos Keeling and Mauritius. It can take several weeks depending on stops.
- The northern route across the Indian Ocean, Phuket to Sri Lanka, is 1,400nm and takes about 10–12 days.
- Sri Lanka to the Red Sea is 2,200nm and takes 2–3 weeks.
- Cape Town to Salvador in Brazil, with a stop at St Helena in the South Atlantic, is 3,600nm and takes 4–5 weeks.
- Brazil to the Caribbean is 3,000nm with many stops along the way in Brazil. It can take 1–2 months.
- The home stretch, from the Caribbean to northern Europe, is up to 5,000nm, with stops on Bermuda and the Azores, and takes 6–7 weeks.

HURRICANE SEASONS

The single most important factor that determines your routes and timescales are the seasons for the tropical storms (hurricanes, cyclones and typhoons). They can be devastating and every sensible sailor should avoid being in the wrong place at the wrong time. The hurricane season in the Caribbean and the Pacific Ocean near the coast of Central America runs from June to November. In the South Pacific, the hurricane seasons are the opposite, from December to March. Because of this, long-distance sailors should plan to reach New Zealand before December. North of the Equator in the western part of the Pacific Ocean, towards the Philippines, the hurricane season lasts from June to December. There are also two big hurricane seasons in the Indian Ocean, one in the northern ocean from May to November, and one in the southern ocean from December to April. With this in mind, it is important for sailors who want to sail from Darwin to Durban to reach South Africa before the end of November.

Other than hurricane seasons, your itinerary is also influenced by the winds. The Trade winds go relatively consistently from east to west: south-east just below the Equator, and north-east just above the Equator. In the northern Indian Ocean, the monsoons also influence the best time to sail. The north-eastern monsoon occurs between November to March; January to February is usually the best time to sail from Phuket to Sri Lanka and on to Africa. The south-east monsoon season occurs between June to September.

VISAS

The different rules for visas mean you need to do some forward planning and research before arriving in some countries. The USA, Australia, Indonesia, New Guinea and Venezuela (among others) may all require you to have a visa before you arrive. Some other countries will give you a visa when you arrive and others require no visa at all.

CLEARING ROUTINES – THE YELLOW 'Q-FLAG'

It is useful to know what happens when taking a boat to a new country: what harbours to choose, the meaning of the yellow Q-flag, how to clear in and out, what to do if you are carrying weapons, what clothing to wear, the costs – and a reminder that you should never argue with a customs or an immigration officer.

CLEARING IN AND OUT

PORTS OF CALL

When you sail into a new country, you cannot simply choose the harbour that is the most beautiful, the most convenient, or the closest. This applies whether or not it is an island nation, or a part of the mainland. You must make your first landing at a Port of Call, an official clearing-in harbour. This is because not all harbours or small islands have customs or immigration authorities.

Normally, on an island the capital city and the larger harbours are Ports of Call. It is illegal to arrive in a small harbour without having cleared in at the capital city or an approved Port of Call first. You risk being treated as an illegal immigrant, possibly being arrested and having your boat confiscated. If you try to get into a country illegally, you'll be suspected of smuggling drugs, weapons, or even worse, being a terrorist. Even if you are completely innocent, the police might take the whole boat apart, and even drill through the hull and the tanks. Everything can be searched without any compensation to the owner of the boat, even if they do not find anything. Once, when I was caught for chartering illegally in Tahiti after a diving accident, eight policemen boarded *Jennifer* and made a careful search. They even had two dogs with them, one searching for explosives and one for drugs. Of course they didn't find anything, and fortunately they didn't cause too much damage to the boat.

THE Q-FLAG

One of the dullest tasks for a long-distance sailor is to clear in and out of every new country. If you have been doing an ocean crossing it might be a novel experience – the customs and immigration officers are the first people you meet in the new country after several weeks at sea. If you are sailing around the Caribbean, you need to remember that nearly every island is a separate nation, and demands to be respected as an independent country. In some countries, you can't even go ashore until the customs and immigration officers have been on the boat. When you enter a new country you have to fly a yellow flag, the Q-flag (quarantine flag), below the starboard shroud. In the past this meant that you were asking for Free Pratique – the authorities had to come out to the ship and declare it healthy, ensuring there were no rats or plagues on board. Today you still have to fly the yellow flag, but you also have to call the harbour captain or customs officer through the VHF on channel 16. You then get instructions on whether you are to wait aboard for the customs officer, or go ashore to clear. In Micronesia we once had to wait two days before an officer came aboard. In most countries the captain goes ashore himself and clears the boat in. After that is done, the crew can also go ashore.

WEAPONS

Sailing with a weapon on board can help you defend the boat against attack from pirates. You don't usually need a special licence to buy or carry a defensive weapon on board a boat (except if your boat is registered in the UK where the firearms laws are very strict, and you will need a certificate). But if you are carrying weapons it takes much longer to clear in and out of a country. In most countries you have to leave the weapon with the authorities when you clear in, which means that you have to fill in new documents with the weapon's serial number and brand, the amount of ammunition you are carrying, and so on. The weapon will be stored with the authorities until you clear out. You normally have to inform the customs officers 24 hours before you clear out, when the weapon is stored elsewhere, for example the police headquarters, and has to be transported back to the harbour.

When you clear out everything is checked again to ensure that no ammunition has been stolen ashore. If you are unlucky, the person who is in charge of the weapons at the customs office might not be on duty the day you want to sail. An alternative is to keep the weapon aboard, but you need to have a proper safe with locks on it that can be sealed by the customs officers. When you clear out, the customs officer will check the seal is intact.

I took my shotgun with me all around the world and undertook all the formalities at different ports. When we arrived in Trinidad in 1997 I was so fed up with the process of clearing in and out that I didn't retrieve the shotgun when we left the island. Looking back, carrying a gun was probably just not worth all the effort. If our boat had been attacked by pirates, I wouldn't have dared to use it and, even if I had, I wouldn't have had enough time to get it ready.

PAPERWORK

The amount of official paperwork required for a vessel is huge. Owner's certificates and proof of registration always have to be shown when you visit a new country. Some countries require you to fill in four or five different documents, often duplicated several times, so a good tip is to always have carbon paper with you. To save time, you can prepare in advance by writing out the crew list by hand, or have it printed out ready. On the top of the page you write the name of the boat and its registered port, gross and net tonnage, where and when the boat was built, the colour of the hull and the model number. Next you list the names of all the crewmembers with the captain's name first and the rest in decreasing rank (ie the first mate as second on the list, and so on). The rest of the people on board are called 'crew'. If you call them passengers you are obviously sailing a charter, and will have to pay a charter fee.

For the entire crew, a great deal of information has to be given: name, date and place of birth, age, visa number (if applicable), passport number, nationality and when the passport expires. Even if you have prepared the list in advance on the boat, you might be unlucky if the list needs to be copied four times and you only did three copies. The clerk might even demand that all the information has to be re-written on the country's forms. If the clerk is agreeable, however, you might simply be able to staple your list together with their form.

The crew list is needed for both the customs and the immigration authorities. They are sometimes situated in the same building, but in some countries you have to take a bus or taxi to get to both offices. If the administration is old-fashioned, you will have to fill out separate papers for customs and immigration, even though they might all ask for similar information.

St Lucia in the Caribbean seems to have come the furthest in the rational handling of official papers. Both the authorities use similar forms that are copied four times. The customs official takes one copy, the immigration official takes two copies and the captain keeps one copy. By contrast St Vincent seems to be still living the paperwork Stone Age. The customs office has one form and the immigration office another, and both have to be filled in. The usual procedure is that you go to the customs officer first, and then to the immigration officer after you have cleared customs (except in the Virgin Islands where we discovered you need to visit the immigration officer first).

In addition to customs and immigration, you may have to visit other authorities – unless they come to see you first. In the bigger harbours you always have to see the harbourmaster and the health authority. In New Zealand and Australia, for example, the health authorities always come aboard and take away any fresh food you have left. They also take away your rubbish, which they burn. Because of this long-distance sailors don't buy more food than necessary when they visit Australia and New Zealand. In Indonesia, Vietnam, and Cuba the coastguard, navy and border police also want to check you out, and they often want to put a stamp on a document. In some countries you have to fill in a customs declaration for all articles of value aboard so the customs can see that you haven't sold something to the residents without paying the appropriate tax and duty fees.

CLEARING OUT

When you are leaving a country you have to clear out. In principle this means that you have to repeat all of the paperwork, ie the crew lists have to be re-presented. There might even be a new list if you have changed the crew. To take a person off a list can be complicated. It is usually only allowed if the crew in question has an aeroplane ticket back home as the authorities don't want to deal with people who can't pay their air fare back. The other alternative is to put a person on another boat. Then both captains and the individual go to the immigration authorities and sign the name over from one boat to another.

When you clear out you have to give the name of the next harbour. When everything is set you get your clearance and you have a stamped document that shows what boat it is, the captain's name, the number of crewmembers and where you are going to next. Without this document you can't clear into another country. Sadly, you can't be a Flying Dutchman and wander the seas without planning your route in advance. When you clear in, the clearance document is filed with the authorities so that Interpol, if necessary, can track where all the boats have been.

You may be able to sail around in the Caribbean without clearing in or out. The inspection system is faulty and has holes. The coastguard occasionally checks out the boats, and if you don't have your papers in order you will have to answer some tricky questions. On average, I have been checked out once a year in the Caribbean. As a last resort, if you haven't had time to clear out, when you clear in at your destination tell them you have been to St Bart's. It is well known by the customs clerks in the Caribbean that you never need to get clearance to leave from the authorities in St Bart's so long as you have paid the harbour fee.

CLOTHING

Most authorities in the countries you are travelling through want you to be properly dressed when you clear in or out – short sleeved T-shirts, ancient shorts and bare feet are simply not good enough. Often you need to wear trousers rather than shorts. My most extreme experience was in Majuro in the Marshall Islands. Here, not only did I have to be dressed in trousers and a shirt, but also a tie! The usual minimum requirement, however, is to wear a decent pair of shorts, a shirt with a collar or a respectable T-shirt, and shoes. There are so many sailors in the Caribbean that the clerks have learned that we do not mean to offend them with our casual clothing. Still, if they become irritated they might send the captain back with orders to get dressed properly.

THE COSTS

Sometimes it is free to clear in and out although most of the time you are charged a fee. If you arrive after 1600 hours or on a weekend there is almost always an overtime fee of around $15. You should therefore plan accordingly when you clear in or out. Usually you have 24 hours to leave the country after clearing out, so if you are sailing on a Saturday, clear out on Friday before 4pm to avoid the extra fee. Even if you plan to sail on Sunday, you might take the earlier opportunity to clear out on Friday.

On most islands in the Caribbean you have to pay a tourist tax of about $10–15 per person. On Grenada, you have to pay a navigation fee of roughly the same amount. Many countries require you to buy a cruising permit. In Anguilla in the Caribbean and Palau in Micronesia, the permits are very expensive, costing up to $100! If you are staying at a marina, it costs $25–80 per day, but if you are anchored off the cost might only be $10 per day.

If you are chartering, there are different regulations. In international waters (ie moving between two countries, where you pick up guests in one jurisdiction and drop them off in another), international laws mean that you do not have to pay charter fees. If, on the other hand, you are chartering within a country's territories (eg within the Virgin Islands), you need a special permit. Either you pay a fee for the whole season, which can be up to $2,000, or you pay per charter, approximately $250. If you are sailing with any paying guests or crew, there are decisions to be made. Friends or guests who are paying only low rates can be signed on as crew (not as passengers) to avoid paying charter fees. But remember, if it is a full charter and you don't pay the fees, in a worst-case scenario you could be arrested for chartering illegally. When sailing charters (ie with guests that pay full price), I pay the fee per charter unless I have a series of charters arranged in that area, in which case it is usually better to pay the seasonal fee.

NEVER ARGUE

Many sailors skip clearing in immediately, and instead anchor at an outlying island a night or two, collect mail from the post office or see friends on a neighbouring boat first. It is better to clear in as soon as possible – many times I have been 'caught' and reprimanded by officials about this. You should never, ever argue with a customs or immigration officer. Always be polite; smile and say sorry if you did anything wrong or if you misunderstood the forms or routines. Most of the clerks are correct, friendly and are there to advise you on what best to do. Even if the bureaucracy is inconvenient it is not their fault – they are only doing their job.

NAVIGATION – THE NEW ELECTRONICS

The GPS system has transformed the lives of most long-distance sailors. Here you will find out about modern electronics – charts, weather fax, radar, the satellite communication system Inmarsat, the latest Iridium system, the emergency locating system EPIRB, wind vanes and electronic autopilots.

GPS AND THE SEXTANT

When Joshua Slocum sailed alone around the world in the 1890s, he did not have many navigational aids to assist him. The sextant, chronometer, chart and leadline were the only pieces of equipment he had to rely on. For smaller boats, navigational aids did not change very much over the following 100 years. It was only in the middle of the 1980s that satellite navigation started to be used on smaller leisure boats, when both size and price had fallen sufficiently to make them a practical choice.

Early navigation systems were developed by the US Navy to give their nuclear submarines precise positioning when they fired their missiles. Satellites orbited the Earth, and depending on the position of the ships and the satellites, the ships received irregular signals, receiving positions every ten hours. In between these position fixes, the ships had to program their navigation systems with their speed and direction, performing a dead reckoning.

The Americans were not satisfied with the limitations of this process, and developed a better system, the Global Positioning System, or GPS. It is based on 24 satellites that are in geostationary orbit over the Earth (ie they are positioned on a fixed point above the Earth's surface) which between them cover the whole globe. The GPS gives signals every second, a huge improvement on the first satellite navigation system. The GPS system is accurate to within approximately 5m.

GPS can not only give the boat's exact position, but also the course, speed and distance to a waypoint (a set of co-ordinates programmed into the GPS that define a position). When you reach one waypoint in a series, most GPS units automatically switch over to the next one. When you steer the boat you can always see if you are positioned on the course line, and in some cases you can see how far from the course you are. Virtually every long-distance sailor today has at least two GPS units on board. The main unit is connected to the boat's 12-volt electrical system, while a portable unit with batteries is used to back it up. I have three stationary units and one portable unit. In 1990 the cheapest GPS unit cost $1,500! Today, the least expensive units can be bought for around $99.

GPS has proven revolutionary for sailors. Increasing numbers of sailors who previously didn't dare to sail the world now feel safer with the new navigational aids. Some long-distance sailors still carry a sextant, nautical almanac and charts aboard, but fewer and fewer actually use them. Today, many long-distance sailors have astronomical navigation programs built into their computers. The advantage is that the computer keeps track of time, dates, the sun's position, and makes all the calculations. You only have to measure the height of the sun yourself, which is a simple enough task compared to the complex calculations that were required years ago.

CHARTS AND CHART PLOTTERS

The limiting factor with navigation today is, strangely enough, the charts. With the precise position of GPS, you discover that islands are sometimes marked incorrectly (on both paper charts and electronic chart plotters), and are out of position by up to 2nm! Considering that James Cook and the older sailors originally made the old charts this is not so surprising. Of course, the charts are continuously updated, but the oceans cover a huge expanse and the job is expensive and time consuming. So if you are sailing among the low atolls in the southern sea, you have to be extremely observant, or have a radar system.

Charts are also expensive. British Admiralty charts cost $25–45, though local charts are less expensive. Although it is illegal (apart from American charts), most long-distance sailors copy the charts, by borrowing from each other and going to an architect's office with big photocopiers. If you don't want to buy a new chart, it costs less than $7 per chart to copy an existing chart, and some shops in developing countries actually specialize in copying charts. They have copies of the whole world and re-sell them for $10 per chart. Again, this is normally illegal and the charts can be dangerous if they are out of date. In the South Pacific, where there are few navigational obstacles or aids such as lighthouses, an old chart is not very dangerous, so long as the islands and atolls have been marked in the correct position. In busy, marked fairways, on the other hand, a copy of an old, out-of-date chart can be a death trap! A long-distance sailor should therefore not compromise too much, and instead research where and when new charts have most recently been re-issued.

Most of the international charts (ie the British and American issues) originally marked depths in feet and fathoms. Now most are changing to the metric system, and most likely being re-measured at the same time (ie islands are correctly positioned and line up with the GPS co-ordinates). In most big harbour towns there is an agent for the British or American charts. They normally have an excellent assortment of up-to-date charts and pilot guides from the whole world, as well as a large number of informative books on sailing around the world and long-distance sailing.

In recent years, digital charts have become more popular and prices are falling quickly. Digital charts are loaded onto a chart plotter or laptop, which display them on LCD screens. In most cases you can buy a CD containing charts for the whole world, but can choose to only pay for a certain area. When you enter a new area it is possible to buy the code for the new area and pay with a credit card online. Most long-distance sailors have a mix of new, original and copied paper charts. Only the richest and most technically inclined long-distance sailors have digital charts, but even then they have a paper chart as a backup.

WEATHER FORECASTING

WEATHERFAX

The weather is the biggest unknown factor for all sailors. Having a reliable method of receiving reports about the weather is therefore important. For many years, there have been special weatherfax receivers on short wave. They can only receive weather faxes and weather maps. In recent years it has been possible to buy a program for your laptop that combines with the SSB (Single-Side Band) receiver. This allows you to receive weather maps and reports. I have this on my computer and can monitor the weather maps daily. You can even choose different stations and compare the details. In the South Pacific, for example, you can choose between Australian, French and American weather stations. By taking in all three of the weather maps, each of which may have a slightly different forecast for the same area, you've got plenty of information to think about. As more and more sailors are equipped with laptops and some kind of either GSM (cellular) phone or satellite communication, it is

also possible to go on the internet and look at all the different weather sites. Also, many marinas have wireless internet, enabling sailors to surf the internet for both weather and all kinds of information for free.

GRIB FILES

GRIB (GRIdded Binary) is defined as 'a free mathematically concise data format used in meteorology to store historical and forecast weather data'. It is standardized by the World Meteorological Organizations's Commission for Basic Systems. Sailors can download a free program and send a request for GRIB by e-mail, satphone, cellphone or SSB. Within a minute a response arrives and the program opens up with world weather information for five days. This is a very popular way for cruising boats to keep track of weather.

RADAR

Sailors that have used a radar system for a long time often say that they wouldn't be without it. If you are sailing in northern waters, in fog, or in heavy traffic with countless beacons, a radar system is indispensable. In tropical waters, it is useful but not absolutely necessary. It can still be a great help, especially when you pass low atolls, adding a measure of security when sailing through the night.

When Johanna and I were alone, we always kept a radar watch during the nights. We set a radar alarm to 'ring' at a certain distance from the boat, maybe 2nm. If an object, such as a ship, broke the circle, the alarm would go off. To save energy you can set the radar to make a sweep every five minutes, rather than constantly. You can also use the radar to measure the distance to an object and compare it with the distance you have calculated by the GPS and chart. If the distances agree you can feel safer; if they don't you should check the date the chart was made. If it is based on surveys from the 19th century you can assume that the radar is correct. With radar you can also spot incoming bad weather on the screen, which is a great help at night.

COMMUNICATIONS SATELLITES

INMARSAT

The Inmarsat satellites are, in contrast to GPS satellites, communication satellites. Like GPS the four Inmarsat satellites are in geostationary orbits: two are located above the Atlantic Ocean and one is positioned above each of the Pacific and Indian Oceans. Inmarsat is co-owned by most telephone and communication operators around the world. There are many different types of unit: A, B, C, E, M and Mini M. A (which is analogue) is the biggest and oldest unit, and was designed for big ships. B is its digital successor, also meant for big ships. Inmarsat C was the first inexpensive unit aimed at leisure boats, and came on the market around 1990. Its antenna is not much bigger than a handball. Later Inmarsat models were called Fleet 33, 55 and 77 and are all digital. In 2008 the newest model was FleetBroadband 250, six times faster than Fleet 77 and a much smaller unit.

When I bought an Inmarsat C it cost approximately $7,000, but today it is half that price. The C unit is, in contrast to all other models, only a text system, ie not a phone. The C system can therefore only handle telex, faxes in one direction (ship-to-shore) and, nowadays, e-mails. All other units are digital units, meant for leisure boats, which can handle all kinds of communication, ie both phone and fax in both directions, and of course data traffic. This means that at any one time anywhere in the world a cruiser can surf the internet, send and receive e-mail and be reachable 24 hours a day while out at sea. While the different units very useful, they are expensive, and the cost per minute is expensive too.

IRIDIUM

The latest addition to the communication family is the Iridium system. This system, owned by the American company Motorola, went into bankruptcy but has re-emerged. It has more than 60 satellites that orbit at a lower height than the geostationary Inmarsat-satellites. The Iridium unit is slightly bigger than an ordinary mobile phone, and functions in a similar way. Instead of land-based relay stations like the GSM system, you communicate directly via satellites, anywhere on Earth. Thus you can get a phone and a number that will last your whole life wherever you are in the world. The Iridium units can also be connected to a computer, allowing access to not only phone systems, but also fax and e-mail even out on the open ocean, although at a very low speed. The price per unit is around $4,000 and the airtime costs are relatively expensive, at about $10 per minute. The advantage for the consumer is that Inmarsat now has a competitor, which should help to lower their prices too. Microsoft and other operators also have plans for similar systems.

EPIRBS

EPIRB stands for Emergency Position Indicating Rescue Beacon. It sends out an emergency signal to either aircrafts or satellites. There are two different models. The cheapest transmits only on the emergency frequency of rescue

and commercial aircraft (121.5 MHz) so this model is not recommended. If no aircraft pass the area from where the emergency signal is sent, the signal will not be detected. An emergency signal in the northern hemisphere will nearly always be detected, due to the frequent air traffic, while a signal in the South Pacific, where there are relatively few aircraft, is less likely to be detected.

A 406 MHz model, communicating with satellites, is definitely recommended. The cheapest 406 MHz EPIRBs cost about $1,000, although the most expensive satellite units with inbuilt GPS cost more. The advantage with inbuilt GPS is that the rescue station can find your co-ordinates faster. Without the GPS, the satellites use the so called 'Doppler effect' to determine your co-ordinates (which takes perhaps 20 minutes extra). All units are encoded with the boat and owner's name, so that the land-based monitoring stations can see who is sending the signal. On the Inmarsat C unit there is an emergency button that can send signals to an Inmarsat Satellite. Those units are also coded. Furthermore, if you have a GPS built in the Inmarsat C unit, the signal also gives the ship's location, speed and course, which can greatly assist the rescuer in their attempts to locate you. Inmarsat also has an E unit, which can only send emergency signals.

WIND VANES AND AUTOPILOTS

Long-distance sailboats are usually equipped with a wind vane that is attached to the stern. It is adjusted for a certain angle against the wind and, connected to a small rudder, can steer the whole boat. If the wind changes direction, the boat will follow a new course, maintaining the same angle against the wind. Wind vanes work surprisingly well in most winds, though when sailing downwind some units have difficulty holding a steady course. They cost between $3,000 and $6,000, but once installed they do not require any power. The disadvantage of wind vanes is that they don't work when it is dead calm. You have to steer by hand when you motor, unless you also have an autopilot.

In recent years, autopilots have become more and more popular. The bigger units are directly connected to the rudder quadrant, and the smaller ones are attached to the steering wheel or the tiller. The most common brand is Autohelm (today called Raymarine), which carries models in many sizes. Due to the excessive wear on autopilots, they often break, so most boats carry one or two back-up units. The cheapest autopilots cost about $1,000, and the most expensive ones about $10,000. The disadvantage of autopilots is the energy consumption. In bad weather, the autopilot might use five amps per hour, which will be 120 amps per day. During a trans-Atlantic crossing lasting four weeks, an electrical autopilot would use 3,600 amp-hours, which is a lot of power for one piece of equipment.

If there are only two people on board, it is important to think about the steering. It was impossible to have a permanent wind rudder on *Jennifer* because of the swimming platform in the stern, but I do have two autopilots, one that moves the steering wheel and one that is attached to the quadrant.

The best solution is to have both a wind vane and a good autopilot, preferably with a back-up unit. It is also possible to connect the autopilot to the GPS, so that when a waypoint is reached and a new course is taken, a signal goes to the autopilot and the course is updated automatically. One of the most advanced big yachts is the 164ft (50m) sailboat *Hyperion* owned by Jim Clark who, among other things, was one of the founders of Netscape. The whole ship is kind of a floating computer, and all the sails and systems are controlled electronically. Clark can even sit at home in the USA and sail his boat from his computer. Everything is connected: satellite navigation, radar, GPS, chart plotters, video cameras, sails, and so on – all of which can be controlled digitally.

ENERGY – SOLAR, WIND AND WATER POWER

One of the most important practical details of a long-distance voyage is the energy supply. Here we look at the battery bank's size and maintenance requirements, the fossil-fuel alternatives, the advantages and disadvantages associated with solar, wind and water power and compare the various costs.

BATTERIES

Every long-distance sailor puts some thought and effort into the energy supply. It is essential to have good, well-kept batteries, preferably in two banks – one for the motor and one for the boat. The usual arrangement is to have a single big 12-volt battery for the engine and two or more 12-volt batteries connected in parallel to supply the rest of the boat. You should be able to connect all the batteries in an emergency, but normally the banks should be separated to avoid accidentally draining the engine battery. Considering that you should not routinely use more than 50 per cent of the battery capacity, you can calculate a total capacity for your boat. If you need 200 amp-hours, the batteries should have a capacity of at least 400 amp-hours. *Jennifer* has had many batteries over the years. The present battery bank consists of four serial- and parallel-connected 6-volt golf cart batteries, each holding 120 amp-hours, which give a total of 480 amp-hours and 12 volts. The most important factor in maintenance of the batteries is to regularly check the liquid level. If any one of the battery's six cells gets destroyed, the whole battery is destroyed. The cables and terminals should always be clean and without rust. A quick inspection of the battery banks gives you a good picture of the state of the whole boat.

FOSSIL POWER

The next big challenge is to charge the batteries. The generator from the engine (modern engines have an alternator) is the most usual way for charging batteries. Many long-distance boats also have dedicated generators of 2–6kW, which are either stationary or portable. Bigger boats, especially charter boats, always have a stationary diesel-driven generator of up to 20kW each. The very big charter boats of 100ft (30m) or more, might even have two or three generators of up to 50kW – or even bigger.

Smaller boats that want to have access to 110 or 220 volts to more effectively charge the batteries have small, portable power generators that are run on gasoline. The generators are normally put up on deck, where they are run for an hour or two. Their noise, however, might cause irritation aboard the neighbouring boats in the bay where you have anchored. *Jennifer* has a fixed 5kW generator that is run by a belt from the main Perkins engine, so I only have one diesel engine on board.

SOURCES OF ALTERNATIVE ENERGY

SOLAR POWER

Probably the best power source for long-distance sailors is solar power. I have three big 50-watt solar panels built into a frame on a high pole in the stern. I can turn the panels 360° and aim them between zero and 90° to the sun. Every panel has an amp-meter, and each gives a maximum of 3.3 amp-hours, or a total maximum of 10 amp-hours.

In the tropics, where it is sunny for most of the time, the solar panels generate many amp-hours a day. To get the maximum effect you may have to turn the panels towards the sun several times during the day. If you have them in a set position, they will only give around 50 per cent of their capacity. Solar cells only require a minimum of upkeep and spares, because they do not have any moving parts. The initial price is fairly high at $500 to $1,000 per panel depending on the capacity. Today, you can find 100-watt panels that give 5–6 amp-hours.

WIND POWER

Many long-distance sailboats have a wind generator on board, and *Jennifer* had one for several years. It blew overboard during a storm in the Pacific and I decided not to replace it, buying a radar system instead. This is because there are many disadvantages to having a wind generator on board.

First of all it contains many moving parts and therefore needs maintenance. Second, a wind generator vibrates and makes a loud noise, especially in strong winds. Third, most of the units are supposed to shut themselves off in strong winds, and this doesn't always happen. In heavy weather, when you should be concentrating on reefing and steering, you have to lock the blades in place, which can be dangerous. If you get one of your hands caught in the blades, you can lose it. Finally, the wind generators rarely work when running with the wind. The relative wind speed becomes too low – the generator tends to constantly increase and decrease in speed and creates an irritating sound.

The wind generator is most useful when you are anchored. The wind comes from a steady direction, there are no waves to disturb the generator and you can generate a great deal of energy both day and night. A good wind generator gives between 5 and 15 amp-hours in the Trade winds, depending on how strong the wind is. If for example you are anchored in Tobago Cays in the Caribbean, where the wind blows consistently at a speed of 15 knots, you will get approximately 8 amp-hours of power. That totals 200 amp-hours every 24 hours, which is excellent (if you can live with the noise and vibrations). The price for a wind generator is typically anywhere between $1,000–2,000.

WATER POWER

If you can use water power when you are sailing, its efficiency is greater than either solar or wind power. The most usual way to harness water power is to use a towed generator. This is a generator with propellers that are driven by the flow of the water, towed with a 20m cable. Even overlooking the problems associated with bringing it in and laying it out, seaweed and ropes can easily get stuck in its propellers. Today there are models that can be used as both water and wind generators, but they require some work to switch them between their mounting places.

Another way to harness water power is to attach a generator to the propeller shaft and let the shaft spin freely while sailing. The disadvantages are the sound and vibrations created (and the fact that the engine might not take a full day of a spinning shaft very well). The best alternative is to have a permanent water generator on the stern. Resembling an outboard motor on a dinghy, the generator can easily be folded up and down and doesn't require any cables or complicated work to deploy. With normal sailing speeds of around five knots, the generator will yield four to eight amp-hours. The price of a water generator is around $1,500–2,500.

COMPARISON

When you are considering how you should invest quite a large sum of money in renewable energy sources, you need to consider the following factors: where you are going to be sailing, how strong and reliable the wind will be, whether you are going to spend a lot of time at anchor and how many hours a day the sun will shine. I think that solar and wind power give you a similar amount of energy for the amount of money you put in, but solar power is best when you consider how easy it is to maintain. Water power only works if you are sailing, and long-distance cruisers are often anchored, perhaps 60–80 per cent of the total time. Therefore, the choice will really be between wind and solar power, with water power as an extra energy source. The traditional fossil fuel alternative is always an option; you just have to start the engine or the generator. However, to be spared the sounds of the engine and the smell of gas or diesel is something every long-distance sailor longs for.

If I built a new boat today, I would put ten solar panels in a row on a high mount on the stern or on top of the Bimini. They could give out 50–200 amp-hours on an average day. I would also install a built-in water generator for use when sailing. With that amount of energy, you could supply the energy demands for the whole boat: lights, instruments and refrigeration. It would be a pity to waste any extra energy that the solar panels would generate. When the batteries are fully charged, you could even run a 12-volt desalinator (water maker). It would not produce as much fresh water as a 220-volt unit (which produces 50–150 litres in an hour), but would still provide approximately 10 litres per hour, using 5–7 amperes per hour.

PART II
THE VOYAGE

THE CARIBBEAN – MY ADVENTURE STARTS

I have made the decision to circumnavigate the world, and in the autumn of 1992 we sail from Mallorca to Gibraltar and the Canary Islands, and then across the Atlantic to the Caribbean. After visiting some of the Caribbean islands, we sail via Venezuela to the San Blas Islands. Finally, we pass through the Panama Canal.

DEBT FREE THROUGH THE PANAMA CANAL?

When I first sailed *Jennifer* in 1988, I planned to sail charters for 3–4 years to get used to the boat, get to know the Caribbean and pay off my debt. After that, I planned to start my circumnavigation. I had promised myself not to go through the Panama Canal with any outstanding debts. The Panama Canal divides the Caribbean Sea and the Pacific Ocean. As long as you are on the Caribbean side, you can always sail back back to your base there. Furthermore, there are better means of communication with the rest of the world in the Caribbean and it is easier to organize spare parts.

Once you pass through the canal, everything changes. It is almost impossible to sail against the Trade winds, and the only real alternative is to keep on sailing around the world. You can sail north towards Hawaii and on to California and from there south to Panama again, but it is a long distance to cover. Those who abandon their circumnavigation for various reasons often choose to sell their boat in New Zealand and then fly home.

By the summer of 1992, we were in the Mediterranean, and my debt was still not paid off. Still, I had two charters booked in the Caribbean over Christmas and the New Year, so I decided to start the voyage around the world that autumn. While the charter industry is well organized – with established agents, charter shows and a well-defined market – the paying-crew concept was relatively new and untried. There are very few boats that make a living doing this sort of business, even though many long-distance sailors pick up hitchhikers in harbours as they pass through. My decision to sail around the world with paying crew was a risky concept. Very few sailors had done it before. To go through an agent and try to convince the paying public to come aboard an unfamiliar boat on a sail around the world, far away from home, was a bold venture.

In the Caribbean for Christmas in 1992, I could have paid off the whole loan, but decided instead to buy a satellite communications unit. To be able to finance my circumnavigation by taking on paying crew, I decided that I needed to have reliable lines of communication with my agents.

The end result was that, against my better judgment, I went through the Panama Canal with debts of $7,000. Now the real adventure had begun – in more ways than one.

THE FIRST CROSSING OF THE ATLANTIC

We started our voyage around the world after charter sailing in Mallorca, Corsica, Sardinia, Malta, Greece and Turkey during the summer of 1992. We departed from Mallorca in October. The crew was made up of six people, including Ylva, who had been on the boat since 1991. She was my girlfriend and was also the on-board chef when we had charters. There was also Bo and Jan, who were both unemployed and came through a yacht charter agent in Gothenburg. David, a lawyer from Chicago, came through an agent in California and Alexia, a student from the dark forests in Sweden, had signed up through an adventure travel company in Stockholm. Alexia was 18 years old, had never been sailing before and wanted to try something different. She had contacted the travel company, received our brochure and decided to sail across the Atlantic.

The first leg was to Gibraltar, a distance of 450nm. On the way we passed the Greenwich (or International) Meridian. Later on, in the South Pacific, we would eventually pass its counterpart, the International Dateline. We struggled on through four days of tacking in hard gale conditions. Most of the crew were seasick, including Alexia. I was absolutely sure that she would quit in Gibraltar after this eye-opening experience. However, when we reached Gibraltar, everything was forgotten and she was happy just to have managed the ordeal. After this long passage she finally developed sea legs and from here on everything could only get better.

Gibraltar, affectionately known by English people as 'the Rock', is a small area with a town but it is also a British military base, well known for its resident monkeys. Legend says that as long as the monkeys are still on the Rock, Gibraltar will remain an English colony. Spain, irritated that England

wouldn't return the Rock, closed the border to Gibraltar for long periods during the 1970s and the 1980s, but has now accepted Gibraltar's status as a British territory.

The voyage from Gibraltar to the Canary Islands was 650nm and was a much easier passage with the wind from behind. It was so calm in some parts that we used the motor. We stopped in the marina in Puerto Rico on Gran Canaria for a week to prepare for the crossing of the Atlantic. At the same time, about 150 other sailing boats, most of them at the marina in Las Palmas, were also preparing for a cruise to the Caribbean. The yachts were taking part in the Atlantic Rally for Cruisers (ARC), which is a cruise in company with an emphasis on the social life, rather than racing. We could not take part, however, because the ARC participants were only aiming to reach the Caribbean just before Christmas, while we had to be in Antigua in the beginning of December for the annual charter show.

During the week on Gran Canaria Jan and Bo helped with the engine before they returned to Sweden to find work. Meanwhile Anders, a medical student from Stockholm, joined the crew. He was a friend of another crewmember who had sailed with *Jennifer* the year before. We also signed on a British couple, who had chosen to take an extended sailing holiday. The total number of crewmembers was now seven.

Finally, after shopping for groceries, topping up with water and fuel, purchasing spare parts, and distributing *Jennifer*'s new 'Around the World' brochure to the agents, we set sail for the West Indies in the beginning of November 1992.

The passage from the Canary Islands to Antigua is 2,700nm. The Trade winds took us there almost directly, even though they were fairly light. In the first week we caught an unusually large amount of fish; mostly dorado (gold mackerel) and tuna, perhaps the best tasting of the deep-sea fish. Every crewmember except the skipper had galley duty on a rolling schedule (approximately once a week) and when we caught fish the choice of dinner was easy. After seven catches the bait was gone, and with it went our luck with fishing. The weather was inconsistent; sometimes it was calm and pleasant, and at other times we hit tough, rainy weather with strong winds when we had to take the sails down.

We navigated with the sextant and 'swam' by hanging onto a long rope trailing behind the boat. I rebuilt the forepeak to be able to fit in a new sailcloth sewing machine and did an inventory of all the charts and spare parts. We had numerous discussions about sail area, and it was the only time during the circumnavigation that someone persuaded me to fly more sails than I thought was suitable.

David had been active in the Civil Rights movement in the USA during the 1960s as a top lawyer and had won many of his cases. But he was also a recovering alcoholic and had had a rough time. He had a lot of experience in racing yachts and seemed to expect to race across the Atlantic. We had long discussions where I explained that this was a long distance cruising voyage, where security and comfort were more important than speed. When we arrived in Antigua, David apologized and said that he understood what I was trying to do.

Halfway across the Atlantic, the main engine's alternator broke. This was the piece of equipment that charged the batteries and powered some of the electronic instruments. However, I could still charge the batteries with the main generator. A few days before we reached Antigua the Trade winds blew into a gale and the mainsail was torn apart. Finally, after 19 days of sailing, we limped into the historical English Harbour in Antigua in the middle of the night – tired, but satisfied to have reached the Caribbean as last.

THE WEST INDIES OR THE CARIBBEAN?

Was Columbus right – if you sail due west from Europe, will you reach Asia? When he went ashore, he was sure that he had reached the western part of India. Hence came the name of the islands; and he even called the people he met Indians. The Spaniards, who only wanted to find gold and spices, didn't find either on the small islands they came to first and kept on going. Eventually they moved on to the Greater Antilles: Cuba, Jamaica, Hispaniola and Puerto Rico and then the American mainland, which they took over and quickly colonized.

The smaller islands – the Lesser Antilles (usually called the West Indies or Caribbean), where today's sailors normally spend most of their time – were left for Britain, Germany, France, Holland and Denmark to share. Many of the islands have changed ownership several times – St Lucia has changed hands some 13 times! When they didn't find gold on the islands, the new colonists were nevertheless anxious to get the islands to give them something. Sugar, the white gold, was the single most important product that generated big amounts of money for the white plantation owners and the colonial government.

Britain and France fought many battles over the Caribbean, and during one of these Britain won Martinique and Guadeloupe, both big sugar producers. The rich English plantation owners on other islands were worried about the competition from the recently captured islands, and they succeeded in persuading parliament in London (partly with bribes) to trade them back

to France in exchange for Canada. France, defeated in war in the 1760s, agreed to abandon its territorial claims in Canada in return for British recognition of French control of Guadeloupe. Later the French regained control of Martinique.

Initially, the native Indians were used as slaves, but the plantation owners started to import black African slaves to get all the manpower they needed. Soon one of the biggest forced transfers of humanity in history was taking place and 10–14 million black Africans were shipped across the Atlantic under inhumane conditions.

After the Second World War the islands started to become independent as the descendants of the former slaves took over and inherited the islands. Today most of the islands are independent, but some have chosen to remain colonies. The French islands, for example, have (with help from massive subsidies) chosen to stay French.

The other remaining colonies belong to Britain and the Netherlands and are unsure about a future as independent nations. Britain, for example, tried to form one independent nation out of the islands of St Kitts, Nevis and Anguilla. With a population of just under 10,000, however, Anguilla refused to become independent and chose to remain a British colony. Denmark used to own half of the Virgin Islands, but sold its rights to the USA at the beginning of the First World War. Even Sweden traded business rights in Gothenburg for St Barts during the 18th century. When St Barts island became less lucrative it was returned to France.

The independent island states, each with a total population of about 100,000, are small units and often lack a sufficient local economy to be fully independent. Corruption and misrule are commonplace, especially in Antigua. This island nation has been notorious throughout history for its corruption and impudence. In addition to accusations of stealing most of the foreign-aid money when they built the international airport, the government has also reportedly been involved in money laundering, drug dealing and the illegal arms trade. The worst incidents occurred at the time of apartheid in South Africa, which then was under UN sanctions. Ironically, the black government in Antigua supplied the white regime in Pretoria with weapons to quell the rebellious people in South Africa. There was also another significant incident in 1990, which agitated both the American senate and the US Department of Justice. Antigua's government, led by the prime minister's son, supported smuggling Israeli weapons to the Medellin-cartel in Colombia – a group of drug smugglers that the USA was fighting against. The affair was a scandal in both Israel and Antigua, but Antigua's family government remained in power and is still ruling.

Beyond the history and politics, the Lesser Antilles, with its long arc of islands stretching about 600nm from the Virgin Islands in the north to Grenada in the south, is the paradise of sailing. The Virgin Islands, St Martin, St Barts, Antigua and the Grenadines archipelago between St Vincent and Grenada are some of the most popular areas for sailing, and *Jennifer* has chartered among these islands many times over the years.

THE ISLANDS OF THE CARIBBEAN

BEQUIA – THE WHALE-HUNTING ISLAND

After sailing charters over Christmas and the New Year in the Caribbean, we started the next voyage to Panama from the little island of Bequia in the Grenadines. Bequia is my favourite island in the Caribbean: small, friendly, unpretentious and with a modest number of bars and hotels. There are lovely beaches, good diving, few tourists and plenty of sailing boats. Over the years, we have spent a great deal of time there, in between charters. Lars and Margit Abrahamson, from Gothenburg, own the Friendship Bay Beach Hotel, the biggest hotel on the island. For many years Margit successfully ran a restaurant business in Gothenburg. At the beginning of the 1990s she decided it was time for new challenges and she and Lars ended up on Bequia. In his book *Don't Stop the Carnival*, published in the 1960s, American author Herman Wouk humorously describes the challenges faced by westerners running a hotel in the Caribbean. Lars' later comment was that the description in the book was 'perfect'.

Bequia has a long tradition of whale hunting, and many of the population are descended from the European whale-hunters of the 19th century. The International Whale Hunting Commission, which tries to regulate whale hunting over the world, has given Bequia permission to catch three whales per year (the first whale caught in four years was caught in 1997) under the condition that they use only traditional methods. This means using small rowing or sailing boats and hand-thrown harpoons. This is similar to the permission granted to the Inuit, or Eskimos of the Arctic. The traditional whaling profession used to be passed down from father to son, but it is now gradually disappearing. The last master harpooner, 70-year-old Olliviere, told us that when he harpooned a whale a couple of years ago, one of the men got caught in the harpoon rope. The angry whale dragged him and the boat underwater. Under the water, Olliviere managed to cut the rope and the boat and the man leaped up to the surface again.

Over the years, we saw many humpback whales in the Grenadines. On one occasion we heard a message on the VHF-radio that told us that a whale

had been caught. Along with nearly the entire population of Bequia, we went to the close-by island of Petit Nevis, where the whales were traditionally butchered. The whale was dragged halfway up the beach and the butchering took place in the water, which became red with blood. There was a big celebration on the island and the families with traditional whaling rights were given the meat, oil and blubber. They gave the meat to friends and sold some to the tourists too – it actually tasted very good. I was surprised that there were no sharks in the water, but the locals explained to me that there are now very few sharks in the area because of over-fishing.

After Bequia we made a short stop in Tobago Cays in the Grenadines. Tobago Cays is made up of four uninhabited islands with white beaches surrounded by big horseshoe-shaped reefs. It is one of the most popular anchorages in the Caribbean with excellent snorkelling and diving. At any given time there can be up to 70–80 boats in Tobago Cays. We spent a lot of time among these deserted islands during the years of charter business.

GRENADA INVADED

Our next stop was Grenada, 40nm south, also called the Spice Island. In 1983, Grenada was in the limelight when US President Ronald Reagan decided to invade it in response to a coup d'état. We stayed for two days while we organized our Venezuelan visas, and explored the green, fertile hills and rainforests, its waterfalls and spice factories.

Grenada gained its independence from Britain in 1974, and was led by its first prime minister, Sir Eric Gairy. Five years later, in 1979, the socialist Maurice Bishop carried off a bloodless coup d'état. He admired Fidel Castro and wanted to turn Grenada into a copy of Marxist-controlled Cuba. Whilst Bishop held power, the health and education system improved but at the price of freedom. Freedom of the press was forbidden and political opponents were imprisoned. However, there was a left wing faction within the socialist party led by Bernard Coard and his wife. With help from the army, they succeeded in putting Bishop under house arrest, although a demonstration in the capital led to his being freed. The Coard faction then asked for support from the garrison in the picturesque town of St George and succeeded in cold-bloodedly executing Bishop, half the government and many civilians. General Hudson Austin's military government then took power.

Together with Grenada's neighbouring states, the USA then decided to take action. Normally this would be a task for the US Marines, which has its own navy, army and air force but the action required the combined strength of the armed Special Forces. What was supposed to be merely show of strength turned into a proper war. One reason for the invasion was that the Cubans had built a large international airport on the island, and the assumption was that the airport was going to be used as a Soviet-Cuban airbase to fly Cuban troops against the USA. When the Americans invaded, they encountered unexpectedly heavy ground resistance from Cuban soldiers, the small Grenadan army and the labourers who were building the airport.

In two days, however, the invading US naval and air superiority quelled the ground resistance. After the invasion, the airport continued to grow, but this time it was with the help of the USA and it helped tourism develop on the island. When boats sail into the harbour of St George, visitors can see a prison on the mountaintop above the city. Here, Bernard Coard and his wife are imprisoned for life. I have never met a single person that felt pity for them.

TOWARDS SOUTH AMERICA

THE CARIBBEAN CROSSING

The crew on the next voyage included Ylva and myself; Barbara, an American publisher who had already chartered *Jennifer* twice (and came back again to Tahiti); Jeff, a financial consultant from the USA, whose parents had chartered *Jennifer* in Turkey during the summer of 1992; Ulrica, a dentist, pilot and diving instructor from Helsingborg who had already worked as a chef on a charter boat in the West Indies, and wanted to sail to Tahiti and Claes; and a friend of mine from Stockholm who runs a factory for boat equipment and was in need of a long vacation. We had many enjoyable musical evenings when Jeff and Claes played the instruments Claes had brought along with him.

Our first night of sailing after Grenada was a passage of 24 hours and 150nm to the Venezuelan island of Margarita. Margarita is best known as a holiday island for rich and famous Venezuelans and it also has a very good harbour for cruising sailors. Here we filled our tanks with diesel for only ten cents per litre; it felt like we were being paid to take their fuel!

The Islas Los Rochas was the most popular of our stops in Venezuela. The Los Rochas is made up of a number of islands within a large reef. There is beautiful light green and blue water in the lagoon and only a few sailing boats.

Some 105nm further west lie the Dutch Antilles, composed of the ABC islands of Aruba, Bonaire and Curacao. Bonaire is the most beautiful island and is mostly known for spectacular diving. The water around the island is an underwater national park. To protect the coral it is forbidden to anchor around Bonaire. Instead, mooring buoys are in place for use by visiting sailing

boats and professional divers. Here we experienced our first real taste of diving nirvana.

Barbara left us in Bonaire, and Chuck, an American oil worker who worked five weeks on and five weeks off, signed on in her place. Chuck wanted to try out life on board a boat, with the idea that one day in the future he would buy a boat and sail it himself. After a short stop in Aruba we began sailing 550nm to the San Blas Islands outside of Panama. We had perfect winds for four days, with 14–26 knots blowing from behind. We sailed without the mainsail but with two sails attached to the forestay, sailing 'wing on wing'. During the passage, both Ylva and I were sick with fever and Claes was hit on the head by the jib. We were also on the lookout for pirates off the coast of Colombia, although fortunately we didn't spot a single ship.

We spent several lovely days on the very beautiful San Blas Islands. About 50 of the 350 islands are inhabited by Kuna Indians while the rest are uninhabited. The Kuna Indians are the last descendants of the full-blooded Indians who lived in the Caribbean before Columbus arrived. The reason they still inhabit these islands is that they did not own any gold, so the Spaniards left them alone. The Kuna Indians are known for their molas, a type of appliqué woven by the women and made up of material composed of several layers and colours. I bought 25 of them that I later had sewed into a bedspread.

The Kuna Indians still live quite traditionally. The biggest problem today is how to adapt to the western consumer-driven society. Probably the greatest change from a traditional to a modern lifestyle has been brought about through the use of electricity. Portable diesel generators can create electricity, but this involves a cost to buy fuel and electrical equipment. At the same time, electricity opens a window to the rest of the world through television, and television often incites a need to consume where none has existed. Young people begin to find their way to the cities in search of a 'better' life – which normally means mopeds, cars, computers, nightclubs – and the traditional social structure starts to fall apart. Electricity will probably be accepted on some islands, but some islands will, as long as they can withstand the pressure, protect the traditional lifestyle.

THE PANAMA CANAL

THE US STEALS THE PANAMA CANAL

One of the greatest construction projects in modern times was the Panama Canal. In the middle of the 19th century, the Suez Canal was built. This was very important because it meant that the European colonists' ships no longer had to sail around Africa to reach Asia. In the same way, if a canal existed across Central America it would make it easier for the commerce and shipping nations to go from the Atlantic to the Pacific Ocean, without sailing all the way around the tip of South America.

Under French leadership, Ferdinand de Lesseps, a former hero in his own country, tried to build a canal over Panama at sea level in the 1880s. Unfortunately there is a difference of several metres in sea levels between the Atlantic and the Pacific, but nobody realized this at this time. The technical difficulties were overwhelming and the project ended in bribery and bankruptcy. A financial fiasco ensued with Lesseps and many others prosecuted and found guilty of corruption.

The USA became seriously interested in the canal project at the beginning of the 20th century. Among other things, it wanted fast transportation of its war ships between the east and west coasts. The Americans were not united on where the canal would go, either through Panama or Nicaragua, but in the end they decided to continue the work that the Frenchmen had started, but now with locks. In his book *The Path Between the Seas – The Creation of the Panama Canal*, the American author David McCullough tells the fascinating story of the construction of the canal.

At that time Panama was a province of Colombia, who placed strict demands on the construction of the canal through its territory. The American president Theodore Roosevelt, having failed to reach an agreement with Colombia, effectively stole part of the Panama province by encouraging a political coup. The coup leaders declared Panama independent, and at the same time granted the area along the planned location of the canal to the USA. To protect the new republic from Colombian troops, the USA deployed naval warships on each side of Panama. After this, the big project to complete the canal began. The biggest problem was malaria and yellow fever, which took thousands of lives. Eventually, the US Army's physicians succeed in solving the problem with malaria, and Roosevelt could tell the army to finish building the canal. After huge costs, setbacks, nearly unsolvable technical problems and thousands of deaths, the Panama Canal finally opened in 1914. The USA built a whole city along the canal and permanently placed soldiers in the Canal Zone. In the end of the 1970s, president Carter decided that, in the year 2000, the Canal and the Canal Zone should be given back to Panama, when perhaps it really should have been given back to Colombia.

When Carter made his agreement with Panama in 1979, I was on board the three-masted schooner *Sofia* in Panama. The Panama National Guard, whose commander was Colonel Manuel Noriega, was celebrating the deal and acted as if they already owned the canal. One evening, they boarded many of the American ships that were at anchor on the Pacific side of the canal, including *Sofia* who flew an American flag. One of the boats was a luxurious yacht owned by President Carter's cousin. The National Guard approached the yacht, which was anchored next to *Sofia*, in a small boat without lights and without uniforms and demanded to come aboard. The Americans refused because they thought that it was pirates, and a gunfight started, causing a huge diplomatic confrontation. It ended badly for us too. Our whole crew, except for me and two others, was taken to the National Guard's headquarters, where they where questioned and had to stay overnight. I had injured my foot and showed them my visible wound, refusing to leave the boat. I still do not understand to this day why the soldiers accepted my excuse or how I even dared to be so cocky. The next day the other crew returned, tired and hungry but not handled roughly.

Later Noriega seized power in Panama and declared himself president. He was captured by American troops in the 1990s and is today in an American prison accused of drug smuggling. Today post-Noriega Panama is similar to pre-Noriega Panama. The pattern in the Third World always seems to be the same. The leaders and the ruling class have only two goals: to remain in power and enrich themselves. Of course they have good examples to follow – historically it is what the European Royal Houses had been doing in their countries for centuries.

THROUGH THE PANAMA CANAL

From the San Blas Islands, it was only 20 hours to sail to Colon on the west coast of Panama. This is one of the most dangerous cities on the entire South American continent. Crime is so high that yachtsmen don't dare to walk in town. If you have an errand to do, you take a taxi and let it wait for you outside a store or bank where they have armed guards and then take the taxi back to the marina. There is a well-fenced yacht club in Colon where visiting boats are safe.

All sailors have to visit the canal office in Colon to pay the fee to go through the Panama Canal. When we went through the canal in 1993, the fee was about $300–400 per boat, including compulsory pilot. The pilot joined us for the whole passage, which normally takes a full day, with locks at both ends. In between the locks the world's biggest artificial lake, Lake Gatùn, is situated where a rainforest once stood.

Although the canal was completed in 1914, there are still dead trees sticking up through the water beside the marked route. Every boat has to have four hands on board to handle the ropes. Because most of the boats have only two people on board, the boats help each other. The train from the Pacific coast back to the Caribbean side only takes 40 minutes, so many of the crews have travelled along the canal maybe two or even three times. In 2000, when the canal came under Panama's control the costs increased. The fee in 2009 for a boat up to 80ft (24m) is $500–$750. The Canal Company does not really wish to handle sailing boats, especially as it means a lot of work for them in comparison to the income. Smaller boats may be taken on a truck over the isthmus in the future. When we went through the canal to the Pacific side, we anchored outside of the Balboa Yacht Club, a pleasant old colonial building on the edge of Panama City. The Balboa Yacht Club was burned down a few years ago, leaving only the area of cement where the wooden building once stood.

THE SOUTH PACIFIC – THE DREAM OF PARADISE

We're in the Pacific now, and sail from Panama to the Cocos Islands, across the Equator to the Galápagos Islands and their famous tortoises, and then embark on our longest crossing to the mountainous Marquesas Islands in Polynesia. We explore the low Tuamotu atolls, sail to Tahiti and via Bora-Bora through the South Pacific to the Cook Islands and arrive in the Kingdom of Tonga. From Polynesia we arrive in Melanesia, on to New Caledonia, and eventually further on south through a storm to New Zealand.

THE SOUTH PACIFIC

SEAFARER'S DISCOVERIES

The distance across the Pacific from Panama to New Zealand is as far as 7,500nm while the distance across the Atlantic, from the Canary Islands to the West Indies, is only 2,800nm. The Pacific is bigger than the Atlantic, Indian and Arctic Oceans combined and covers a third of the Earth's surface. The Spaniard, Vasco Núñez de Balboa, was the first white man to see this wide ocean after a tough crossing of Panama by foot in 1513. The path that Balboa cut through the rainforest crosses nearly the same stretch as the canal today. Its direction was not east-west but more north-south. For this reason Balboa named the ocean south of Panama the South Sea, and the ocean north of Panama the Northern Sea. Only the name South Sea is still used today.

The Spanish seafarer Ferdinand Magellan was the first to cross the new ocean between 1519–21 during the first ever circumnavigation. After sailing against hard storms and toiling many weeks to round South America through the strait that today bears his name, he finally ended up in a smooth new ocean and gave it the name the Calm Ocean (the Pacific Ocean). It is hard for today's cruisers, equipped with charts, GPS-navigation, radar, e-mail and engines to understand the difficulties that the famous seafarer faced. Magellan didn't have a clue about the shape or the size of the Pacific – or if it was possible to sail around Australia – or if even Australia and New Zealand were attached to each other.

Captain James Cook found the answer to all these questions. His reputation was so impressive and his achievements so groundbreaking that even when Britain was at war with America, France and Spain, all these nations gave orders to their navies not to interrupt Cook on his scientific voyages. The big seafaring nations realized that his discoveries would be useful for them. All of them wanted to find the huge continent that, according to the scientists, must exist 'down there' to balance the big Eurasia continent on the northern hemisphere. The belief was that the nation who won this huge continent would control the world.

Today, the Pacific States include three of the world's biggest economies, USA, China and Japan, and are the most important economic area in the world. The Pacific region has surpassed the Atlantic region in terms of economic activity and businesses. The small Pacific nations that lie in the ocean between Japan and the USA are not at all rich or big. They are incredibly small – 22 independent states and colonies – with two million people on a land area smaller than Cuba (not including Hawaii and New Guinea). Maybe it is not so strange that in the 19th century the Western world felt free to annex these small states or in the 20th century to carry out nuclear testing: the USA on Bikini atoll, Britain on Christmas Island, and France on Mururoa atoll. Bearing in mind that only two million people live there and they do not even have the right to vote, a well-known American politician remarked 'who gives a damn?' The sad truth is that these small Pacific nations remain a part of the Third World, with corruption, high unemployment, poverty and sometimes plundering of their natural assets. It was this Pacific Ocean that we prepared to sail into from Panama.

THE PASSAGE FROM PANAMA

CRAZY WOLFGANG

We were fully booked, which means eight people aboard, but the number was soon seven, and later six. In addition to Ylva and myself there was Ulrica who had been sailing with us from Bequia; Ulrika's new boyfriend William, from Ireland; Lisa and Jan who were friends from Sweden; Terry from Canada and Wolfgang from Germany. The last two had contacted us through my agents. Lisa had her own boat and owned a fashion store in Stockholm where she told clothes to the rich and famous. She communicated with her employees during the trip with the help of the satellite fax. Jan was a civil engineer and well-known Swedish television chef who arranged dinners and parties at castles around Sweden. A big refrigerator company wanted him to take part in a commercial for a new refrigerator. Jan had refused, saying that the refrigerator was not environmentally friendly enough. Six months later the company got back to him with an improved version, and they also used the satellite fax to negotiate details for the new campaign. Terry was an experienced sailor and a professor at Edmonton University in Canada. She conducted research, including diving in tropical water for underwater algae, searching to find a cure for cancer.

Wolfgang was a strange person, with little social competence. He was pale, almost sickly, and ate only fresh food, rejecting anything from a jar. Wolfgang had never been on a boat before and his goal was to emigrate to the Marquesas Islands, in French Polynesia, although it was almost impossible to get permission to do this. He insisted that as a member of the EU he had the right to settle down on the Marquesas Islands, so I took him to the French Consul General in Panama City. The Consul confirmed what I had already said, but Wolfgang was still going to sail with us to the Marquesas Islands. I made sure I took a deposit from him to cover the airfare from Tahiti back to Germany. Ulrica's boyfriend couldn't join us because his mother was sick, a situation that naturally made Ulrica unhappy.

Jennifer had made seven crossings of the Atlantic, where each time we had provisioned for a five-week voyage, but now we had to provision for a three-month passage to Tahiti. Ylva, Ulrica and Terry had the important task of coming back with a truck full of food in the evening. For the first time since I bought *Jennifer*, I was worried about how we were going to store everything on the boat. Four hours later, everything was stowed, under the sofas in the saloon and in the forepeak. Our shopping trip cost $4,000 including: 150 rolls of toilet paper, 140 litres of milk, 120 litres of juice, 900 tea bags, 60kg of apples, 40kg of oranges, 40kg of potatoes, 20kg of onions, 45kg of flour, pasta en masse, 400 jars of food, lots of fresh vegetables and a big stock of bananas.

At the end of February we finally began our sail towards the Cocos Islands, and soon the problems began. The generator broke after two days. Without the generator, we couldn't run the desalinator or, even worse, the diving compressor. Now we couldn't dive in the South Pacific, at least not before Tahiti anyway. Everybody except Wolfgang had diving certificates and had been looking forward to the diving. At the same time, Wolfgang refused to do his night watches. He would not work at night and came up with a serious suggestion that we should anchor every night so the crew could sleep. I tried to explain that it was impossible to anchor because we did not have 10,000m of chain aboard. If he did not take his night watches then someone else had to do it and he would be on the boat as a charter guest and not 'paying crew'. Over the first 24 hours since coming onboard, Wolfgang had argued with everyone else and was also eating all our stores of fresh fruit and vegetables. For example he took a banana and rinsed it in fresh water (of which we had a limited quantity), peeled it and rinsed it again with more fresh water. Both Terry and Ulrica had long talks with Wolfgang, and silently wondered if he might have escaped from a mental hospital.

With those two incidents in mind, it was not hard to decide to return to Panama. Jan found the problem with the generator; a ballbearing had broken. We bought new bearings in Panama, and the generator was soon working fine again. Even after a long discussion with Wolfgang about the night watch, he still refused to do it so I asked him to leave the boat. Not until I started to carry his bags off the boat did he realize how serious I was about him leaving. After returning his deposit, we left him at the dock, to everyone's relief, and continued on our voyage to the South Pacific. Now, we had six crew members. That was the first and last time that I ever asked anyone to leave *Jennifer*.

TO THE GALÁPAGOS ISLANDS

HAMMERHEADS AND TURTLES

The passage from Panama to Cocos Island was 550nm, with a further 450nm to the Galápagos Islands. The trip went through the Doldrums, an area on both sides of the Equator with little or no wind. With only light winds, we were forced to motor. It became very hot in the middle of the day with the sun continuously beating down on us. We really began to appreciate having the Bimini (the sun cover over the whole cockpit). We started taking long swims every day. We caught so many fish that we even had to stop fishing for a couple of days.

Cocos Island belongs to Costa Rica, and must be one of the largest uninhabited islands in the world. In 1991, a marine park was established, and there is now a small park station. Its high mountain is covered by thick tropical vegetation, and fabulous treasures are supposed to be buried here from the pirate era. Until a couple of years ago, treasure hunting was permitted on the island, as long as any successful treasure hunters agreed to a 50/50 share with the government. We took a hike through the rainforest along a river to a waterfall, where we took a refreshing swim in the pool below the falls.

Today, Cocos Island is most known for its diving and hammerhead sharks.

Here we did one of our best dives ever. On the edge of the island there is a cliff, and here we dived off it into the crystal clear water below. At about 30m depth we started to see hammerhead sharks, and even further down at 40m we saw 50–100 hammerheads in big schools. Most of them didn't care about us, but some came to check us out. We also saw reef sharks, manta rays, lobsters and big shoals of other fish, which meant that there was plenty of food for the sharks. We were careful to not dive in the afternoon, which is when the sharks catch their food.

Early one morning in the beginning of March, we crossed the Equator for the first time – we would do it six times in total – and celebrated with hot chocolate, rum and a birthday cake for Ylva's 33rd birthday. Tradition says that when you cross the Equator for the first time, King Neptune and his court will baptize you. When I crossed the Equator for the first time aboard *Sofia* in 1979, several memorable things were done to us, one of which was being dipped in oil and rolled in feathers!

The Equator cuts through the Galápagos Islands and we had only a couple of hours before arriving at the main island of Santa Cruz. Here we were met by playful dolphins, and sea turtles floated carelessly in the water. Two pelicans landed on the boom and hitchhiked with us almost the whole way to the harbour at Santa Cruz. We also passed an island where sea-lions lay sunbathing.

We arrived in Galápagos without a permit, which is supposed to be mandatory. One of my agents informed me that it would be possible to obtain a permit for $1,000, which I clearly did not wish to do. Without the permit, boats are only allowed to stay for three days to make emergency repairs. To our surprise, the harbourmaster asked us how long we wanted to stay, and gave us the week I had been hoping for at a price of only $270. The reason for this gesture, we heard later, was that he pocketed the money himself. Although we were not allowed to sail between the islands on *Jennifer* – as all the excursions had to be done on expensive local charter boats – we sailed to a nearby island on one occasion.

On Galápagos, we dived with sea-lions and penguins, hired horses and rode up on the highest peak of the island and explored a kilometre-long lava tunnel in complete darkness. The animal and plant life is spectacular; the most fascinating being the giant land tortoises and lizards. The tortoises can weigh up to 250kg, live for 200 years but cannot defend themselves. Pirates and whale-hunters captured many thousands in earlier centuries, until they were almost made extinct. They were taken aboard and kept alive for several months by the crew as a source of fresh meat. In 1835 Charles Darwin also visited the Galápagos Islands with the ship *Beagle*, and observed the giant tortoises. Later, he published *The Origin of Species*, his theory about the evolution of species (see the chapter *Indonesia – Dragons and spices*). Through the building of a national park and the Charles Darwin Research Station, the tortoises became a protected species. At the research station we observed the birth and growth of the tortoises and how they were later set free. On the other side of the Earth, on the Aldebra atoll in the Seychelles, we later visited another island with huge tortoises. They had some 160,000 turtles, compared with only 4,500 on Galápagos.

Other than the animal and plant life, the Galápagos Islands were not quite what we had expected. There were approximately 20 charter boats in the harbour that took groups to the different islands. The little town, Puerto Ayora, is full of tourists, T-shirt stores, bars and restaurants. We even met two Swedes who had travelled to the island to pick up women.

It is not easy to find a balance between the generation of tourism income and the protection of the islands' sensitive ecosystem. Cruise ships with more than 500 tourists are now forbidden. According to the research station's boss, the station had almost no money, and the Ecuadorian government would not give them any finance from the 1993 budget. A couple of years after we had been there, a group of fishermen occupied the station to protest that they could not earn their livelihood without being disturbed. The whole thing was portrayed as if the local people could not live traditionally because of the tourists, and that the environmental interest of the rich world was a priority. The government gave in and approved their devastating fishing methods. The problem for western visitors, at least some of us, is that we wish for an untouched, exotic and non-commercial environment – one without any other tourists.

GALÁPAGOS TO THE MARQUESAS ISLANDS – THE LONGEST PASSAGE ON EARTH

The voyage from the Galápagos Islands to the Marquesas Islands is a distance of 3,000nm. It is the longest passage on a circumnavigation (ie without a stopping point). You sail south/south-west from the Equator and find the south-east Trade wind. Eventually the wind came from behind, and we ran with the wind (or at an angle from behind) on a beam reach. The weather in the Trade wind belt is usually warm and pleasant, with small pillow-like cumulus clouds that are occasionally interrupted by heavy wind and rain. For long periods the wind was dead calm.

How do you spend three or four weeks at sea? The most important thing is to complete the watches. Depending on the size of the crew, the watches

vary. After Terry signed off in Santa Cruz as planned we had five people left in the crew. This gave us two hours on and eight hours off with one daytime watch and one nighttime watch per person. The second most important thing is galley duty. The skipper is free from galley duty on *Jennifer*, which means that the crew has galley duty every fourth day. With Jan as a pro chef and the two charter chefs Ylva and Ulrica, the meals were always more than satisfactory.

On the westbound voyage we could observe the Big Dipper pointing to the North Pole in the sky to starboard, the Southern Cross pointing to the South Pole on the port side and Orion on the hemisphere's Equator directly over the boat during our night passages. It was also fascinating to watch the fluorescent plankton in the wake – it looked like a long neon tail trailing behind the boat. In the daytime we could see big surges that rolled in from a distant storm somewhere down in the Roaring Forties. They were 100m long but only 2–3m high and therefore hard to identify. Often dolphins came up to the boat, playing and jumping.

Most of the days we had contact via the SSB-radio with a big French catamaran who had left the Galápagos at the same time as we did. We listened to BBC and the Voice of America to keep up to date with the rest of the world, while the Swedish overseas program was difficult to get in this part of the South Pacific.

There was always something to fix aboard. In the middle of the Pacific, the gennaker broke in two. With a surface area of 140m^2 it took three days for Ylva and myself to repair it (I had to start by learning how to operate the heavy-duty sewing machine). *Jennifer* normally had a good handyman on board and on this voyage it was Jan. One day the stove broke, the next the sewing machine, followed by the outboard motor, the fishing equipment, the heads and so on.

Ylva made colourful jackets out of the sailcloth, which she hoped to be able to sell when she returned to Sweden for the summer vacation. Lisa made small necklaces out of leather and tin thread. One of the most popular pastimes on board was reading, and all the crewmembers read several books during any ocean crossing. We always had a long fishing line for trawling behind the boat. The biggest fish we caught was a 1.5m swordfish that weighed 25kg and supplied us with fresh food for four days. Sometimes even bigger fish like blue marlin made an attempt on the trawling line, with the risk that the line would break.

At sunset, when the temperature became a little cooler, the deck became a gym. Members of the crew occupied every available space, and everyone had their own program: yoga, meditation or regular gymnastics. After time in the gym, there was a line-up to take a salt-water shower on the stern platform before dinner. Every Saturday evening was treated as a special evening, and we dressed up in the best clothing we had. Finally, after three weeks at sea, we arrived in the Marquesas Islands – we had reached the legendary Polynesia.

POLYNESIA – THE MARQUESAS ISLANDS

The Marquesas Islands are volcanic, with wild and spectacular mountains, some more than 1,000m high. Since the islands are geologically relatively young, coral reefs have not yet begun to develop. The beaches are therefore not white, but black from the volcanoes. Our first harbour was Hiva Oa, where we cleared into French Polynesia. The island is famous partly because the French painter Paul Gauguin and the Belgian singer-songwriter Jacques Brel are both buried there. We visited their graves.

We also got three new crewmembers on the Marquesas Islands: Mary, Jamie and Dustin; all of whom had booked through an American agent. *Jennifer* now had a full crew of eight. Mary and Jamie were travelling around the world and had just been to Australia. Dustin was a certified nurse who worked with criminally insane patients and owned a 30ft (9m) sailing boat of his own.

We rented a jeep and drove across the island on the small roads to see the tall tikis (stone statues) hidden in the rainforest. Interestingly, similar statues have been found in South America.

On Hiva Oa Ulrica celebrated her 30th birthday. We invited the crews from all the other boats in the harbour to join in the party. There was an American couple in their 40s who were ski instructors from Colorado and were taking time off for a couple of years, two Canadians in their 20s in a very small 27ft (8m) boat, two Americans both around 25 years old on a slightly larger boat and two single-handed sailors in their 30s. Everybody had sailed either from Panama, Mexico or the USA and planned to sail around the world. New Zealand was the next safe place to stay for the hurricane season. We would meet up with these crews again in other harbours.

On most of the islands that we visited we took hikes in the mountains, hired horses and rode or walked in the incredibly green fertile valleys full of fruit: bananas, mangos, oranges, papayas, lemons, avocados and the main foods of Polynesia – coconuts and breadfruit. Captain Bligh sailed to Tahiti on the *Bounty* just to pick up breadfruit plants to bring to the West Indies as cheap food for the slaves. With plentiful fishing around the islands it seems impossible that the people of the Marquesas Islands would ever starve. Since

I had visited with the ship *Sofia* in 1980 the biggest difference I found was the huge number of jeeps on the island; everybody had one. The irony is that there are almost no roads. In the little village of Atuona on Hiva Oa, I counted up to 50 jeeps outside the church during a Sunday mass – and no one lives further than 15 minutes away!

THOR HEYERDAHL'S EXPERIMENTS

After Hiva Oa we sailed to Fatu Hiva, which is probably the most beautiful of the Marquesas Islands. Fatu Hiva became famous when Thor Heyerdahl spent a year on the island with his wife Liv. Thor was fed up with the modern civilization of the 1930s and wanted to escape back to nature. He chose the island of Fatu Hiva as his retreat. They spent only a year on the island and suffered sickness and food problems. They both returned home, a bit wiser, but still believing that modern civilization was wrong. Thor wrote a book, *Fatu Hiva*, about their life on the island.

When I visited the island in 1980 onboard *Sofia*, I had befriended two young girls who were seven or eight years old, and had photographed them. When I returned in 1993 I had all my photos with me, and the locals could easily identify the girls. One of them had gone on to become Miss Tahiti. I also visited another family that I had stayed with in 1980. The father, who was now dead, had helped Thor and Liv to build huts and shown them how to get food. There are two villages on the island. When I was there 1980 there was only a path between them and it took several hours to hike over the hills to the other village. Now, in 1993, there was a small road between the villages and quite a few jeeps on the island. I definitely preferred the old path.

THE TUAMOTU ISLAND ATOLLS

If there is anything on Earth that can be described as a paradise, it is an atoll. The Tuamotu Islands form a giant archipelago, with 76 atolls covering an incredible distance of 1,000nm. An atoll begins as a volcano on the bottom of the sea that grows big enough to form an island. Over thousands and thousands of years, coral polyps, each smaller than the head of a needle, build numerous 'limestone houses' or reefs around the island. After many thousands of years, the original volcano island has decomposed and collapsed into the sea, leaving only the surrounding coral reef with a lagoon in the middle where the island was before – the atoll. In French Polynesia, the Marquesas Islands are the youngest volcanic islands without reefs, Tahiti is a little older but with high mountains and surrounding reefs and the Tuamotu Islands are the oldest, consisting only of atolls.

The human inhabitants of the atolls lead a hard life. They live only on fishing and coconuts, but they are also very inventive. For example, they have learned to utilize the coconut palm in every way they can. The wood is perfect for building material, the leaves are used to weave roofs, baskets and rugs and the bark is used as fuel. But it is the coconut that is the secret to life on the atolls. When it is young and still green, it gives sweet, tasty and nutritious milk that can substitute both cows' milk and water. When it gets brown and ripe, the milk inside the shell turns into a white flesh that can be eaten and the liquid becomes a tasteless water. The last step is to remove the nut from the shell and dry it in the sun – it has now turned into copra (the dried kernel). In the refinery in Tahiti, copra is then turned into oil that is used to make margarine, soft soap and perfume.

The biggest event on the atolls is when the copra boats arrive. In the past they only picked up the copra sacks and the dried fish, and dropped off a colonial administrator or missionary. Today they carry food, fuel and other consumable goods and equipment: diesel generators, televisions, chainsaws and outboard motors.

We visited the atolls of Manihi, Ahe and Rangiroa. Most of the inhabitants on Manihi work on pearl farms, spread out around the lagoon. The most valuable pearl, the Mother of Pearl, is worth approximately $1,000. Ahe is one of the smaller atolls while Rangiora, the third biggest atoll in the world, is almost 60nm long.

It is difficult to see an atoll at night, particularly when it is only 2–3m high with trees on top, so yachts should always plan to arrive in daylight. The distance from the Marquesas Islands to the atolls is 500nm and can take 3–5 days. With that in mind, we started our journey in the evening, planning to arrive in the morning. We got stronger winds than expected, the sail broke again and we had to slow down in the last 24 hours because of the partly reefed genoa. Early one morning, we sailed into the narrow opening in the Manihi atoll. The tide was on its way out and a large amount of water from the lagoon was moving against us at a speed of 6 knots. Without a powerful engine we would not have been able to reach the lagoon and would have been forced to wait until the tide had turned. The water seemed to boil in the atoll opening, and it was a very nervous entrance.

The atoll entrances have the most interesting diving. At a depth of 10–20m you can float in (or out) of the atoll at a speed of 2–5 knots in a drift dive. The water in the opening is very nutritious and attracts many fish. There are also plenty of sharks that patrol the entrance (we saw up to 10–15 per dive). On the outside of the opening, where the depth is around 40m and the deep sea begins, you meet a wall of sharks and a huge shoal of barracudas that

are all waiting for something edible in the waters that are moving out of the atoll. It is not as dangerous as it sounds; the sharks are not interested in divers as long as they are not provoked. Nevertheless, your pulse races and you get a rush of adrenaline whenever a shark gets close.

The distance from Rangiroa to Tahiti is only 180nm. We arrived in Tahiti at the end of April, perhaps one of the most famous destinations in the world.

TAHITI – A PARADISE?

Why do westerners see Tahiti as a paradise? The island was first discovered by Europeans in 1767. Almost immediately it became famous around the world. The main reason for this was the pleasant climate, but another was that the men got a very warm welcome from the women. For them, sex was something totally natural, fun and enjoyable and when the sex-starved white seamen arrived, the women willingly offered to be their lovers. They even paddled out to the boats naked. It was one of the reasons for the mutiny on the *Bounty*. While the ship waited several months for the right season to dig up the breadfruit plants, the men got spoiled by the comfortable life full of enjoyment on land and only very reluctantly left Tahiti. The mutiny was probably inevitable and Captain Bligh's harshness was merely the straw that broke the camel's back.

After its discovery by the early explorers, many well-known authors and artists spent long periods in Polynesia, including Herman Melville, Robert Louis Stevenson, Jack London, Somerset Maugham, Paul Gauguin, Charles Nordhoff and James Hall (*Mutiny on the Bounty*). In modern times, James Michener and the Swede Bengt Danielsson (*Villervalle of the South Pacific*) are perhaps the most well known. They spread the myth about paradise to the westerners through their books and paintings, but except for the very first explorers, they all search for something that was lost a long time ago, the Original Paradise.

One of the first visitors to Tahiti was Melville. As a crewmember on a whale-hunting ship, he stayed on the Marquesas Islands. As the inhabitants were still cannibals he feared that they were giving him food to fatten him up so they could later eat him. But in his books he describes many things from the 'civilized' world that were missing on the island: no one in debt, no childless people, no orphans, no poor people, no lovesick women, no complaining bachelors, no discontented youths, no spoiled children and – the reason for much of this – no money.

Melville, Gauguin and London all criticized the missionaries and the colonial authorities. According to them it was a catastrophe when the white man arrived. When Cook first visited the Marquesas Islands in 1774 the population was around 50,000. A century later, the population was reduced to 2,000, decimated by sickness, murder, forced labour and slave hunting. And as if that were not enough, the missionaries forced the survivors to drastically change their lifestyle, with the result that many of them lost the will to live.

The Polynesia of today has adapted to the western culture of consumer goods (in contrast to the San Blas Indians), with jeeps, televisions, videos and even lawnmowers.

THE KON-TIKI RAFT

Polynesia is a big triangle in the Pacific, with the northern corner by Hawaii, the eastern corner by Easter Island and the southern corner by New Zealand. It is thought that the Polynesians originated from Asia, but Thor Heyerdahl believes that they might have come from South America. To prove his thesis, he sailed a crew (including the Swede Bengt Danielsson) from Peru to Polynesia on a raft called the *Kon-Tiki* and landed (or stranded) on the Raroia atoll in the Tuamotos archipelago in 1947.

After the *Kon-Tiki* voyage, Bengt and his wife Marie-Therèse settled down on Tahiti and wrote an excellent book, *Mururoa Mon Amour*, about France's testing of atomic weapons in Polynesia. His book was extremely critical of the French experiments. After its publication the French government informed the Swedish ministry for foreign affairs that Danielsson was no longer allowed to be the Swedish consul on Tahiti. But they could not deport him because he was married to a French woman. First in 1980 on *Sofia* and now in 1993 on *Jennifer* I visited Bengt and Marie-Therèse in their home in Tahiti. He was still active within both the anti-nuclear weapon and independence movements, and he told me about the tactics the French used to maintain control of Polynesia. At the same time he gave me a copy of his latest book, *Poisoned Reign: French Nuclear Colonialism in the Pacific*. By then Bengt was 70 years old but still alert and very active. One day, Marie-Therèse came down to the harbour with a pile of books that she wanted to send to Sweden. I thanked her but explained that I was going to be out sailing for several years and that the books might not get to their destination. Four years later on the South Atlantic in 1997 I heard on the radio that Bengt had died; the person who had been a very active and strong advocate for the people of the South Pacific was gone.

ATOMIC WEAPONS TESTING

The population of French Polynesia is only about 240,000. Tahiti, and its capital city of Papeete, is a small island that you can drive around in about

three hours in a jeep. Our first task in Papeete was to clear in. We had already cleared in at Hiva Oa, but this was only a preliminary clearance. Through the years Tahiti has seen many fortune hunters who have sailed in and wanted to stay, but without enough money to live on or to cover the airfare back home. In the 1970s the French made a rule that every sailor had to have a ticket to his or her home country or pay a deposit equal to the airfare. Since the rest of the crew was planning to fly home from Tahiti, I was the only one who had to pay the deposit.

There is one event in recent history that has changed Tahiti completely. When France was forced to give up her former colony and leave Algeria in 1962, they had to find another place to test their nuclear weapons. They chose the little Mururoa atoll in French Polynesia. A huge construction project began and people started to move in from the outer islands to work on the military sites. When the tests were eventually stopped the economy fell into crisis. Other than the tourist industry, the enormous military infrastructure was the biggest employer on the island. To compensate for the loss of jobs the people were promised an investment that would change the structure of the economy. But with a negative-balanced budget in France, and a corrupt government locally, France hesitated to give them more money. The whole colony is very expensive to administer. It was even suggested that Polynesians could be offered their freedom. However, my view is that France wished to maintain her honour at any price. The French look at themselves as a great power, with colonies and military bases around the whole world in an empire where the sun never sets: Martinique in the West Indies, Tahiti and New Caledonia in the South Pacific, Réunion and Mayotte in the Indian Ocean and French Guyana in the Atlantic.

BORA-BORA, HUAHINE AND TAHAA

THE SOCIETY ISLANDS

Much of our time was spent on islands 100nm to the north-west of Tahiti, Moorea and the Leeward Islands. These consisted of Bora-Bora, Raitea, Taha, Huahine and Maupiti. They are all green, hilly and incredibly beautiful, with surrounding barrier reefs and small passages into the blue/green lagoons. Moorea with its lovely Cook's Bay and Bora-Bora with its lagoon are two of the most beautiful and best-known islands. Jack Nicholson, Meryl Streep and many other famous actors have from time to time owned bungalows here. Marlon Brando even had his own atoll, Tetiarora, close to Tahiti, which he bought in the 1960s when he filmed *Mutiny on the Bounty*.

The best hotels are found on Bora-Bora and the Hotel Bora-Bora, close

Top The three-masted schooner *Sofia* was built in Sweden in 1921 as a Baltic Trader. She was the last floating hippy/co-op traditional sailing ship. I joined her for a year in 1979–80 in the South Seas. *Sofia* capsized and sank in the Pacific the year after I left her.

Left *Jennifer*'s first day at the Beneteau boatyard in France in April 1988. The mould is cleaned and sprayed with gelcoat, after which fibreglass is applied. After drying, the fibreglass hull is lifted out from the mould, which is then cleaned and prepared for the next hull.

Top My god-daughter Jennifer at six years old in 1989, between the wheels of *Jennifer*. I named the yacht after her.

Right *Jennifer* from the top of the mast. Note the bimini top over the cockpit, the footsteps on the mast, the two large deck mattresses, solar panels and diving platform.

Bottom A nice passage in the South Seas. The crew is bagging sunrays and reading. We are sailing wing-on-wing, two foresails on each pole and no mainsail. We're keeping fruit at the foot of the mast.

Top I've held aerobics classes with guests and crew on many beaches over the years. Here we're on the small islet of Mopion in the Grenadines, Caribbean.

Bottom *Jennifer*'s crew land on Mopion, for snorkelling and diving.

Top *Jennifer* sailing in the tradewinds wing-on-wing with genoa and gennaker.

Bottom By an old aeroplane from World War II on Butaritari atoll, Kiribati, Micronesia.

Top Another wreck from the war, also on Butaritari. We encountered numerous aircraft, guns and tanks during our stay in Micronesia, reminders of the brutal fighting between the American and Japanese forces.

Bottom Pulawat lagoon in Micronesia, seen from *Jennifer*'s mast. Only one other boat visited during the weeks we stayed there. Paradise on earth!

Top Me and Johanna among the locals on the small Pulawat atoll. The women here are bare breasted, the men wear loincloths, the canoes are built by hand and the last of the old master navigators are still alive.

Bottom Canoe houses on Pulawat atoll. These buildings not only housed the canoes; they were also the 'pub', and women were barred from entering.

Top A turtle party on Pulawat. Turtles are the inhabitants' most important source of protein after fish. They are caught and turned upside down, and can live like this for several weeks. We pitied them and put coconuts under their heads. The islanders thought we were nuts.

Bottom The Pulawat men have an easy existence. Here they are building a canoe while smoking and socializing. The women on the other hand have to do the hard and dirty jobs – working the fields and doing the cooking.

Opposite page

Top A large canoe under construction. The wooden planks are joined using natural glue from palm trees.

Bottom Two small kids in an outrigger canoe in Pulawat lagoon.

This page

Top The Darwin Research Station in the Galapagos is a must for every visitor. Here they nurture the giant land turtles and try to protect the environment from the encroaching tourism and mainlanders who are moving to the islands from Equador.

Bottom Entering the Galapagos Islands we had these two hitchhikers onboard for hours. We also met sea turtles, dolphins and sea lions.

Top The Kuna Indians from the San Blas Islands outside Panama in the Caribbean board *Jennifer* and offer the crew 'mulas' (traditional cloth panels) for sale. Among the Kunas the women are in charge: the men play an inferior role.

Bottom Between the wheels on *Jennifer* in the South Seas. I am at 'work', dressed in a suit and tie and holding my handbag.

Top The former sultan's palace in Zanzibar. We were anchored just outside this magnificent old building, close to town.

Bottom The entrance to Salomon atoll in the Chagos archipelago, Indian Ocean, on an early morning. Johanna is at the wheel and Lori watches out for coral heads.

Top *Jennifer* anchored outside Lamu Island in northern Kenya. The fishermen are doing what they have done for thousands of years, oblivious of us.

Bottom Johanna in front of the International Donkey Protection Trust on Lamu. This non-profit organization saves and takes care of worn out donkeys.

Top Provisioning in Cape Town before the South Atlantic crossing. We bought enough food to feed eight people for five weeks. From the left: Baxter, Sue, Johanna and Wolf.

Bottom Johanna and I steering together, each on one of the two wheels. Above us you can see the solar panels and radar dome. The combined GPS/Inmarsat-C antenna is on top of the radar, and enabled us to use satellite communications like fax and e-mail.

Top During Antigua Sail Week at the end of April each year there are races every day, apart from 'Layday', when there are games and parties instead.

Bottom *Jennifer* in Antigua in 1997, just before the important Agents' Week, when about 200 agents fly in to inspect the charter fleet.

Top *Jennifer* under sail in the Caribbean in a good beam wind. Note the large deck mattresses, solar panels, wind generator and champagne fenders behind the genoa.

Bottom With a working elephant on the Andaman Islands in the Indian Ocean. The elephants work hard all day, pulling large hardwood trees through the rainforest and lifting them onto trucks.

Top When *Jennifer* sailed down the Amazon river in Brazil, the villagers usually hid when we approached: thoughts of the slave traders from the last century were still in their minds.

Bottom Some of the inhabitants of North Sentinel, one of the Andaman Islands. Over hundreds of years, they have (wisely) avoided contact with modern civilisation – when anthropologists or government officials try to go ashore they are greeted with a shower of arrows and stones.

to where we often anchored, is the oldest. Many other expensive hotels and apartments were later built with Japanese money and American management – it costs $1,500 per night to hire a bungalow constructed on poles over the water.

The most frequented bar among cruisers used to be the Bora-Bora Yacht Club. In 1980 on *Sofia* and in 1993 on *Jennifer* sailors from all corners of the world – including California, Panama, Hawaii, New Zealand and Australia – met there and swapped stories and charts. Quite a few beers were also consumed on the large wooden dock. By 2007 the atmosphere of the yacht club and the bar had gone and there was only one expensive restaurant left, although yachts could still fill their water tanks and use the buoys outside.

On the picturesque island of Huahine we visited the most exclusive hotel I have ever seen, built by an eccentric American. The hotel consisted of 14 Indonesian-Polynesian bungalows spread out in the rainforest with their own hot tubs outside. The bungalows had total privacy with a view over the lagoon, up to the hills and down to the beach. The cost of staying at the hotel was $2,000 per day. Unfortunately the hotel was destroyed during a hurricane in 1998 and today only the lovely beach is left.

On the island of Tahaa we met the Frenchman Alain Plantier. He sailed from France in 1978 and arrived in Tahiti in 1983. He soon settled down with his new wife and bought a small property in Hurepiti Bay on the west coast of Tahaa. Alain then built a house in traditional Polynesian style using natural materials, something the average Polynesian does not do any more because they prefer European houses. The drawback with traditional houses is that the roof has to be remade every five years or so. Alain, who is a very congenial and friendly person, guides visiting sailors around the vanilla plantations and drives them high up into Tahaa's rainforest in his jeep.

What made him even more interesting was the fact that he was a good friend to the legendary French long-distance cruiser and author Bernard Moitessier. Bernard participated in the first ever solo nonstop circumnavigation, the Golden Globe, in the late 1960s and was the leading yacht. With only the last leg from the South Atlantic to England left to be completed, he decided to quit and returned to Tahiti, so receiving neither the fame nor the prize money in the likely event that he would have won. 'I have decided to sail back to the South Seas because I am happy at sea and perhaps to save my soul', he later wrote. He moored his yacht *Joshua* for a few years at Alain's dock, worked on his books *The Long Way* and *A Sea Vagabond's World* in the mornings and helped Alain on his property in the afternoons. Moitessier died in 1994 in Tahiti but Alain was still alive and kicking when I met him again in 2007.

THE DIVING ACCIDENT

During our month in the Society Islands, we had several charters. Of those, many on board had already sailed with *Jennifer* in the Caribbean and now came to visit us in the South Pacific. After five years without serious accidents, I ran out of luck in Tahiti; during a scuba dive a crewmember died.

An American group of six guests, most of whom had already been on board three times, had flown into Tahiti for a ten day charter in the area around Tahiti and Bora-Bora. All of them had diving certificates, and four of them had been diving with me before in the Caribbean. The diving accident happened during one of the first dives by the island of Tahaa. Five of us were supposed to dive in an atoll-passage into the lagoon. I had chosen a time when the tide was slack, so we wouldn't have to dive in the strong current. *Jennifer* was anchored inside the lagoon, and we took the dinghy out to the opening and tied it to a navigational marker on one side of the passage. One couple dived together and I dived with two of the women.

There was no current at all when we started the dive. There was no problem during the dive, and at the end the two women and I surfaced just beside the dinghy. The women were diving 'buddies', which means that they would stay together during the dive. They continued to dive at a depth of only 3m around the marker where the dinghy was attached, while I surfaced to wait in the dinghy. I was not worried, and I knew that they always wanted to get the most out of their time and dived as long as there was enough air (ie 50 bar on the meter).

Both the women had weight belts on. Divers who use aluminium bottles normally need weight belts because aluminium bottles are relatively light, but I have steel bottles, which are heavier, so you normally don't need weight belts. On the way out to the dive site in the dinghy I made it clear to them that they did not need the weights, but both of them were stubborn and wanted to keep them on.

Soon I heard screams for help. One of the women came up to the surface 20–30m away, screamed, and then disappeared under the surface again. I debated whether I should swim over there just with snorkelling equipment, or take on full diving gear. A few seconds later she surfaced, screamed for help again, and went down. I went into the water with the snorkelling equipment since it was the quickest thing to do, taking for granted that I would find her at a depth of 3–5m. After a couple of minutes I realized that I needed diving equipment and quickly swam back to get it. The other woman had surfaced, not knowing what had happened to her friend. Together, we took the dinghy to the spot where I last saw her and went down. The current was slowly forming.

After only a few minutes I found her, lying on her side on a slope some 15m down. I have never seen a dead person before, but presumed that she was dead already. First I tried to inflate her buoyancy vest (BCD), but discovered that she had run out of air. She must have been so preoccupied with her diving that she forgot to check the air supply and in her panic forgot to detach the weight belt, which is one of the first things you do when you run out of air. I attached my own air tube to her vest, filled her vest and then my own vest and brought her up to the surface. Together with her dive buddy we got her up into the boat. The other couple had now reached the surface. Luckily, the man was a heart specialist and immediately began CPR, including cardiac massage.

We went back to *Jennifer* and called the police via the VHF radio. A police boat came quickly and we went to the nearest village, where a doctor waited. He realized that it was too late but gave her an adrenaline injection without result and declared her officially dead. The following police investigation – after detailed questioning and checking of the dive equipment – led to the conclusion that this was an accident.

The mood on board was now very low. After a day, the group turned on me and claimed that it was my fault: I should not have dived in a passage where there was a current; I should have been with the women for the whole dive; I should have had better equipment in the dinghy and a rope should have been thrown to her. One of the group in particular, an American lawyer, took a real dislike to me. When you dive anywhere in the world, divers have to sign a form where they make it clear that they dive at their own risk. The lawyer wanted me to return this form, and I refused.

They stayed aboard for three more days after the accident and then flew to Papeete, where they went to the local paper and accused me of illegal chartering. The paper made a big deal about the case and the next day the police came and forced me to sail back to Tahiti, where they seized the boat and took my passport.

In most parts of the world it is forbidden to sail charters without permission, but most authorities are very relaxed about it. If you only stay a couple of weeks in each place the bureaucracy is too slow to give you permission in time to stay. I was asked to pay a fine of $20,000 but explained to the chief magistrate that it was impossible for me to find that kind of money. After some negotiation, he agreed on a fine of $10,000. I had to ask my family back home in Sweden to help me out and after a couple of days the fine was paid. I also had to leave French Polynesia within a week (and was of course forbidden to sail any more charters).

The whole incident cost me $18,000; $10,000 in fines and $8,000 in lost income. On top of everything, the chef had left the boat along with the guests. She had come from Sweden to replace Ylva over the summer months. Those weeks were very difficult. I was totally empty, both emotionally and financially. Only a couple of months earlier in Panama, the boat had finally been paid off and I could start to save a little. Instead, it was like being back at square one. I was totally alone, and have never felt so abandoned and miserable.

TO THE COOK ISLANDS

THE INTERNATIONAL DATELINE

Fortunately, Ulrica was still on Tahiti. She had left *Jennifer* back in May to try her luck on other boats, and then started a relationship with a single-handed sailor. Their relationship was a little complicated at the time so she signed up to *Jennifer* for the voyage to Tonga. I had to leave the French territory before 1 July, and would miss the festivities during the Bastille Day, which is a big event in Polynesia.

We needed a crew to sail to Tonga, or at least to the Cook Islands. On Bora-Bora we found two Frenchmen who signed on. When I cleared out, the police wanted me to contact the authorities in Papeete, where they had heard that I was still doing charters. As a matter of fact, I did do one more charter with friends from the USA. It was a big risk, but a calculated one. I did not want to turn them down and I couldn't afford to return the prepaid charter fee either. Of course, I was not interested in any further contact with Papeete and claimed, and received, my clearing-out documents. It was a relief to leave the French authorities behind.

The voyage to the Cook Islands, which was some 550nm, was a hard one. It blew a heavy gale the whole way in the strong south-east Trade wind, and we sailed under a reefed mainsail and jib. Day after day sea water splashed up into the cockpit and salt irritated our eyes. We were just four crewmembers and steered for two hours each. It was warm and wet below deck because we had to keep all the hatches closed. There was not much to do while off-duty other than stay in bed and try to read.

The entrance through the reef into Rarotonga was hard to identify in the bad weather. When we finally discovered it, I hesitated to enter. But there were not many options available so we made a run for it and entered the small harbour. It was full, with about ten cruising boats and two commercial ships, all crowded in together. The harbour was not well protected against the wind and the gale continued for two more days. *Jennifer* lost two of her lines in the swells, which rolled into the harbour. She also got some scratches on the hull, but nothing serious.

RAROTONGA

Rarotonga is the main island of the Cook Islands. It is volcanic and almost circular with a big mountain in the middle. The Cook Islands consist of many small atolls beside the main island spread over a large area in the Pacific. The closest atoll is Aitutaki, where larger sailboats cannot enter the lagoon and have to anchor outside the reef. But the most famous atoll amongst circumnavigators is Suvarow atoll, situated in the northern Cook Islands. Here the New Zealander Tom Neale lived alone for 16 years and become an icon for passing circumnavigators who visited him. He died 1977 after having written a book *An Island to Oneself*. The irony is that the book made him famous and so more visitors arrived. This was something he had not foreseen and he genuinely wanted to live there alone. In 1978 Suvarow was declared a National Park and a caretaker now resides on the island. But sailors still visit the island and keep his garden and house in good order.

When I visited Rarotonga while on *Sofia* 1980 I posed as a freelance journalist and asked for an interview with the then Prime Minister, Tom Davies. The answer was no, the Prime Minister was very busy. But on the tenth day, when I was working on *Sofia*, a limousine drove up next to *Sofia* and asked for me. I had been granted an audience with the Prime Minister. I quickly changed clothes and was driven to his office in a small cottage-like building in town. I soon understood that the reason for granting me an audience was that there had been an article in the American magazine *Time*, which he thought was unfavourable about the Cook Islands. He thought that perhaps I could correct the facts and write something more encouraging!

We got a new crewmember in Rarotonga; Jane, a lawyer from San Francisco, had been booked through an agent in California. We sailed on to the little island of Niue (some 585nm away) in better weather than we had recently experienced. Niue is one of the smallest 'independent' island nations in the world, with a population of only 2,000. The island 'sort of' belongs to New Zealand, which gives it economic support. It is clear that a nation with 2,000 inhabitants can't possibly be economically independent and the whole situation is absurd. However, Niue's water is crystal clear and the diving is excellent. One evening at sunset a whale breached only 25m away from us! This fantastic experience happened several times during our stay on the island. On Niue I visited the Minister of Tourism and had a long talk with him about possible improvements for visiting sailors. I told him that there was no pier or harbour on Niue and all visiting ships and yachts had to anchor off the reef. If the wind changed direction, all the boats had to leave in a hurry. I proposed that the government could install a number of buoys on the reef so the yachts could feel safe in any wind direction. Later I heard this had been implemented. During the mid-1990s the government printed a few stamps to commemorate the fact that foreign yachts often visited the island. One of the stamps ($1 Niue) pictured *Jennifer* from the photo in the brochure I gave him.

From Niue to Tonga was a distance of 250nm and took only two days to sail. However, on the way, a whole day disappeared – we passed the 180° line of longitude, the International Dateline. Tonga is the first country on Earth that sees the new day. More correctly, the 180° line of longitude passes straight through Fiji, not Tonga. But when Fiji was a British colony and Tonga a British protectorate, the British governor in Fiji wanted to have the same time zone in all his domains, and moved the date line east, so that the day began in Tonga instead of Fiji. A look at the globe shows the exact curve the date line takes around Tonga.

TONGA – THE KING'S COUNTRY

Tonga is one of only a few non-European countries that has never been a colony, a distinction that is shared only with Japan, Thailand and Ethiopia. Tonga, with a population of about 100,000, is still led by a feudal king who, together with nobles and priests, controls the country with a hand of steel, just as in Europe centuries ago. Democracy does not really exist. The castle is a Victorian house from the turn of the century in the capital city of Nukualofa. When he was young and strong the former king was one of the world's largest men at 2.10m (6ft 5in) tall and weighed 200kg. When he died he was relatively popular in Tonga. The son who succeeded him in 2006 is a notorious playboy, which is not popular in a country that is both religious and conservative. The king's daughter is well respected and a driven businesswoman. Both children are successful within Tonga's economic life. It is easy to make a comparison with Indonesia in the 1990s under Suharto, the second President. The aged general let his children monopolize most of the economy in his country.

The best sailing in Tonga is in the northern Vava'u archipelago. This area contains a large number of reefs and small islands with white beaches and palm trees, all protected by a huge reef. Because we had had to leave French Polynesia ahead of time *Jennifer* stayed for almost three months in Neiafu, Vava'u's sleepy capital village. Unfortunately, the weather was very poor with rain, strong winds and cold seas – only 24–25°C when I was used to 27–28°C.

Friends from Sweden came to visit us in Tonga. For the rest of the time we did some diving and snorkelling in the caves. Whales played and jumped in the water beside us and I snorkelled next to a female and her calf. They watched me as I stayed away at a respectful distance of about 10m. We also worked on *Jennifer* and spent time with other around-the-world sailors.

Among the other boats was *Elsie Rose*, a 21ft (6m) sailboat belonging to a single-handed American sailor, Steve. The boat had so little equipment on board that I would hesitate before sailing her any distance. But Steve had sailed from the Caribbean to Panama, crossing the Pacific to Easter Island, Tahiti and Tonga without major problems and we had run into him many times before. Steve wrote about *Jennifer* in his newsletter:

'In Tonga I sailed around the Vava'u's islands and reefs. One morning, in a calm bay, I was interrupted during my breakfast by the sight of four 50ft (15m) sailboats. One of them was the Swedish boat *Jennifer*, where I had been invited to dinner twice before when we shared a mooring in French Polynesia. Lars did not waste any time. As soon as he had anchored *Jennifer* he went around all the other boats and organized an aerobics session. "The session starts in ten minutes on the beach," he announced when his dinghy passed in the stern of *Elsie Rose*. A Tongan family was kind enough to let us use part of the beach in front of their hut and watched us with big eyes as Lars, a former aerobics instructor, led 25 sailors from the ages of 3 to 65, accompanied by music from Madonna on his boom box.'

In the middle of September Ylva returned from Sweden, which made me feel much better. I had been pretty lonely during the months in Tonga and I was glad not to be a single-handed sailor any longer. At the beginning of October the rest of the crew that were coming with us to New Zealand arrived. They were seven university students from Sweden: Peder, Jonas, Lars, Kristian, Fredrik, Mattias and Filip. They were going to be on board for ten weeks. All of them were friends of Filip who had crossed the Atlantic with *Jennifer* before.

SUPER-YACHTS, NORMAL YACHTS AND LONG-DISTANCE SAILORS

We met many different boats in the South Pacific, from the biggest private luxury yachts to the smallest single-handed sailboats. Among the biggest was *Marilyn IV*, a 201ft (61m) power yacht with a crew of eight. One of them was a Swede who worked on board as a deckhand. The owner was an American who owned ten big cruising ships in the West Indies. *Marilyn* has two gyms (one for the guests and one for the owner), Picasso paintings on the walls and a library of 800 films. Another boat was *Andromeda*, the

biggest sailing boat in the world at that time – a 140ft (43m) ketch. It had a crew of eight and a 'flying bridge' over the cockpit, where it could be sailed by just one person with an electronic joystick. *Virginian*, a 210ft (64m) power yacht, was another giant with a crew of twelve.

We got invitations to all of these boats when the owners weren't on board, and their crews were invited on board *Jennifer*. The smallest boat we met was *Elsie Rose*. Another interesting boat was the 50ft (15m) Viking ship, built by a Dane who dressed up like a Viking or pirate, day and night. He was always on the front page of the local papers in every place he visited.

Most of the other boats were 30–42 ft (9–13m). A few were smaller. I estimated that 80% of the crews were couples, 10% were single-handed sailors and the rest were a mix. These included big private yachts like *Andromeda*, sailboats that took paying crew like *Jennifer* or families with children. Hardly any charter boats sail around the world. *Blaze*, a 50ft (15m) American sailboat, had four children between the ages of six and ten on board. The mother, a former stockbroker in her 30s, organized lessons for the children for four hours a day, five days a week. I was impressed by the discipline among the families – we even met a boat that had been out sailing for 18 years, with the whole family still on board.

Among the long-distance cruisers there were some who were retired and others who were wealthy professionals – lawyers, businessmen or doctors – who had taken a few years off but kept their house/apartment at home waiting for when they returned. Most of the people had sold their belongings to sail for a couple of years, return home, sell the boat and start all over again. Many had to work and earn some money along the way to maintain their travelling funds. They always seemed to find work, even when the times were bad – you can always find a job if you really want to.

There is one final group that you meet while out sailing – hitchhikers. Hitchhikers try to find a place on board a boat to get from one place to another. Sometimes they travel as paying crew, although at other times they contribute only to the cost of food. Many are women, and although most single-handed sailors are looking for female crew (not because they need help, but because they want to start a relationship) the women hitchhikers usually just want to get from one port to the next. Decisions need to be made, as most of the single-handed sailboats are small, and do not have room for two people in separate cabins. In Tonga I had four women come on board as potential paying guests while they were checking out the different alternatives. Unfortunately, I was already fully booked from Tonga to New Zealand.

MELANESIA – FIJI

FIJI'S CANNIBALS

We sailed from Tonga to Fiji at the end of October, a distance of 450nm that took us only three days in steady wind, with the gennaker up the whole way. When we left Tonga we also left Polynesia ('the many islands') and came to Melanesia ('the black islands'). The year after that, we sailed to Micronesia ('the small islands'). The borders between the three are simple and clear. Both Melanesia and Micronesia are situated to the west of the date line, with Melanesia to the south of the Equator and Micronesia to the north. Polynesia lies to the east of the date line.

Fiji was a pleasant surprise. It consists of 300 islands in several big archipelagos, and is the most populated nation in the South Pacific (other than Guinea), with a population of 700,000. The Fijians used to be cannibals. They captured their sacrifices in tribal wars (or took white men) and tortured them brutally (curiously, this was mostly done by women) before they ate them. Parts of the body, such as an arm, were torn off while the victim was still alive and being tortured, and were eaten in front of the victim before he was boiled alive.

THE MILITARY COUP

Because of the incessant, bitter civil wars between the tribes, Britain was more or less asked to take over Fiji as a colony in the 1870s. To finance this, the British started up sugar plantations. The Fijians refused to participate – the work was very labour intensive and to be forced to work ten hours a day didn't go together at all with the South Pacific lifestyle. Britain therefore imported a workforce from India to work on the plantations. Today more than half of the inhabitants of Fiji are Indians. The society is divided so that the original inhabitants (the Fijians) own all the land and control the army, while the imported Indians control the economy.

Fiji became independent from Britain in 1970. It has had four military coups in two decades, most recently in 2006. Led by Fijians these coups overthrew a legally elected Indian-dominated government. The issue centred on the Fijian chiefs' rights to their feudal and inherited privileges. In contrast to Tonga, the king of Fiji has been replaced by an elected government, but the nobility (ie the chiefs) still cling to the past. The Indians in Fiji feel threatened by the native Fijians, who in turn feel threatened by the Indians – the same situation as in Trinidad.

THE OLDEST BAR IN THE SOUTH PACIFIC

We chose to clear in at the old capital of Levuka on the island of Ovalau, east of the main island, Viti Levu. At the end of the 19th century the capital of Fiji was moved to Suva on the main island and Levuka became a forgotten city, frozen in its era of greatness. To walk among the old colonial buildings in Levuka is like travelling back in time. The exotic Ovalau Club is the oldest club and bar in the South Pacific and it became our retreat and meeting place. The next stop was the capital Suva, where we anchored by Suva's Royalty Yacht Club and met up with crews from many familiar boats. From Suva, we sailed on to the Beqa Lagoon just south of Viti Levu (and world famous for its diving) and then continued to the west side of Viti Levu. We sailed for several weeks in the Yasawa and Mamanuca archipelagoes, snorkelling in the waters and visiting the various villages. Our favourite place to go was the Muscet Cove Yacht Club on Malololailai Island, which was designed for long-distance cruisers. We spent most of our time among the Yasawa Islands, where the movie *The Blue Lagoon* was filmed in the 1970s.

When you visit a village in Fiji, you always have to bring a kava root (the pepper plant's dried root) as a gift for the chief. Mixed with water, the ground-up kava is served as a drink in a ritual practice. The kava looks like dish water and it makes your tongue and lips go numb, but it is a calming non-alcoholic drink. If you drink a lot of it, it also affects muscle control in your arms and legs. Kava plays an important social role in Fiji, rather like beer does for us at home. If you don't like it you shouldn't visit the outer islands, as it is impolite not to take part in the kava ceremonies. Eventually I learned to tolerate, but not love, the kava drink.

SAILING PERSONALITIES

Few sailors have succeeded in making a living out of their hobby – other than the ones who sail the Whitbread or Volvo Ocean races, the America's Cup, or charter or write about sailing. However, a few people have succeeded, among them Jimmy Cornell, who organizes cruises around the world and Dick Smith, who built a yacht club in Fiji after sailing in the South Pacific for several years.

Jimmy realized that long-distance cruisers enjoy sailing together, and in 1985 he organized the first Atlantic Rally for Cruisers (ARC). Note that the word 'rally' is used instead of 'race', to make the point that it is a social voyage rather than a competition. The ARC, which starts during November in the Canary Islands and ends in the Caribbean, has become a tradition, with up to 200 boats in the fleet every year. Seven years later in 1992, Cornell's next project was an around-the-world rally: Europa '92, followed by Europa

'94, which crossed our path in Tonga and Fiji. The rally takes only 17 months, starting in Gibraltar in January and returning to the Rock the following May. For the millennium, he organized a giant rally with multiple starting places and several routes, with options to travel either through the Panama Canal or around Cape Horn, and through the Suez Canal or around the Cape of Good Hope. Cornell has also written the famous *World Cruising Routes*, as well as other similar books, which are all good sources of information for planning a long cruise.

We met Jimmy and many of the 30 sailing boats from the Europa '94 rally in both Fiji and the Caribbean. Most of the sailboats were European, particularly Italian, but many American sailing boats joined the flotilla in the Pacific Ocean. Almost all the boats were privately owned and sailed by the owner and his or her friends. Two sailing boats sailed with paying crew, at a cost of $35,000 per person for the whole voyage. The entry fee was $10,000 per boat, which initially sounds like a lot of money, but this included the cost for both the Panama and Suez Canals, free berths in the marinas where you stayed, organized clearing-in procedures with customs and immigration authorities as well as many parties and events. Most of the crews enjoy the camaraderie with other cruisers, not to mention the feeling of security that comes with daily radio conferences on the SSB-radio.

Many men and women have travelled to the South Pacific in search of happiness and adventure. Many did not find what they were looking for and eventually returned to the western world, but some did succeed and make a living, either through doing odd jobs or as entrepreneurs. Some 50 years ago, the Australian Dick Smith decided to head to the South Pacific. He piloted his powerboat *Stardust* to Tahiti, where he became involved in the movie *The Mutiny on the Bounty*, which starred Marlon Brando and Trevor Howard. After that he chartered his boat around the South Pacific and on Christmas Island taught British seamen how to water-ski during their holidays from nuclear weapons duty. Eventually, he ended up in Fiji. He built two of Fiji's first hotels on the islands to the west of the main island of Viti Levu. He later sold them and built the Muscet Cove Yacht Club on an old copra plantation on Malololailai. Muscet Cove has several bungalows, a marina and even a small airport. Around-the-world sailors can become lifetime members in the yacht club: $5 for the crew and only $1 for the skipper: 'they have already paid a lot to get there...' In September, Dick hosts the annual Muscet Cove Regatta, perhaps the most unusual and entertaining regatta in the world – to win you must prove that you have cheated! There are many barbecues and happy hour gatherings in his Two Dollar Bar on a tiny island connected to the marina by a footbridge.

During our many visits to Muscet Cove, we got to know Dick pretty well. One evening, he explained how he became the host for Jimmy Cornell's around-the-world-stop in Fiji. Jimmy and Dick initially negotiated with Suva Yacht Club to have all the participating boats stay at the marina during their time in Fiji. The chairman of the club began to outline the fees to Jimmy, including the dock fee, extra security costs, water, electricity and so on. When Jimmy tried to explain to the chairman that *he* was the one who would have to pay *Jimmy* for the privilege of hosting the boats, the negotiations quickly broke down. Dick then offered Jimmy $10,000 in cash plus free spots at the dock, in return for making the Fiji stop at Muscet Cove Yacht Club, which Jimmy accepted. Dick chuckled and remarked, 'Hell, I earned that money back in two days in my Two Dollar Bar'.

As well as being the owner of a hotel, the president of Fiji's hotel society and a central figure in the sailing culture in this part of the South Pacific, Dick also owns areas of rainforest on Fiji's mainland. Dick's plan is to protect the rainforest by building a small number of houses in one part of it and giving the rest of the land to a society managed by the house owners, on the condition that the forest would never be sold, cut down or otherwise exploited. Compared to the fate of other rainforests in the Third World, this seems to be a reasonable and realistic compromise.

NEW CALEDONIA

New Caledonia, like French Polynesia, is a French colony. It has approximately 250,000 inhabitants and is commonly referred to as the Pacific's Riviera.

As recently as 1988 the native Melanesian Kanaks attempted an armed revolt against the French colonial government. The French regarded them as rebels, while the Kanaks honoured them as freedom fighters. During the revolt many were captured or killed by French paratroopers, the French just managed to avoid having this massacre brought before the United Nations. A referendum on the question of self-government was promised for 1998, but that date is now postponed until 2014. New Caledonia has one of the biggest nickel mines in the world, and partly because of this it will probably never become fully independent. Historically, France has never freely given any of its colonies their independence.

It took us five days to sail from Fiji to New Caledonia's capital Nouméa, a distance of 675nm. After a half-gale at the start, the wind settled down towards the end of the voyage, allowing us to put up the worn-out spinnaker. We stayed a week in New Caledonia, mostly in the rather sophisticated city of Nouméa, where we reprovisioned and found some spares for the boat. After a few days we sailed to a lagoon south-east of the main island where the beautiful Ile des Pins ('isle of pines') is situated, with one of the most glorious beaches I have ever seen.

THE PASSAGE TO NEW ZEALAND

We wanted to reach New Zealand before the start of the hurricane season in early December. We set sail in late November, heading south-east, with 875nm to cover before reaching New Zealand. The forecast had promised pleasant winds from the north-west, but instead we got a strong headwind, gusting at 45 knots, which made most of us (including myself) seasick. Within an hour the genoa was torn and we had to change to a smaller jib. The next day the mainsail was damaged and it took us over six hours to repair it. On the third day, we lost our steering. One of the helms fell off, we had to use the emergency tiller and it took us three hours to re-attach the steering wheel.

This is the type of passage that I can happily live without. During a typical watch the helmsman is continually drenched by sea water. You hardly eat and it is difficult to sleep. Everything on board is in a mess. There are times during rough passages when I wonder what I am doing. However, I am also aware that it is the price I pay for all the good things we have experienced.

We kept four watches, with two people doing two hours each. This meant spending two hours on and six hours off. On top of that, two crewmembers had galley duty. After four days, the gale calmed down, but we still had headwinds and it grew progressively colder. Eventually, the wind died out completely and we motored for three days under a sunny sky until a wind on the beam carried us into The Bay of Islands on New Zealand's northern island. On the final day big killer whales, with their characteristic back fins, welcomed us to New Zealand.

NEW ZEALAND – THE LAND OF THE KIWIS

We stayed for four months in New Zealand during the South Pacific hurricane season. Because of the diving accident, I had very little money, but *Jennifer* had a detailed inspection and I got to see the Whitbread Race boats finish. Ylva signed off in December and Johanna signed on in April. We then set off across the Tasmanian Sea . . .

THE WHITBREAD RACE BOATS FINISH

The Whitbread boats were due to arrive during the night in Auckland, and we watched the race finish with some new friends from New Zealand. Some 40,000 people were out on the beach and thousands upon thousands of boats were out to welcome the Whitbread racers. There was a confused collection of red, green and white lights out on the bay and the waves made it difficult to follow what was happening. Helicopters with searchlights suddenly appeared in the sky and illuminated the sails of the leading boats. It was truly an impressive sight, with the tall, gleaming white sails almost looking as if they were on fire in the night, like angels from heaven.

The wind was only 12 knots, but the Whitbread boats travelled at a speed of 8–9 knots, which we could barely match, even with the motor. The New Zealand boat *Tokio* was in the lead just before the finish line, when the even bigger maxi boat *Endeavour* passed it in an exciting duel and won by only 2 metres.

During their month-long stop in Auckland, the Whitbread Race boats were in the Whitbread-village, a newly built harbour in the centre of Auckland. They were visited by more than 800,000 people. In February, the race's fourth leg to South America started, with 6,000 spectator boats and 15 helicopters on hand to see them off. There were 15 paying friends aboard *Jennifer*. It was windy, and we joined the spectator fleet towards the start. Suddenly, the leading boat *Tokio* tacked straight towards us, and a second later 6,000 boats had to change direction. You had to be extremely awake – or risk being run over by one of the many other spectator boats.

THE OVERHAUL OF *JENNIFER*

Jennifer was now a little more than five years old, and had been used almost every day. It was time for a solid inspection. Our most important piece of equipment was the engine, an 80hp Perkins that had so far been running like a Swiss clock for more than 9,000 hours. A compression test showed that the engine was in good condition, although the heat exchangers and some other related parts needed service and a few parts needed to be replaced. Other projects on board included: replacing the refrigerator, freezer, wind indicator and ground tackle; repairing and servicing the dinghy and outboard motor; adjusting the propeller shaft, the forestay and the two compasses; and galvanizing the 30kg heavy anchor. In addition, we replaced the transmission and throttle controls, installed new cables to the engine panel, replaced the batteries, installed new ball bearings in the generator, cleaned the water machine, sewed new covers for the furniture and bought new charts for the Pacific and Indian Oceans, plus a new mattress for my cabin. The sails were also properly repaired after the tough voyage from New Caledonia and I bought a new software program for the satellite unit.

I also repainted *Jennifer*'s hull. I did this by placing her in a special dock where I could paint below the waterline. When the tide went out the keel rested on the bottom and I had six hours to work before the water rose again. The first time I attached lines to the hull, as well as to the masthead and secured those lines to different places on the dock. The second time I secured only the hull and the third time I just put the boat into the dock and waited for the tide to go out. The reason for my increasingly careless methods was that I realized that *Jennifer*'s keel design made her stand very securely as long as the bottom was firm. I tried to rock her by running from side to side but she stood totally still.

Over the years I have spent a lot of time arguing with the manufacturers of boat parts. I tell them that I have chosen their brand because of their good reputation, and that I expect the parts to remain intact throughout my circumnavigation. It certainly pays to complain – I received a brand new wind generator worth $1,500, and Brooks & Gatehouse agreed to share the $900 cost of a new computer card for the wind instrument. *Jennifer's* overhaul took two of our four months in New Zealand and the total cost for the inspection and refit was $7,000.

NEW ZEALAND

We reached the Bay of Islands in early December 1993. The relationship between Ylva and myself, ongoing since 1991, was coming to an end. On top of the usual arguments about the day-to-day things, she wanted to start a family (she turned 33 on the Galápagos) and have a more steady relationship. As I wasn't in a position to give her any of this, we decided that she would stay aboard just as far as New Zealand, and then cast off and look for happiness there. It didn't take her long to find a job and after a month she found a new boyfriend, which made me very happy. She got married six months later and we still keep in touch. Although it was often very lonely for me in New Zealand, and I was also short of money, there were some other long distance cruisers that we had got to know, and I could spend time with them.

Geographically, New Zealand is part of Polynesia. When the Europeans discovered the island in the 17th century it was already inhabited by the Maoris, a Polynesian tribe that had arrived several hundreds of years before. Today they make up 15 per cent of the total population and are somewhat marginalized, although not to the same extent as the Aboriginals in Australia.

I am very impressed by New Zealand, especially the BYO (bring your own) restaurant, where you can bring your own alcohol. New Zealand has already managed to alter and update the structure of their society, something that Sweden and the rest of Europe are doing slowly. The welfare state is changing and more and more companies and authorities that were originally run by the state are becoming privatized. It is the first country in the world that has started to use a more realistic system for tracking and managing its economy. All the assets of the country (such as natural resources) as well as all liabilities (such as pensions) are included, just as a business would be required to do. If businessmen did as most politicians usually do, all the chief executives would be in jail.

The coast of Auckland, the 'city of sails', is perfect for sailing. Every day after work many boats leave the Westhaven Marina in the middle of the city to race just outside. Within 20nm there is a small archipelago, and the Bay of Islands is 125nm further north. This is another archipelago and many of the islands are beautiful, green, nature reserves with excellent hiking trails up to volcanoes and peaks. Both Ylva and Ulrica worked in restaurants in the village of Russell on the archipelago.

Most around-the-world cruisers sail to New Zealand and stay there to wait out the hurricane season in the South Pacific, which lasts from December to April. In 1993, some 450 sailing boats cleared in to New Zealand and stayed in one of the four marinas on the North Island. Relatively few make the passage to the South Island.

During the 4–5 month stopover, some take the chance to travel home over Christmas and New Year. Many buy a used car and explore both the North and South Island, later selling the car for almost the same price. Others find work to increase their travel funds. I don't think I have ever met a sailor who hasn't succeeded in finding some sort of a job – strawberry seller, apple picker, dishwasher, diving instructor or repairman for other boats and engines. During our stay in New Zealand, many people sailed with us as paying crew: Lars-Göran and his girlfriend Tina as a part of their around the world trip; Terri, who had sailed with us from Panama to the Galápagos; Maryse, a sailor and diving instructor from Montreal; Peter, an environmental engineer from Los Angeles who sailed with us in the Virgin Islands and came back with two friends; and Linda, a nurse and horse rider from Britain. Linda was supposed to be taking part in the 16-month circumnavigation, Europa '94. She had paid to crew on a boat but the owner went bankrupt so her agent suggested *Jennifer* as a substitute. Later Linda came back for more sailing.

JOHANNA

Johanna was born in Holland and made her first crossing of the Atlantic when she was seven years old, when her parents immigrated to Canada by ship. She took a Bachelor's degree in botany, and also became a diving instructor. In 1979, she left Canada with her boyfriend to set up a diving centre and hotel on an uninhabited island in what was then British Honduras.

When British Honduras became independent in 1981 it changed its name to Belize. Neighbouring Guatemala threatened to invade Belize, claiming that it belonged to them. The hotel and diving business foundered because of this political instability and Johanna started to work as a deckhand, crossing the Atlantic and sailing in the Mediterranean on different yachts. After that she worked as a diving instructor in the Red Sea and Mexico. In 1992, she decided to sail around the world on different sailing boats and try to earn a living as a diving instructor.

I met Johanna for the first time in Tahiti, just days after the diving accident. At the time, I was too upset to think much about her. As fate would have it, I met her again in Tonga. We ran into each other several times and I became interested in this beautiful woman. We talked about the possibility of her sailing aboard *Jennifer* from New Zealand. With her experience in the diving business, she thought that she might get many of her former diving customers to sail aboard *Jennifer*. We didn't see much of each other on New Zealand as Johanna took the opportunity to travel across South Island and

I did not even know where she was. Eventually, in late March we met again and continued to plan a trip together. Johanna had made some enquiries to see if any of her former diving guests were interested in sailing with *Jennifer*, but without any luck.

Johanna's finances were not very secure. On the four boats she had been sailing with so far, she had paid for her own food but couldn't save much for the future. Most of all, she wanted to find a job aboard a sailboat. She had been offered a place aboard *Galaxy*, an 80ft (24m) charter boat owned by an unfriendly and arrogant American. *Galaxy* was headed towards Fiji where it was going to be stationed. There would be no salary but the opportunity to work as a diving instructor if any of the future guests so wished. He did not have very many bookings, so the *Galaxy* idea was not very interesting. My finances were at their lowest point since the voyage began and I could not afford to pay very much either. But Joanna was welcome to sign on without paying anything for food, work as a chef when we had charters and also do as much diving instruction as was possible with *Jennifer*'s equipment. For the diving instruction I offered a 75/25 deal: 75% to her and 25% to me, as I would be providing the equipment. She accepted. Prior to that, I had invited her for dinner on board one night – I wanted to test her cooking knowledge. She was a bit perplexed about the test, but did very well, and teased me often about it later.

We soon began a relationship. To live, sail and work together on a boat has its problems, as I had already discovered with Ylva. We had two relationships: one as man/woman and one as employer/employee. The limits were not always clear as to the latter, and we had many confrontations, sometimes not speaking for days. One of those times we were lucky to have only one, very tolerant, guest aboard, Lori, a Canadian who was very understanding when it came to confrontations. Despite this our relationship worked, even if it increasingly became a friendship rather than a man/woman relationship. It worked financially too – Johanna could survive with her income from the diving instruction and the charter weeks.

TOWARDS AUSTRALIA

CROSSING THE TASMAN SEA

After four months in New Zealand, it was time to sail on to Australia. I had put up flyers in sailing clubs and youth hostels to find a crew for the passage across the Tasman Sea and I eventually had a full crew. The problem was that none of them had any sailing experience. During the three days sailing to the Bay of Islands, we practised steering a compass course, taking down the sails, using the GPS, and working in the galley. The crew consisted of: Johanna; Dan, an artist from Britain who helped me when I painted the hull of the boat in Auckland; Jean-Pierre from France; Juanette and Karen from South Africa; and Adrienne and Nancy from USA. All of them were backpackers and had travelled the world for 6–12 months.

The Tasman Sea, spanning 1,350nm from New Zealand to Australia, is as notorious as the Bay of Biscay, ie you can expect gales and storms. The first day was fine, but after that a hard gale hit us from behind. During the night Adrienne, who was steering, made an accidental gybe and the main sail was torn apart (to be fair, this can happen to even experienced helmsmen). The rest of the time we sailed either 'wing on wing' – with foresails on each side of the forestay supported by the two spinnaker booms – or we sailed only with the genoa. After ten days we reached Bundaberg, north of Brisbane in Queensland. We had arrived 'Down Under'.

SUBMERGED CONTAINERS

On arriving in Bundaberg we learned that a boat we had met in Auckland (that had sailed the day before us) had collided with a cargo container and sank. The crew was lucky and had been rescued by helicopter, as the accident happened close to Australia. Submerged cargo containers are the biggest threat for sailing boats. Containers do not sink, but float mostly submerged close to the surface and are nearly impossible to detect. Because the international rules defining the number of containers a ship is allowed to carry and the way they must carry them are unclear, ships under pressure to make a profit often transport too many containers. In bad weather they lose them (or worse still dump them) overboard. During our crossing I got a message on the satellite unit that warned all ships that there were 16 abandoned containers close to Fiji. A few weeks earlier, six containers went missing close to Australia. It is scary to think that all these invisible containers could float around for years.

AUSTRALIA – THE WORLD'S LONGEST REEF

We sailed along Australia's barrier reef using our new autopilot, then realized that we were in the wrong place for bookings and decided to return to Tonga to pick up more crew, sailing against the Trade winds and along the edge of a killer storm.

THE GREAT BARRIER REEF

The longest reef in the world stretches for 2,000km (or 1,100nm) along the east coast of Australia. Here you find the biggest ecosystem of the world; even bigger than a tropical rainforest. The reef is considered to be one of the best places in the world to dive and is included on UNESCO's World Heritage List. To our disappointment, we never experienced the full beauty of the reef.

During our five-week stopover the weather was terrible – strong winds and a great deal of rain. We did several dives and understood that the potential was there for spectacular diving, but the water was not clear. Even so, we saw many fish and because of the strong wind even a few of the famous giant mussels that can be up to 1m long. As we sailed between Bundaberg and Cairns (half of the length of the reef) we picked up a few passengers, mostly backpackers, along the way. Tomas, a Swedish friend who worked as a ski instructor in Vail, Colorado, also joined us for two weeks, to try out the charter life. In 1997 he bought the 53ft (16m) *Servisen* and is currently successfully sailing charters in the West Indies and Sweden.

ARNOLD – THE NEW AUTOPILOT

When I ordered *Jennifer* in 1988, I had planned on installing an autopilot. But after the delivery, with all the extra equipment that was going to be installed, I couldn 't afford the $5,000 cost of the autopilot. Since I usually have a crew of 6–8 on an ocean crossing, there had always been enough people to steer. Still, out of all the long distance cruising boats I met, *Jennifer* was probably the only one that lacked both a wind vane and an electrical autopilot. The surprised comment from other skippers was usually: 'You really mean that you are actually sailing the boat?' Before the upcoming voyage to Tonga against the Trade winds, and with the possibility of only a small crew, I decided that it was finally time to invest. One deciding factor was that there was a good value autopilot out on the market for only $1,500. It was belt-driven, in contrast to the more expensive models that are geared directly onto the rudder quadrant. We called it Arnold, as it was pretty strong. When Arnold is working, he is the best helmsman I have ever had – he steers with small, exact movements, never complains and only eats electricity. The downside of a belt-driven autopilot is that it can only steer in about 75 per cent of the wind conditions and cannot be used in large waves.

TO TONGA

23 DAYS AGAINST THE TRADE WINDS

I didn't have any bookings in Australia, so when my agent in California told me that there were requests for charters and paying crew in Tonga and Fiji, I realized that I was in the wrong place at the wrong time. It was easy to make the decision to sail back to Tonga. Once again I put up flyers at the marinas and found two new crew members: Normand, an engineer from Scotland; and Michel from Holland, a former soldier with the Special Forces, and a Dutch champion and black belt in judo. Michel had been injured whilst in the military and now had a lifelong pension. Linda, who had sailed with *Jennifer* in New Zealand, flew in for the trip to Tonga, and Anders, who had been on *Sofia* and now lived in Australia, also signed on. With Johanna and myself, there were now six people to sail the 2,800nm from Cairns to Tonga – the same distance as crossing the Atlantic.

A voyage around the world normally follows the Trade winds, from east to west. Most of the time the winds are comfortably from behind. Our sailing from Australia to Tonga was going in the wrong direction, against the Trade winds, which was hard for both the boat and the crew. The best way is to first sail south to go under the Trade wind belt and reach some westerly winds, and then sail north to meet the south-east Trade wind at a better angle. At the end of May, we began by motorsailing south against a head wind towards the lonely, beautiful Lord Howe Island – also on UNESCO's World Heritage List. The island is 1,200nm and 10 days from Cairns, situated between Australia and New Zealand. We stopped here for a couple of hours to fill up with diesel. We then passed Norfolk Island, where the British had moved descendants of the *Bounty* mutineers from Pitcairn Island in June

1856. Some of them later moved back to Pitcairn Island, and 53 people still live there today.

THE KILLER STORM

Within sailing circles, including long distance cruisers and competitive sailors, there are two big storms from modern times that are etched into people's memories – the Fastnet Race storm in 1979 and the storm in the South Pacific in 1994. In the Fastnet storm, crews learned the lesson that they should not go into the liferafts too early, ie before the sailboat is really sinking. After that storm, several boats were found floating and intact, but without either crew or liferafts.

Fifteen years later, we found ourselves on the edge of the South Pacific storm. Several boats had left New Zealand together, en route to Tonga. The forecast was good and the hurricane season was over. After a few days, without warning from the meteorologists, a killer storm blew up and surprised the whole fleet. For the next two to three days, the fleet fought for their lives. Several boats experienced a 'knock down' and rolled through a full 360°, often losing their masts in the process and resulting in severe damage to both the boat and the crew. If any of the heavy lead-acid batteries were not secured properly they became deadly projectiles and could even damage the hull itself.

Some boats pitch-poled, ie made a forward somersault. This can be disastrous – especially for catamarans, which once capsized can never right themselves again. Many boats were dismasted and one entire crew was lost. Some crews were lucky and were rescued by freighters and warships. One of the abandoned boats was found six months later, still floating in the Pacific Ocean, and was towed back to a thankful owner. He had abandoned ship after injuring himself during a 360° roll. We were on the edge of the storm, which for us was a strong gale. Our main damage was the loss of the wind generator overboard. The masthead wind indicator also decided that it had had enough and jumped overboard. During the voyage from Australia to Tonga we kept in touch with a private radio station, Kerikeri Radio in New Zealand, every day. They contacted sailing boats that had registered with them on their SSB-radio and gave them weather forecast updates. During the storm, we followed the whole course of events, and we could hear the MAYDAY calls transmitted over the radio. If *Jennifer* suffered an extreme emergency, I could simply press the emergency button on the satellite unit. A land-based station would then identify *Jennifer*, as well as our position, course and speed. At the end of June we finally arrived in Tonga – we had returned to the South Pacific. It had been the longest passage of our voyage around the world so far – 23 days at sea.

TONGA AND FIJI AGAIN – *JENNIFER* AS A 'LOVE BOAT'

After sailing back to Tonga and Fiji, I returned to Sweden for a short visit and took a working vacation in San Francisco to see my agent. We got new equipment for the boat, faced a seasickness drama with an American family on board and made an emergency stop on the beautiful island of Rotuma. Johanna and I sailed on to Tuvalu, in the Marshall Islands, the smallest nation in the world.

SAILING IN TONGA AND FIJI

During the summer and the autumn of 1994, *Jennifer* sailed the South Pacific around Tonga and Fiji, hosting both charter guests and paying crew. We had many interesting people aboard, most of them from the USA and Sweden: a famous hair stylist from New York, a fireman, a goldsmith, a couple on their honeymoon, a church organist, a journalist, two physiotherapists, and several teachers and computer consultants. Also, for the first time, we had a family with children on board.

Many of the crewmembers were experienced sailors, who wanted to live their dream of sailing in the South Pacific. Others hadn't sailed before and wanted to try it out. For four weeks there were nine of us aboard and it was one of the nicest months we had. Through the years at least five couples have come together on board, ie they came aboard without knowing each other, but left together. Two relationships were formed during this month and both couples later got married. Out of the five couples, one is no longer together but the other four are still married.

We filled the days sailing, snorkelling and diving from *Jennifer*'s stern platform. The diving is best in Fiji, on the reefs around Taveuni Island in the east and the Kadavu Islands in the south. Johanna taught five people to dive and gave three recertification courses. Other activities included aerobics on various beaches, hiking through the rainforest to waterfalls, meeting other sailors during happy hour, visiting the small islands, reading and thinking about life. During one of the visits to the islands we noticed something unusual when it came to cultural definitions of beautiful women. We often had women on board who were blond, tanned and slim. On this sailing we had a big American woman aboard – somewhat overweight by European standards. The Tongan men were crazy for her and totally uninterested in the others. Most Polynesian men and women are big and sturdy and this is their ideal body form. I was asked several times by Tongan men if I could fix a date for them with the large American woman.

Sailing around Taveuni (a tall, hilly island covered with rainforest) we crossed the 180° longitude meridian several times and noticed how the GPS changed from east to west each time. We also hiked through the jungle to three beautiful waterfalls. The rainforest in Taveuni is an interesting example of how international aid can be used to support a positive development. The village that owns this part of the rainforest got an offer from a logging company wanting to cut down all the trees. The New Zealand government then made an alternative offer of $60,000 to turn the rainforest into a nature park and recommended that the village charge tourists a fee to walk to the waterfall. The village chose the park alternative and we paid $5 each to take the walk – a sum that felt completely right to pay. This way, the rainforest will generate an ongoing income instead of a one-time payment.

If we anchored close to a village on a Sunday we would often go to mass. It was astounding to see the usually half-naked fishermen and farmers (or planters as they call themselves) dressed up in a shirt and tie and the women in their best dresses. There are sometimes up to six different churches in a village that might not even have electricity – a sign of the hard competition between the missionaries and their various religions. The visiting sailors normally get to sit in the first row, close to the chief of the village who sits alone facing the crowd. Most of the chiefs are very elegant, like a director or a politician. I left the Swedish church a long time ago, but still find it interesting to see the villages come to life on Sundays, and I enjoy listening to the harmonious singing. Their God seems to be an angry God, or at least that is my conclusion after I have seen and heard the priests' wild gestures and yelling during the masses.

Most evenings we ate dinner in the cockpit underneath the stars, and had long and interesting discussions. Sometimes we dressed up and had hat parties, or went to a kava party in one of the villages. Some nights we sailed from one group of islands to another, or even from one country to another. On one pleasant four-day crossing from Tonga to Fiji we caught two of our biggest fish, a tuna weighing 16kg and a dorado weighing 14kg.

WORKING VACATION

With the income from the charters and paying crewmembers, my financial situation was much improved and I could pay off my debt from the diving accident. I could also afford to travel home for a short visit, see my agent in California and buy new equipment for *Jennifer*.

In September I flew from Fiji to Stockholm for a week. I had not been in Sweden since 1991 and it was exciting to come home to meet family and friends. My nephews and nieces were now teenagers, and when I saw them I realized how quickly the years had passed. The days were filled with lunches and dinners, as well as meetings with agents. I also did an interview with a Swedish boat magazine and met future crewmembers through an advertisement I had placed in a sailing magazine.

On my way back from Stockholm, I stopped in San Francisco and visited Mary, the owner of Ocean Voyages, an agent who sent many paying crews to *Jennifer*. The office is in a houseboat in Sausalito, San Francisco's sailing centre on the northern side of the Golden Gate Bridge. It was fun to meet her employees and see how they worked. Mary also took me to the St Francis Sailing Club and to other events, and I saw the famous musician Booker T. Jones. The leading sailing magazine in northern California, *Latitude 38*, also interviewed me. One thing that struck me when I visited civilization was how easily and naturally my siblings' children and Mary's daughter used the microwave oven. They no longer made tea by boiling water on the stove; we had reached a new era.

NEW EQUIPMENT

In San Francisco I took the opportunity to buy new equipment for *Jennifer*. West Marine, based in the USA, has a fantastic catalogue that I have used while abroad. Even if I was sitting on my boat out in the Pacific, I could fax my order over the satellite, pay with my credit card and arrange a shipment via courier to meet me in Fiji, for example. This system worked well and was an enormous help. This time, I bought new foul weather gear, wine glasses and two more GPS units.

When I got back to Fiji, I had a new genoa made. The old one had already sailed some 60,000nm and was totally worn out by the sun's ultraviolet rays. I also mounted new spars on the mast. This meant that the two spinnaker poles could stand against the mast, instead of lying on the deck, with two up- and down-hauls permanently attached. With this in place, it became easy to put out the booms in tailwinds and sail with two foresails, without using the mainsail.

OUT OF POLYNESIA

A SEASICKNESS DRAMA

In November 1994, after three months in the Fijian archipelago, we left the beautiful group of islands. We had an American family of four aboard, including two sons aged six and twelve. Corby, the younger son, was a real character and we really liked him. This family had had lengthy negotiations with our agent to sail as a paying crew for an extended time in the South Pacific. Eventually, a voyage of two months had been booked aboard *Jennifer*, spanning the whole distance from Fiji to the Marshall Islands in Micronesia. The deeply religious parents had, according to the agent, hesitated over the fact that Johanna and I were not married; they were not sure if they wanted to expose their sons to a non-married relationship.

As soon as we got out onto the open sea, the mother Rita became seasick and seriously dehydrated. Because of this, we had to make an emergency stop on Fiji's northernmost island, Rotuma, about 250nm from the main island of Viti Levu. Rotuma is not an official Port of Call, ie it is not a clearing-in harbour, which meant that boat could not come into Fiji via Rotuma without special permission from Fiji's capital, Levuka. After we anchored in the bay in front of a small island village we were immediately picked up and driven to the police station. We explained the situation, and the family asked permission to clear off the boat and fly back to Fiji, while we got permission to stay for a couple of days.

The local doctor's examination of Rita determined that she could not continue her journey at sea. The family had to wait for five days for a flight to Fiji's main island, a delay they really came to appreciate. The island of Rotuma is so far away and so isolated that its inhabitants are not accustomed to the usual stream of western visitors. Like Molokai on Hawaii, visitors also require special permission before they can land. This makes it almost like a reserve and means that Rotuma only gets visits from about five sailing boats per year. The people who live on the island are very kind, friendly and curious.

Rotuma is beautifully green and the water is crystal clear. Where we were anchored we did some amazing snorkelling from the boat, and saw some huge mantas, barracudas and sharks on one of the best coral reefs that we had ever seen. On the fifth day, in pouring tropical rain, we waved good-bye to the American family that had so unfortunately had to give up their long distance cruising plans. Still, they were grateful for the days at Rotuma and their taste of paradise. Towards the end of our visit the chief of Rotuma, a retired UN officer who'd served in Lebanon, invited Johanna and myself over for dinner.

We learned that despite the protected idyll on the island, some people were critical of the limit on the number of tourists allowed to visit. They felt that tourism would stimulate the economy and create more jobs. The never-ending conflict between development and the protection of a traditional lifestyle continues.

THE MARSHALL ISLANDS

Johanna and I were now unexpectedly alone, facing the long voyage to the Marshall Islands, a distance of 1,400nm. It was the first time ever that *Jennifer* had had such a small crew for a long ocean passage, but our new autopilot Arnold more than compensated for the lack of hands.

Our first stay was at Funafuti in the state of Tuvalu in northern Polynesia, 400nm from Rotuma. Tuvalu is one of the smallest nations in the world, with a population of only 10,000. It was once a part of the British colony of the Gilbert and Ellice Islands. When the colony got its independence in 1978, the Ellice Islands chose to go their own way and changed their name to Tuvalu, while the Gilbert Islands changed their name to Kiribati in 1979.

Because of its small size, Tuvalu is a very poor nation and can only survive with the help of foreign aid. However, Britain, its former colonial master and source of funding, is gradually leaving the Pacific. The only British colony left is Pitcairn Island, and British foreign aid to the region is gradually disappearing. Its financial support now comes from several other countries including Australia, New Zealand, the USA, Japan and South Korea. The people of Tuvalu say that they may as well belong to Japan as Japan's foreign aid in the area increases every year.

One of the country's most important exports is well-trained seamen, educated in the Tuvalu Marine School on one of the small islands on the Funafuti lagoon. Every year, 40 young people pass through the school, and after leaving they are able to find jobs aboard cargo and commercial ships. Not only are they extraordinary seamen, but they are also an inexpensive workforce. They send a large proportion of their salaries back home to Tuvalu. This totals approximately one million dollars per year and represents an important part of the small island nation's economy. However, the school only gets a small amount in funding, and its German principal has complained about the lack of equipment. When he showed us around, I understood the problem – there were rusty diesel motors and pumps more suited to a museum than a training workshop. No computers or other modern equipment was to be found. While in the village I decided to investigate the problem further and visited an ugly old former concert building where the ministry of education was situated. I managed to get a meeting with the minister for education, and he assured me that the government's commitment to the school was substantial. However, his response to my questions about the future budget of the school and future investments sent me to his assistant for more information. After an interesting and occasionally lively discussion in his office, more and more people got involved. Many questioned my impudence in challenging them. My concerns were confirmed: there was no new money for the school; it had to be run with the assistance, if any, from other industrialized countries.

The country's capital is Funafuti, on the island of Fongafale. It is essentially a village on a coral island in a big atoll, where everything is a five-minute walk away: the post office, the airport, the police station, the customs office, the only hotel on the island and the government buildings. The parliament is a building with a thatched roof and open walls, where the inhabitants can see and hear the debates between the nine (later twelve) members of parliament.

I listened in on the parliamentary discussions one day and then walked over to the government building. I managed to get hold of a minister and asked for some figures from the budget. I got some very interesting but disturbing facts. This small island nation imports goods of $16 million but exports goods worth only $1 million. This equation does not work out and the balance is covered by foreign aid. But everything has a price. Japan tells Tuvalu which way to vote at the International Whaling Commission, for example. Of all the imported items, canned tuna is the most perplexing. There is plenty of tuna in the waters around Tuvalu. The fish, however, is caught (sometimes illegally) by large fishing fleets from South Korea and Taiwan, canned in faraway places and sold back to Tuvalu. Besides income from fishing fees and copra, Tuvalu also sold its coveted internet domain suffix .tv in the year 2000. We left Polynesia from Tuvalu by sailing north, crossing the Equator and entering Micronesia.

REFLECTIONS ON THE SOUTH PACIFIC

THE FUTURE

One morning in a little bay in Tonga, some local women waded out into the water and started to fish in the traditional way. Some of them formed a half circle and held a net between them, while others hit the water and threw rocks to scare the fish into the net. They did not notice us at all; we could have been on another planet. Our lifestyle was so far away from theirs.

This traditional way of living is changing fast. An alarming report, *Pacific 2010: Challenging the Future*, has been published by the Australian National

University. It gives a frightening forecast, including the rising problem of unemployment, slums, unrealistic demands on social services, increasing lawlessness and a worn-out environment. The capital of New Guinea, Port Moresby, has already faced a frightening growth of lawlessness. The population of the South Pacific is increasing quickly but economic growth is so slow that a demographic and financial catastrophe is unavoidable. The economic growth per capita has been negative or close to zero. This means that small island nations cannot provide jobs, education or healthcare for the rapidly expanding population. All the islands are in desperate need of foreign aid, to cover their perennial budget deficits.

Foreign aid, especially from Australia and New Zealand, diminishes as the two nations direct their attention towards Asia. Furthermore, so does their willingness to absorb the excess workforce of the island nations – for example half of the population of the Cook Islands and Niue already live and work (or live on social welfare) in New Zealand.

The grim truth is that the mentality of the island nations perfectly suits their traditional lifestyle, but it is a poor match for the modern consumer-driven society. According to traditional patterns, large extended families share everything, for example the fish that are caught, or the wages earned at work. In their language, the difference between 'mine' and 'yours' does not exist. This does not encourage individuals to work for a salary, when the family will ask for its share. We met a storeowner who was eventually forced to shut down, because his family came and picked up things for free all the time, and it was hard for the owner to stop them. On top of that, the political leaders are either incompetent or hopelessly corrupt. Most of the foreign aid money pays the excessively high salaries of the many bureaucrats. The World Bank has identified the problem as a top-heavy official sector, old methods and lack of encouragement for free enterprise.

THE PLUNDERING OF THE SOUTH PACIFIC

Do the islands have any resources? Yes, they have fishing and they have tourism. By international convention, they now have control over a 200nm radius around their islands in an ocean that has a lot of fish, especially tuna. The big fishing nations such as Russia, Korea, Japan, and Taiwan with their floating fishing factories are anxious to exploit this. And exploiting is what they are doing; they pay almost nothing for the privilege of vacuuming the sea and even then some of them do not accurately report their catches.

The small island nations have made attempts to negotiate together as a group with the big fishing countries, but these have been unsuccessful. For example, Japan refuses to talk with them as a group and will only negotiate

with one country at a time. Reducing foreign aid is used as a weapon if the negotiations get too tough. Worst of all, according to the UN organization, the Food and Agriculture Organization (FAO), almost all commercially interesting fish species are nearing the brink of extinction.

Some of the Pacific nations have undeveloped rainforests that are now being logged – mostly by Malaysian companies. At the present rate of logging, the rainforests will disappear before 2050. The reason that this can happen is that many of the politicians are corrupt and the governments have limited resources to control the large and powerful forestry corporations. Like the fishing industry, the forestry industry gives inaccurate reports when it comes to how much timber they have harvested; sometimes they do not report their business at all.

Tourism is all that is left after the fish are plundered and the rainforests cleared out. The small nations hope for some income from this. Still, only 700,000 tourists travel to the South Pacific paradise every year, with Fiji and Tahiti as the most popular destinations. That number is small compared with Hawaii's six million visitors per year. Foreign companies own most of the hotels, and the profits are leaving the island nations. Out of the foreign money that comes in via tourism, approximately 70 per cent goes on imported food, construction supplies and so on, just to meet the needs of the tourism industry. On the other hand, the tourism industry creates some spin-off jobs, even if these are often the worst-paid positions such as cleaners, porters and dishwashers.

This is a very dark picture, but the numbers are taken from official documents and books. Considering the other problems facing the Earth – flooding, hurricanes, earthquakes and civil war, this is a relatively small issue. Excluding Hawaii and New Guinea, the population of the entire South Pacific area is only two million. Again I repeat what an American politician once said: 'Who gives a damn?'

MICRONESIA – THE SMALL ISLANDS

We sail on to Micronesia and further through the South Pacific. The whole region seems to be a paradise, one of the most beautiful and least spoiled places on Earth. Our visit to Micronesia is one of the high points of my sail around the world. We cross the Equator, sail over the deepest place on Earth, have one of our most exciting dives ever in the Bikini lagoon, and meet a president, chieftains, missionaries, Peace Corps activists and master navigators. We are also guests of honour at a village feast.

WE CROSS THE EQUATOR

Sailing the 700nm from Tuvalu in Polynesia to Kiribati in Micronesia includes crossing the Equator. The winds in a high-pressure system blow clockwise on the north side of the Equator and counterclockwise on the south side. The Trade winds change direction from south-east south of the Equator to north-east north of the Equator.

Around the Equator there is an area with very little wind, the Doldrums, which are the dread of many sailors. In earlier times sailing ships could be left floating for many weeks in the Doldrums waiting for wind, with their rations of food and water slowly running out. Above and below these Doldrums lie the 'horse latitudes'. It was there that the horses on board these ships were often slaughtered when the remaining food stocks on board were only enough for the crew.

The satellite messages we received also changed in character from one side of the Equator to the other. On the southern half of the globe not much happened – a few missing containers, some warnings about storms, hurricanes and oilrigs and a few MAYDAY calls. On the northern half of the globe the satellite messages were much livelier. I was quite struck by the warlike element to many of them. Nearly every day there were warnings about bombings, cannon firings and missile launches. Furthermore, and maybe scariest of all, there were plenty of warnings of pirate attacks, especially in the South China Sea and the Malacca Strait.

KIRIBATI – OUR FIRST STOP IN MICRONESIA

Before we left Funafuti in Tuvalu we got permission to visit Nanumea, the country's northernmost atoll. Three days after setting sail we reached our destination. Arriving early in the morning, the tide was on its way out of the atoll's lagoon, which caused large, steep waves to nearly block the entrance. Faced with the choice of waiting half a day for higher water or continuing on to Kiribati, we chose the latter alternative.

An American boat that we were in daily contact with via SSB radio sailed to the atoll at high tide the day after us. Due to strong winds they wound up 'trapped' on the atoll for ten wonderful days before they could get their boat out through the passage again.

Kiribati prides itself on being the only country in the world that is on both sides of the Equator *and* the International Dateline; it also covers a vast area of water. It was here that we saw the first signs of the Second World War: big Japanese cannons and burned-out tanks on the beach. The capital city, Bairiki, is situated on a small strip of land on the Tarawa atoll's south side.

The people of Kiribati still live in traditional houses – wooden structures on stilts with straw roofs and open sides (no walls). Some houses have steel wire around them instead of walls, which makes them look like cages. We never dared to ask what the wire was there for, but we guessed that the purpose was either to prevent their few earthly possessions from tumbling out or to stop the chickens and dogs from getting in.

One day Johanna and I climbed up on the enormous Japanese cannons and searched for an old Japanese bunker. We met a young man who invited us to follow him home to meet his family. When we got there we climbed up into their cage and were presented to his extended family, a group of 30 people. That evening there was a feast where we, as guests of honour, sat on handmade pandanus rugs (made of dried leaves) on a podium where we could watch young boys and girls doing traditional dances while we were served a superb meal of taro, fish, coconut meat, breadfruit and bananas.

Just before the feast we saw a few of the women go out to the nearby food store – a little kiosk half-full of canned food, Coca-Cola and potato chips – and buy a few cans of corned beef. We realized to our embarrassment that they were buying it for us, as we westerners were apparently known to love the stuff. It was not just that they were spending some of their very limited funds on western canned food for us; what made it worse was the fact that we actually hated corned beef – it is hard to think of anything less wholesome, saltier or fattier. We really felt like colonial dignitaries and the party made a very strong impression on us. The next day we invited all of them on board *Jennifer*. They had never been on a modern sailboat before.

THE MARSHALL ISLANDS

BUTARITARI ATOLL

On our sail from Tarawa to the Marshall Islands we stopped alongside the Butaritari atoll. This distant and isolated atoll gets very few foreign visitors and is very sheltered from the outside world. Yet it was another place in the South Pacific with innumerable aeroplane and shipwrecks from the Second World War.

It was on Tarawa and Butaritari that the American offensive began in 1943, when Admiral Chester Nimitz and his 3rd Fleet drove the Japanese out of Micronesia while US General Douglas MacArthur with his 7th Fleet opened the Japanese southern flank via the Solomon Islands, Papau New Guinea and the Philippines. The war between the Japanese and the American forces in the Pacific Ocean was long and brutal.

The Americans captured island after island with enormous losses on both sides. The inhabitants of the islands also suffered terribly, of course. While sailing in Micronesia we were nearly consumed by the history, since some of the Second World War's most decisive battles took place in this part of the world.

'SHANGHAIED' IN PARADISE

Most of the small countries in Micronesia are in desperate need of skilled workers – electricians, mechanics and computer experts. In spite of the fact that it is generally very difficult for cruising sailors to get work permits in these island states it is often the case that those with special competencies get 'shanghaied' (ie businesses use coercive techniques to make them stay).

We met many such sailors who had been called upon to stay and help with different tasks – to operate the radio station, run the local newspaper, install electrical systems or teach computer skills. On one island a Swedish sailor spent four years running a fish freezing factory where the Russian and Korean fish fleets froze and stored their catches until they were air-shipped to markets in Tokyo and Hawaii. Although he tried to train local men to run the factory there was no one who wanted to take over so, every year

when he wanted to sail off to somewhere new, the government raised his salary in desperation so that he wouldn't leave the island.

On the really isolated islands in Micronesia the situation is less complicated. Even a fairly non-technical person like myself is considered competent. David, who sailed with us for two months in Micronesia and who is very handy, became the most sought-after man on the islands. Like many other long-distance sailors we met in Micronesia we helped install solar panels, check batteries, fix clocks, repair chainsaws and drill and cut metal, as most boats are relatively well equipped with tools that the locals don't have.

As thanks for our help we were allowed to wander freely on the islands, take pictures of the inhabitants (one should normally ask the chief for permission), pick bananas, breadfruit, papaya and catch fish. It ended up being a great trade-off.

THE BIKINI ATOLL

The world's first three atom bombs were all set off in 1945. They were 'Trinity' in Alamogordo in the New Mexico desert, 'Little Boy' over Hiroshima and 'Fat Man' over Nagasaki. In the summer of 1946 the Americans exploded the world's fourth and fifth atom bombs over the Bikini atoll, which were given the names Able and Baker. Able and Baker were tested on a fleet made up of 95 battleships, cruisers, destroyers and submarines and one aircraft carrier.

All of these ships were veterans from the great sea battles of the Second World War – Pearl Harbor, Coral Sea, Midway, the Solomon Islands and the breakout attempt in the North Atlantic of the German warship *Bismarck*. So was USS *Saratoga*, the American aircraft carrier that was once the biggest in the world; *Nagato*, the Japanese warship that was Admiral Yamamoto's flagship during the Japanese attack on Pearl Harbor; *Prins Eugen*, the heavy German cruiser; and USS *Nevada*, the American battleship that sank at Pearl Harbor but was later salvaged.

The size of the fleet on which the A-bombs were tested was at the time the fourth largest in the world. All of the ships were anchored in the Bikini lagoon in the northern area of the Marshall Islands. A total of around 43,000 American sailors and soldiers, journalists from around the world, observers from the UN and American senators and congressmen were there to witness the historical event.

The whole course of events, named Operation Crossroads, is extraordinarily well described by the American lawyer Jonathan Weisgall. He represented the inhabitants of the Bikini atoll against the American government in his book

Operation Crossroads: The Atomic Tests at Bikini Atoll. The photographs in the book are incredible. The A-bomb tests were really about a bitter rivalry between the American Navy and the Army (which included the Air Force at that time).

The Army/Air Force maintained that the naval fleet was now obsolete due to the arrival of the nuclear age and thus they hoped to sink as many ships as possible. The Navy, on the other hand, just wanted to find out what effects atom bombs would have on battleships and wanted to save as many ships as possible. At stake was the enormous funding from the American Congress to the two service branches. Many boats, of course, were sunk. As a result of the lack of skill of the pilot who dropped Able from a B-29 Super Fortress bomber many of the big ships were indeed sunk, but significantly fewer than had been expected, so the Navy's survival was assured.

Before Operation Crossroads began, the US government convinced the 167 inhabitants of Bikini that their island and lagoon were needed for the good of humankind. The islanders were temporarily moved to Rongerik, an uninhabited atoll nearby, with promises that they would soon be able to move back to Bikini.

So began the tragic story of how the Bikini inhabitants became nuclear nomads. It was soon clear that they could not survive on Rongerik – the island could not produce enough food for them and the 167 Bikini refugees nearly starved to death (this may have been the reason the atoll was uninhabited). After two years they were moved from Rongerik to Kwajalein, the world's biggest atoll, and shortly thereafter to the little island of Kili, which lacks both a lagoon and a reef, making it virtually impossible to fish there. The Bikini people call Kili the 'prison island'.

In 1954 the United States exploded Bravo (a fifteen-megaton hydrogen bomb that was 1,200 times stronger than the Hiroshima bomb Little Boy) over the Bikini lagoon, pulverizing one of its islands. Bravo was the most powerful and dirtiest bomb that had ever been detonated and when it exploded it spread radiation to all the surrounding islands.

Bikini was left extremely radioactive and the inhabitants of the nearby atolls, Rongelap and Utirik, were forced to evacuate. A Japanese fishing boat that didn't hear the warnings was also badly exposed to radiation. The evacuation was not carried out until two to three days after the test, however. The government of the Marshall Islands asserted that this delay occurred with the full knowledge of the American defence authorities and that the inhabitants of the area were used as radioactive guinea pigs in order to test the effects of radiation exposure on human beings.

The inhabitants of Rongelap, were moved back to their homes in 1957 without any radiation sanitation taking place, in spite of the fact that the United States had found that the atoll had higher radiation levels than Bikini. The population of Rongelap thus began to suffer from radiation-related illnesses. Yet despite many appeals to the American government that they be re-evacuated, they got no assistance. In desperation the people of Rongelap turned to Greenpeace, who evacuated the whole population to Kwajalein with their ship *Rainbow Warrior* in 1985, in a widely publicized media event. (*Rainbow Warrior* was the same ship that was sunk by the French intelligence service in New Zealand later the same year.)

But the Bikini inhabitants' living situation was still not solved. In 1969 the Americans asserted that Bikini was sanitized and safe, so its former inhabitants moved back. But, ten years later, the United States realized that Bikini was not safe at all. The inhabitants had been exposed to the largest dose of plutonium ever measured in any population group, and so the nuclear nomads were moved again, this time to the 'prison island' of Kili. Many of the people became seriously ill and when no compensation was offered from the US they chose to sue the American government, with Weisgall as their lawyer.

Eventually, the American government offered a fund of $100 million. It is being used to clean up and put the Bikini atoll in order so that its native population can return home. But the fund is not used only for this purpose. Every living Bikini inhabitant was supposed to receive about $2,000 annually in compensation from the fund. From the original 167 inhabitants there are now more than 2,000, as many men from the Marshall Islands rushed to marry Bikini women when the fund was established.

WHOSE RESPONSIBILITY?

It is easy to take the side of the people of Bikini when one learns about the way they were treated by the United States and to a certain degree by the international community. But there is another side to the story. The Bikini people, with Weisgall's help, are constantly trying to get more money from the American government. They argue that the $2,000 annual compensation is not enough to live on. It would have been enough for the 167 people who lived there in 1946, but of course it is not enough for the several thousand people living there today or for the rapidly increasing population of the future.

The fact is that the people of Bikini today do not want to work and they believe that the United States has a responsibility to take care of them forever. With the original $100 million in the fund they have meetings in Las Vegas, travel far and wide, buy consumer goods – and avoid working. In 2001 the fund was supposed to be increased to $500 million and there are still lawsuits pending in the United States courts to obtain that money and more from the

American government. When a proposal was put forward to build a hotel and diving centre with completely modern equipment, the people of Bikini originally voted down the project when they found out that it would only generate $100,000 in revenue per year. One could say that the people of Bikini have gone from being nuclear nomads to being welfare abusers. The fund has also created internal conflicts in the Marshall Islands. The national government has no overview or influence over the Bikini fund, which is instead controlled by the Bikini islanders themselves. The president of the Marshall Islands is persistent in his attempts to change this with various political manoeuvres, however.

The construction of a nuclear waste dump for Japanese and American reactors' waste on the Bikini atoll has been under discussion. According to the project's advocates, Bikini is still radioactive anyway. The money generated was said to be about a billion dollars. Greed knows no boundaries. Nearby countries were strongly protesting against this proposal, as one might expect, and nothing came out of it.

In the Bikini atoll the island of Eneu is now sanitized and ready for people to move home, according to the Americans, and a new airport and harbour were under construction when we were there. The problem is that you can't eat anything that grows on the island, such as coconuts, vegetables and fruit because there is still caesium (a radioactive metal) in the soil. The likelihood of the original inhabitants wanting to move back under such conditions is not high. But I have heard that the diving station has opened.

THE OTHER BIKINI

The other bikini is the famous bathing suit that got its name when a French clothing designer presented his new creation in Cannes in 1946 – 'the Atom', the world's smallest bathing suit. He was quickly overshadowed by another designer, who asserted that his 'bikini' was tinier than the smallest bathing suit in the world. The second designer used the name bikini to symbolize the explosive appearance of the new bathing suit. He could not get any models to wear the new bikini, so he was forced to hire prostitutes to model them instead. Eventually, with the help of Brigitte Bardot, the bikini's enduring success was assured.

DIVING TO AN AIRCRAFT CARRIER

Early on New Year's Day in 1995 *Jennifer* sailed into the Bikini lagoon. The sun was just coming up and it looked like a big, glaring red ball hovering above the horizon in the first minutes of the early morning. It was a gloomy reminder to us of the enormous fireball that man had created 50 years earlier.

The reason for our early arrival was that we wanted it to go unnoticed. The plan was to dive on the sunken aircraft carrier USS *Saratoga*, which required permission that we did not have.

We hoped that on New Year's Day the personnel at the American research station would be tired and hungover, and less likely to notice us. We had also been unsuccessful in our attempts to obtain the co-ordinates to the USS *Saratoga* from the Marshall Islands' authorities, so we got them instead from the June 1992 edition of *National Geographic*, which featured a story called 'Bikini's Nuclear Graveyard' (see also 'Gray Reef Sharks' in the January 1995 edition).

For two days we were anchored above the sunken ship in strong winds and choppy seas in the middle of the lagoon, 4nm from the Bikini Islands. It was a giddy feeling, being anchored over a part of world history with USS *Saratoga* 50m below us.

When the atom bomb Baker was detonated underwater in 1946 somewhere beneath us, USS *Saratoga* was lifted 13m upwards by one of the largest waves the Earth has ever seen – 32m high. At the same time an enormous mass of water was thrown up in the air and crashed down on her flight deck. Eight hours after the explosion she sank and today she lies astonishingly intact 50m under the ocean, with Navy Hellcats aircraft and battle-ready torpedoes and bombs on board. The reason for this is that the Americans wanted to make the circumstances as realistic as possible during the testing. USS *Saratoga* has since become one of the world's most spectacular places to dive.

Johanna and I made four exciting deep dives to check out the huge ship, but only two per day because of the enormous depth. Down on the flight deck we ran into five big reef sharks that seemed to be patrolling the ship. By this time in our travels, after two years of intensive diving in the South Pacific, we were fairly used to meeting sharks on our dives so we weren't especially excited. We just ignored them – we didn't have time for them, quite frankly. Due to the depth our time underwater was limited and we wanted to spend as much time as possible inside USS *Saratoga*. We were totally fascinated with her and swam wherever we could. We explored the tower on the flight deck, the hangar deck (the deck under the flight deck) where we were able to sit in the airplanes' cockpits and check out the bombs and torpedoes and the huge cannons on the ship's sides.

Those two days' dives were undoubtedly the most amazing we have ever done. Thanks to the clarity of the water we could even observe how the flight deck had been powerfully compressed, the result of the enormous mass of water that had fallen on the ship after the detonation. We also noticed that the ship had very little coral growing on it and thought this may have been due to radiation.

At the end of the second day a boat came out from the research station and asked if we had permission to dive. We pretended not to understand and said that we had permission to sail to Bikini, which we had got in the capital city of Majuro. We were asked to motor in to Bikini Island, where the American Department of Energy (DOE) carries out scientific tests on the area's radioactivity. Rather than being reprimanded we were invited to dinner and shown around the rather shabby buildings. On the nearby island of Eneu an American construction company had built a new airport and harbour, and we stayed there for ten days as their guests, ate in their cafeteria, borrowed videos and drove around the island on three-wheeled motorbikes. Ours was the only guest boat there since few sailors go so far north in the Marshall archipelago. When we left many of the US crew on the island wanted to join us, but I did not feel like having the US Navy chasing us for letting their sailors 'flee' Bikini atoll.

SAILING THROUGH MICRONESIA

Johanna and I had been sailing alone for three weeks among the Marshall Islands and visited many atolls. We never saw another sailboat other than at the main island, Majuro. Just before Christmas we had anchored near the Ailinglaplap atoll. Shortly afterwards a man in a canoe paddled out and invited us to the island's Christmas celebrations.

We took the dinghy in to the main village that evening with high expectations. It turned out to be a double celebration. It was a Christmas party, but more importantly it was a celebration of the birthday of the chief's one-year-old son. The chief of the atoll was also the finance minister in the Marshall Islands' government and therefore a very important person. Furthermore, he was married to the president's daughter – one of many examples of the widespread nepotism in this part of the world (family/clan ties being of the utmost importance).

Three hundred of the atoll's residents had gathered for the party, most of them children. Palm-covered wooden structures had been set up as shelter for all of the food and drink that was served in abundance. Yet there was something artificial about it all. The food looked professionally catered – we found out later that part of it had actually been flown in from Majuro.

The chieftain was, naturally, curious about us and we talked with him that evening. He told us that he was now most comfortable in the 'civilized' capital Majuro with its air-conditioned offices, homes, cars and superior food. We got the impression that this event had been arranged mainly as a courtesy visit on his part to keep in contact with his clan (and maybe also to defend/protect his title and position in the community). It is rather like the way our politicians in the western world make their obligatory visits to their voters before every election. He could hardly wait to get on the plane back to Majuro – by six o'clock the next morning he was already in the air.

In January 1995 a new crew was assembled aboard *Jennifer*, all Americans except for one Swede. Computer expert David and policewoman Brenda, both divers from California, sailed with us for eight weeks, all the way to Guam. Eugene, a 65-year-old retired business executive, was with us for a month. He was about to start a new career as a volunteer in the American Peace Corps and his assignment was to teach free market economics in the former Eastern Bloc. Judy, a 40-something woman with a PhD, worked for Apple Computers and sailed with us for two of her five weeks of sabbatical. Grace, 50, was a sailor and a diver who had taken a month off work before starting a new job as a research assistant. Finally there was 40-year-old Eva from Stockholm, a computer programmer and diver who sailed with us for a month.

On our sail through Micronesia we visited many islands and atolls, including Kwajalein, the world's largest atoll. The Kwajalein atoll is 60nm long – nearly all of Stockholm's archipelago could fit inside it – as could both the American and British Virgin Islands. The American Army rents the larger part of the atoll for its Star Wars tests and countless radar installations of different sizes cover many of the atoll's islands.

We witnessed an Inter-Continental Ballistic Missile (ICBM) that had been fired in California – 3,800nm away – drop down in the lagoon. It looked like a gigantic fireworks display. First it was a rocket that got closer and closer and then it suddenly split into many smaller rockets (multiple re-entries). It was both impressive and scary to think that all of these smaller missiles could be armed with their own nuclear weapons. Against these incoming rockets the United States was testing its Anti-Ballistic Missiles (ABM), whose development is the focal point of the Star Wars program.

KWAJALEIN AND EBEYE

On the largest of the atoll's islands, Kwajalein (the same name as for the whole of the atoll), the American Army has built a mini-America for the personnel of the base. Everything is just as it would be in an American suburb – well-groomed lawns, golf courses, supermarkets, swimming pools, clubs and so on. We had hoped to get some supplies at the base but we couldn't get permission to enter. We were only able to visit the neighbouring island of Ebeye, where the conditions are very different from those on

Kwajalein – bad roads, old car wrecks, rubbish everywhere and homes built out of sheet metal and plywood. It was to Ebeye that the original 450 inhabitants of Kwajalein were forcibly relocated when the American Army base was built. The problem is that Ebeye is 13 times smaller than the island of Kwajalein, which only contains about 1,500 people. When we visited, more than 10,000 people were living on Ebeye in very cramped conditions. Today more than 25 per cent of the Marshall Islands' population (about 60,000 in total) lives on Ebeye.

A few of the inhabitants of this little island have found work at the Army base, but the rest of the population gets by on support payments from the United States as compensation for losing their home island. Being on Ebeye was bizarre, with unemployment, slum conditions, melancholy and the Cold War right in the middle of paradise. The population has long since abandoned their old way of life – fishing and living on the copra trade.

Most of the young people from nearby atolls go to Ebeye for the American payouts, possible job opportunities on the base and the temptations of a consumer society. Those who don't receive any money in compensation live off their rich relatives who do. The only ones who seem to have the possibility of getting out of this sad situation are the Marshallese women who have American boyfriends on the base. But when the boyfriends take them back to the US they face an array of different problems. This is a place where one can see the contrasts between the First and the Third World just 2nm apart.

At Kwajalein we dived on the German heavy cruiser *Prins Eugen* – the smaller sister ship to the German battleship *Bismarck*, one of the Second World War's most feared and advanced warships. *Prins Eugen* was captured by the Allies and taken to the Bikini atoll where it survived Able and Baker. The ship was then towed to Kwajalein where she was sunk in 1946 as a result of the high radiation to which she had been exposed. She now lies upside down in the lagoon, her large hull and propellers relatively intact. The wreck lies in shallow water, so we were able to swim and dive around inside the ship without difficulty.

THE CAROLINE ISLANDS

KOSRAE AND POHNPEI

From the Marshall Islands we sailed 300nm south-west to the garden island of Kosrae, which has 7,000 inhabitants. It is a high, green, fertile island, thick with foliage. We stopped for a few days and then continued to Pohnpei, an additional 300nm west. Both islands are part of the Federated States of

Micronesia (FSM) in the archipelago of the Caroline Islands (or the Carolines). We sailed mostly on a broad reach (with the wind from behind at an angle) and seldom at more than 20 knots. A few of the crew got seasick. As usual, we caught fish – we always trailed two lines behind the boat and we sometimes caught as many as two or even three fish within minutes (usually tuna, gold mackerel or barracuda). They were quickly made into delicious Japanese-inspired sashimi and sushi.

Like the island of Kosrae, Pohnpei is high, green and thickly foliaged. It is also very, very wet – with powerful and frequent rain. Pohnpei is the main island of the FSM. On the south end of the island is the old ruined city of Nan Madol, from an earlier civilization, 1,000 years ago. The city consists of a series of 80 artificial islands linked by a network of streets in the form of canals – not unlike Venice. It is only possible to get to Nan Madol by boat or small aeroplane. It is impressive that a civilization so poor in materials could build such a city. If Nan Madol was more easily accessible to the rest of the world it would probably be as famous and as well visited as the ruins of the Inca and the Maya.

During our stay on Pohnpei we anchored at the sailing club, which is the natural gathering place for westerners working in the country. Through them we got a good picture of the state of affairs on the island. During one restaurant visit we met the FSM's president from 1991–97, Bailey Olter, with whom we exchanged a few words. He was in the middle of an election campaign and since his face was on so many election posters we recognized him immediately.

TRUK LAGOON

The next place we visited was the Truk Lagoon, or Chuuk as it is now called. During the Second World War the Japanese made this big and well-protected lagoon their most important naval base in Micronesia. This was mainly due to its having very good sites for anchoring. In 1944 Admiral Nimitz's aircraft carrier-based planes bombed the Japanese fleet here, and although the Japanese ships frantically tried to get out of the lagoon, 60 were sunk.

Nearly all of the shipwrecks are unmoved. This now means that Chuuk is probably the world's Mecca for diving on wrecks. We dived down to ships where we found aeroplanes, tanks, bicycles, gas masks and human bones. The diving was fascinating but also made us reflect on the horrors of the Second World War.

Chuuk is probably the most neglected and mismanaged of all the islands in Micronesia. Its lawlessness is seen at all levels of society. One afternoon, while we were visiting a neighbouring boat, two young men drove up in a small motorboat and asked for gasoline. Before we realized what was going on they had untied our American friend's dinghy and driven away with it, with the outboard motor and everything else – right in front of our eyes. We were all very upset but there was nothing we could do. The skipper rushed below to get his gun but when he came up again the range was too great to shoot. He was enraged and would have undoubtedly shot the perpetrators if he could have done. A long-distance sailor is totally dependent on his or her dinghy – and all the more dependent on the outboard motor. With hardly any marinas, cruising sailors always have to anchor their yacht and take the dinghy in to shore to clear in and out and to get supplies. Sometimes you need to anchor quite a long way from land and if there is a strong wind it can be very difficult to row in to shore.

The thieves also took the gas canister from *Jennifer* while I watched helplessly from afar. To lose a gas canister is not normally a problem – you can buy a new one for about $25. But if you are outside the civilized world it's a whole different ballgame. It turned out to be nearly impossible to get a new gas canister in Chuuk – after looking everywhere I finally found a canister in one store – for $125.

OUTER ISLANDS OF THE CAROLINES

Up until this point we had only visited the larger islands in the FSM. Now we wanted to visit the outer islands in the central Carolines. These islands have between 70 and 500 inhabitants each and only a few sailboats come through each year. The local people eat mainly what the islands provide them with – taro root, breadfruit, bananas and, of course, fish. When they want to eat meat they catch large turtles. After the turtles are captured they are kept alive, lying upside down, sometimes for many weeks. We felt sorry for them, so we put coconuts under their heads so that their necks wouldn't hang down towards the ground. The island people thought we were crazy. But I suppose if the islanders had come to Sweden or the USA and tried to make things more comfortable for our pigs (many of whom do, after all, spend their lives squeezed into iron cages) we would probably question their sanity. In any case, when they prepare a meal with turtle meat they boil the turtles alive. Despite this I must admit that the meat tastes very good.

The islands' inhabitants live mainly in airy huts that are covered with palm-like leaves. The huts look very picturesque – healthy and airy. But after a catastrophic typhoon in 1990 the American defence department gave the islanders small, ugly, closed-in cottages made of cement and plywood. After just a few years these new cottages looked like slum dwellings – the plywood cracked and the cement seemed to suck up water, turning black. Inside they are cold, dark and cheerless. The only advantage to these structures that I could see is that they can apparently survive typhoons.

The people of these islands live in a matriarchal society – when the men get married they move in with the woman's family. In spite of this, the women have low status. For the most part they speak little or no English, work in the taro fields (a hard and dirty job) and do all the cooking. Women still go bare-breasted – the breast having no sexual meaning. The thigh, on the other hand, does have a sexual meaning, so women keep them covered. The men wear only loincloths, a custom that I took up while in the tropics because it felt good and much airier.

Men sit together in the canoe houses, which are both storage places for the islands' canoes and gathering places for men (like pubs) where women are not allowed. In the canoe houses the men talk, smoke and drink 'tuba', the fermented sap of coconut flowers. Unfortunately, the men often get quite drunk. Every so often the women on one of the islands stage a revolt and force the chieftain to forbid the drinking of tuba. The result is that the men have started drinking other fermented drinks instead – ones that taste even worse than tuba, if that is possible. We spent a lot of time in the canoe houses and were 'forced' to drink both tuba and other such drinks.

Sometimes the men go fishing, or they build beautiful out-rigged canoes by hand, according to their ancient traditions. They use coconut twine (made from coconut shells) to lash together the planks of wood from breadfruit trees. Those who commit crimes on the islands are given as punishment the job of plaiting together the twine, and large coils hang from the canoe houses' ceilings. The planks' joints on the canoes are then sealed with strips of twine soaked in the sticky sap of the breadfruit tree. The typhoon of 1990, destroyed most of the breadfruit trees on the islands. This has meant that the wood must be bought elsewhere at high prices and thus canoe building has declined dramatically.

Most men still use traditional sailing canoes for fishing and transportation, but the use of GRP boats and outboard motors is increasing rapidly. More money is now reaching the outlying islands, which allows the inhabitants to buy new boats and engines. However, on the southernmost island, Kapingamarangi, the islanders have decided to outlaw outboard motors in order to protect their traditional way of life.

The men lay claim to the few paid jobs on the islands. All the teachers are men, for example. A kindergarten was recently started up with American initiative and financing. Even there the men laid claim to all the best jobs. It is the same with the few jobs in healthcare. We didn't see a single woman in an occupation that recieved a salary from the government. It may be paradise for men – but it is hardly so for women.

Near the Caroline Islands we came across the missionary ship *Sea Haven*, which was well equipped to work among these isolated islands. The ship was run by a young American couple who in the span of a couple of years had equipped the ship themselves with the help of an assortment of churches in the US and in Europe.

There were a few volunteers on board who had financed their stay through the sponsorship of their own churches. The missionaries had collected together and brought, among other things, used spectacles from the US, and they sailed around helping those who were vision-impaired. We witnessed just such an occasion on one island when an older woman recieved a pair of glasses. I don't know how much or how little she could see before, but it was touching to see how happy she was that she could finally see clearly. She bubbled with joy and surprise and her relatives' elated voices echoed all around. That project is one of the best missionary activities I have seen and we were very impressed by the couple leading it.

On many of the islands in Micronesia (and around the world) we became acquainted with members of the Peace Corps. The Peace Corps was set up by President Kennedy in 1961. Although financial support for the organization has fluctuated over the years – particularly when the Republicans were dominant in Congress – the Peace Corps is still a vital organization that undertakes international projects, especially in former American colonies and other areas of interest. The projects are carried out by young volunteers who commit themselves to working in a developing country for a period of at least two years. During our travels, we also met independent young Swedish men and women with a similar mission. For the most part they taught subjects such as English or agricultural techniques in local schools. They were often placed totally alone on far-flung islands, which meant that it was easy to get to know them, as they were keen for contact with others after months of being the only westerner on their island.

PULUWAT ATOLL

Puluwat and its wonderful lagoon became our favorite atoll. It is made up of five islands, with a tight passage that opens onto the beautiful, sheltered lagoon. About 500 people live here. We spent ten days at Puluwat in the company of three other boats. We also spent a great deal of time on land with the local people, following their way of life and helping them with different technical problems. David, being very handy, was immediately popular with everyone. We visited homes and schools, and spent many hours in the canoe houses drinking tuba with the men. Even Johanna and Brenda were allowed in on the grounds that they were foreigners. David took a video

camera along with him and filmed the island's children. At the end of our stay David played his video on the village's only VCR, which seemed to enchant the islanders.

With the help of the dinghy we explored the lagoon and dived, snorkelled and fished. On one of the five islands there was an old Japanese lighthouse with a 50m-high tower that we were able to climb and enjoy an incredible view over the atoll. One evening we invited the island's chief, Ersin, to dinner on board *Jennifer*. He was between 30–40 years old and very good-looking. A well as being the chief he was also a teacher and a priest. In addition to Ersin's small Protestant congregation the island also had a Catholic congregation and a group of Jehovah's Witnesses. Ersin was in the process of building a new church – a project that really engaged him and made him proud.

The church was to be quite large in spite of the fact that the congregation was both small (perhaps 50 people) and poor. A touch of megalomania, some might say, but you can see the same phenomenon in Europe too, where small towns have built huge cathedrals. With financial support from western churches, Ersin's church has surely been built by now.

Ersin was one of the most harmonious, positive, content and happy men I have ever met and it was a pleasure to have him on board that evening. He told us that he had visited the larger islands as well as the United States. But he had obviously seen what western consumer societies had to offer and come to the conclusion that things were better at home.

THE LAST OF THE MASTER NAVIGATORS

In a small group of islands in the Carolines – Puluwat, Satawal and Lamotrek – travellers can find what might be the last of the world's seafaring cultures. What has been preserved here is not just the legacy from Micronesia and Polynesia but that of the whole world, of mankind, from innumerable generations of seafarers and navigators. Long before the Vikings set out on their journeys of discovery from Scandinavia, the people of the South Pacific had learned to sail thousands of nautical miles without a compass, sextant or chart.

Through observing the rise and fall of 150 fixed stars, as well as the currents and wave patterns, they could read the sea like a map. Two western sailors have followed these last navigators and documented their knowledge – Dr David Lewis in his book, *We, the Navigators: the Ancient Art of Land Finding in the Pacific* (also see *National Geographic*, December 1974 for an article about 'Isles of the Pacific') and Stephen Thomas's book, *The Last Navigator*.

Dr Lewis, a New Zealand explorer, started his research on traditional navigators in the 1960s. By this time most of the old navigator sailing canoes had been dragged up on land and put away in the canoe houses. In 1965 he sailed with the Pacific navigator Tevake (meaning 'tropicbird') on many long ocean journeys, without the use of instruments. At the end of one of these journeys, the old navigator pointed at a seabird that was flying overhead and said with pride and regret, 'My name, Tevake, is the same as that bird's. Once I was as young as he is, was as free, and I could travel as far.'

A few years later, when this proud old man felt that he was becoming a burden to his family, he said goodbye to his relatives and friends and paddled out on his beloved sea in a fragile one-man canoe, never to return. We met Dr Lewis on Fiji in 1994. He was then in his 70s and still sailing. At the yacht club where we had anchored we listened as he spoke eloquently about the art of traditional navigation and the old master navigators.

Stephen Thomas learned from the master navigator Mau Piailug from Satawal in the Caroline Islands. Today Mau is the best known of the master navigators. He became world famous when he sailed *Hokule'a* – a 65ft (20m) copy of a Polynesian double-hulled canoe 2,800nm from Hawaii to Tahiti in 1976, without the help of modern navigation equipment. Stephen Thomas and Mau lived and sailed together between 1983–4. In 2007 Mau presided over the first Pwo ceremony (a sacred initiation ritual in which students become master mariners) for navigators on the island of Satawal in 56 years. At the initiation five native Hawaiians and eleven others were inducted into Pwo as master navigators. The Polynesian Voyaging Society presented Mau Piailug with a canoe, the *Alingano Maisu*, in recognition of his vital role in reviving traditional wayfinding navigation in Hawaii.

We tried to track down the surviving master navigators on the islands we visited. This was the primary reason for our visit to Satawal, the main home of expert navigators. Unfortunately, we were disappointed. When we got to the village, ready to present ourselves to the chiefs, they demanded $20 as a landing fee from each of us. It was a fee that they had started collecting from cruise ship passengers. We tried to explain that we were sailors who had come a long way with gifts for the island's school and with the desire to meet the master navigators. But the chiefs were implacable. We tried to negotiate a $5 anchoring fee, but they wouldn't settle for that either. I felt it was important that we didn't set a precedent and therefore refused to pay more.

The visit to Satawal left a bitter aftertaste in our mouths. Later, on the island of Lamotrek, I met one of the Satawal chiefs's sons as well as one of the Peace Corps activists that had paddled out to meet us when we first arrived. They told us that it was jealousy and rivalry between the chiefs and the master navigators that was behind the demand for a landing fee.

Our request had evidently stirred up those feelings. Apparently, the crew of another sailboat that landed the day after we did was treated much better and they were not asked to pay a landing fee.

The art of traditional navigation is at risk of dying out within a few generations. Unfortunately, there are not many young men who are interested or ambitious enough to devote many years of their lives to intensive study in order to become a 'palu', a navigator with status higher than that of the chieftains. The education begins at the age of five. A 'star compass' made up of 32 stones is laid out on the floor of the canoe house where the master navigator teaches his skills to the young students. Leaves are placed inside the ring of the compass, representing swells coming from different directions and in the middle of the compass is a canoe made of leaves. Each of the stones represents a constellation on the horizon.

The stone furthest north is the North Star and the one furthest south is the Southern Cross. The stones on the right side of the circle represent the stars that rise in the east, while the stones on the left side are the same stars when they set in the west. The navigator navigates, therefore, through setting his course towards particular stars when they rise or set on the horizon. When a star has risen too high in the sky it can't be used anymore and the next star takes its place. The best navigators learn the star patterns between almost all of the Caroline Islands.

During the day, when the stars aren't visible, it is the swells that are the navigators' foremost aid. To demonstrate how a particular swell can affect the boat when it is on a particular course, the navigator puts the palm leaf representing the swell under the leaf representing the canoe so that the student can see how the canoe moves in reaction to the swell. The navigators know, of course, that the islands stay fixed and that it is their canoes that travel over the sea, but when they sail they imagine that the situation is the reverse. The canoe is the fixed point, while the islands are moving. Beyond the horizon, alongside the canoe's path through the water, are islands that will come under new star patterns after the canoe moves forward.

A third aid to the navigators is the study of seabirds. Certain kinds of birds that breed on the flat coral islands set off on daily fishing trips as far as 20nm from land. Thus, if a navigator is unsure about his position and catches sight of these birds, all he has to do is wait for sundown and then follow the birds' trip back to land in a line as straight as an arrow. Long ago, the king of Tonga was sailing back from Samoa, where he had been at a tattooing ceremony. On the way home the king's navigator got lost. An elderly, blind navigator of lower rank, Kaho, directed that the canoe be turned into the wind and then had his son lower him down to the water so that he could feel it with his hand. Kaho then told the king that they were in Fiji's waters. 'What will we do?' asked the king. 'We have nearly run out of our supplies of food and water.' The old blind man then asked what the sun's position was. Then he answered, 'When the sun is in the middle of the sky we will see land.'

A few hours later they saw one of Fiji's easterly islands. The grateful king knighted Kaho and appointed him chief navigator. Many years later one of Kaho's descendants revealed that his forefather's show of dipping his hand in the water was just a trick to impress the king. Kaho knew that land was near because his son had told him that a particular type of bird had been sighted. Cloud formations and reflections on the underside of clouds can also reveal the position of islands long before they are visible to the naked eye.

THE MARIANA ISLANDS

GUAM – MINI-AMERICA

To the North of the Caroline Islands lie the Mariana Islands (or Marianas), made up of island of Guam and the Northern Mariana Islands. Guam is an American territory, with military bases and hotels that mainly seem to attract Japanese honeymooners. This unincorporated island has some typically American characteristics – it is an ugly, spread-out and uninspired settlement without a centre. It is impossible to say where the town begins or ends. There is virtually no public transport so visitors are forced to rent cars, but it is a great place to buy provisions, do repair work and find replacement parts.

We set about doing some maintenance on the boat. Our mainsail, which had been damaged when we were shortening it in a strong half-gale on our way up to Guam, needed to be sewn up and our outboard motor and windlass (the anchor-raising mechanism) needed to be repaired. The dinghy was about to fall apart so we bought a new one, our fourth since 1988 – the others had been lost, stolen or worn out.

We bought a pressure cooker, which significantly reduced meal preparation time and saved propane. (It only took us six months to recoup the cost of the pressure cooker in terms of saved propane.) In addition to these tasks we also had the usual errands that need to be carried out when sailing boats come into a well-stocked harbour – top up on diesel, oil and gasoline; refill the propane canisters for the stove; do the laundry and buy provisions.

We anchored at Mariana's Sailing Club in Guam, where everyone was very friendly and helpful. We ran into old friends and acquaintances and made new ones too. Some of the boats were ones we had known in different places over the years but not seen for a long time – *Dana* from California

with Jim and Linda, for example. Jim is a former fireman and world-class surfer who built their 36ft (11m) sailboat and Linda had previously worked in the media. They were also divers and we were to meet them again many times in the Indian Ocean. At the sailing club we met Bob Bullock, who was the club's president. He was an American stationed on Guam and he did a lot of sailing in his free time. When I told him about my plans to sail to Vietnam he became very interested. He had travelled a great deal in South-east Asia for his work, including Vietnam. He offered to help me with contacts who might be able to help me get permission to sail there.

We also took the opportunity to buy tear gas pistols, which can be bought legally in the US. We would soon be sailing to Papau New Guinea and we had been warned both by other sailors and newspaper articles about its high rate of crime. We bought five pistols that we hid in strategic places on board (we never had to use them). After five days we were happy to leave Guam – we had had enough of western civilization, with its traffic jams and shopping malls.

YAP – THE COUNTRY WITH STONE MONEY

Some 450nm south-west of Guam, back in the Carolines, lies the island of Yap, which we returned to in a three-day passage. In between Guam and Yap is the Mariana Trench. This is supposedly the deepest place in all of the world's oceans – at almost 11,000m – although this figure varies according to the source. It is thus much deeper than the height of Mount Everest at 8,848m. In spite of its great depth, in the 1960s an expedition succeeded in lowering down a manned deep-sea diving submersible to the ocean floor.

Yap is one of the most traditional islands in Micronesia. It has fewer than 10,000 inhabitants and is the only place in the world that gives its chiefs veto rights over national laws relating to culture and tradition. The situation obviously creates conflicts between the politicians and the chiefs.

One of the most interesting characteristics of Yap is its stone money. Their currency is made up of big, flat, round stone coins – big wheels, some of which are up to 3m in diameter. They have a hole in the middle so that two or more men can carry them on a pole. The money is very seldom moved since everyone knows who owns which coins. At different locations on the island visitors can view 'banks' with as many as fifty big coins standing upright. We wandered around in these banks and felt very rich.

One day on Yap we visited the Micronesian Maritime and Fisheries Academy, where a Swede from Gothenburg was headmaster. The school was well equipped with machines and instruments but had virtually no resources to cover its operating costs and only 17 students were studying there at the time of our visit. We felt that it was here that funds should be invested. Yap's economic zone is 200nm long and one of the world's richest areas for tuna fishing. The country is in desperate need of educated fishermen and seamen. They currently lease their fishing grounds out to western countries' fishing fleets who pay ridiculously low fees (when they don't fish illegally) and as a result no job opportunities are created.

PALAU

DEMOCRACY RUN AMOK

Palau is the westernmost archipelago of the Caroline Islands, and could easily be listed in the *Guinness Book of World Records* – for two reasons. The first is that the country is one of the most beautiful places on Earth, with hundreds of small, green, umbrella-shaped rock-islands that seem to be randomly scattered in the azure blue and emerald green water. Each of these islands is well sheltered by the immense Palau reef that stretches over 20nm and has many wonderful places to anchor.

The second reason is that Palau is the most over-governed place on Earth. The nation has only 20,000 inhabitants but it still has an executive, legislative and judiciary branch following the American model. What is even more difficult to believe is that Palau is also made up of 16 independent states, each with its own constitution and under the leadership of its own governor and parliament. The average population of the small states is 1,000 inhabitants. The politicians collect salaries but don't seem to produce anything except words.

This is democracy run amok, and is funded by the United States through the Compact of Free Association agreement. The agreement gives Palau hundreds of millions of dollars in exchange for the United States being given the right to have military bases in the country and nuclear weapons on those bases. All this easy money makes the people of Palau reluctant to work unless it is for the government, where they will receive very high wages and many benefits. One of the worst abuses of the American money is the new trend for importing maids from the Philippines for just $100 per month.

The agreement was not finalized without serious internal disputes. The residents were split on the question of whether or not Palau should permit nuclear weapons on their territory. In 1979 Palau had become the first country in the world to amend its constitution to ban nuclear power, with a 92 per cent popular majority behind the decision. But after 12 referendums, appeals to the courts, the murder of a president in 1985, the suicide of another in

1988 and violent riots, the powers in favour of the agreement with the US (including allowing nuclear weapons) finally won. That happened in 1994, a year before we arrived in Palau.

DIVING

THE QUIET WORLD

Palau has some of the best diving in the world and attracts devoted divers from around the globe. We sailed from Yap to Palau (a distance of 250nm) in two days and spent another ten days in this beautiful diving Mecca. We visited countless diving spots along the reef during the day and anchored among the beautiful rock-islands at night.

On the way to the diving areas in the southern part of Palau we passed the German Channel, which is very narrow and only a few hundred metres long. It is also very shallow so deep-keeled sailboats can only go through it at high tide. When we came towards the channel the tide was on its way out and it was doubtful if we would be able to get through. I took a chance, entered the channel at high speed and hoped for the best. Soon we started to bounce along the bottom and eventually we were stuck. It was very embarrassing when the shallow-going diving boats passed us in the channel – all we could do was smile happily and wave back. It was interesting, however, to be able to observe at close range big groups of huge stingrays swimming through the channel from one side of the reef to the other.

It is a dizzying and tingling feeling to start a dive in shallow water on a reef, swim out over the edge where you can't see the bottom any more and then just fall down along the wall in the crystal clear, blue water. When you dive down a reef wall it feels like you are jumping off the Empire State Building. You pass schools of fish of different colours and sizes that swim up and down along the wall until you meet sharks further down.

In Palau's famous Blue Corner (literally a corner that juts out from the reef then drops off sharply) we dived and swam alongside sharks, turtles, manta rays and barracudas. Another exciting place is the Blue Hole – four connected openings in the reef's upper side, 10m deep. Here you can sink down in one of the openings and then swim out through a tunnel that opens onto the side of the reef wall, 20m further down. You get a fantastic view up through 30m of water that is enhanced by the sun's intense rays, which have the effect of bright spotlights shining down into the deep blue sea. Besides the tunnels, caves and walls you experience the shifting colours and rich bio-diversity in fish and coral of this silent world. And of course you have the ability to move three-dimensionally. When you see something interesting higher up you just have to swim there. This is why astronauts practise weightlessness in water.

If the current is strong you can do a drift-dive, and it is possible to float with your arms and legs spread out at a speed of 1–3 knots and just relax and observe all that passes by. Drift dives can, of course, be dangerous. They must be well planned so that a boat is ready to pick up the divers at the end of the dive. When we were in Palau a Japanese diving group disappeared while drift diving. The diving boat lost contact with the divers and didn't know where they would be coming up. A few days later they found the bodies, floating far out at sea. One of the women had kept notes in a little notebook that divers often use to communicate underwater. Her last note was written 24 hours after the dive began, stating that she didn't have the strength to go on any longer.

When we dive on *Jennifer* we always have a 60m-long line fastened to a big red diving buoy. The buoy can then be easily followed from the accompanying boat. When Johanna and I dive alone, we fasten the dinghy to the line instead and I then pull the dinghy along with me during the dive. In reality it actually works the opposite way – it is the dinghy that takes me along, since we tend to go where the current or the wind takes us.

Our most memorable diving experiences during the circumnavigation were the following: the dive to the aircraft carrier USS *Saratoga*; the dive with the hammerhead sharks at Cocos island; the dive at Palau; drift diving in French Polynesia; and the dive at Manta City at Yap where about ten big manta-rays let us swim up close to them. I would add to this the dive in Papau New Guinea on a mini-submarine. This diving location was made up of two ships on the bottom surrounded by countless numbers of brightly coloured coral fish. One of these ships was an armed Japanese merchant ship that had transported submarines and had been sunk by the Allies in the Second World War. The two ships were 25m underwater and 20m away from each other. On Australia's Great Barrier Reef we dived in one of the most famous locations, Cod Hole. A large family of very similar looking codfish (weighing up to 300kg each) live here and swim around with the divers, even letting the divers stroke them.

MODERN SCUBA DIVING

Modern scuba diving was largely developed by the French diving expert Jacques-Yves Cousteau. Although there were other daredevil pioneers who also risked their lives, Cousteau survived all of the dangers and died in the 1990s at the age of 83. Today scuba diving is a global industry. Divers used to go out in small boats and dive two, maybe three times a day. Now things are different. Today there are 'live aboard' boats; floating diving facilities with air-conditioning, video, fast dinghies and unlimited diving of up to seven dives per day! All this, of course, is at a cost of about $2,000 per week. It used to be usual for people to learn to dive at diving clubs or non-profit diving associations that gave out their own diving certifications. Over the past decade a private American company called the Professional Association of Diving Instructors (PADI) has become the most popular diving certification organization largely through aggressive marketing. PADI is based in California with local branches around the world.

The first certification level is 'Open Water' which costs about $500; the second level is 'Advanced Open Water' which costs about $250; and the third level is 'Rescue Diver' which costs about $375. After that follows the professional levels of 'Dive Master' (about $750) and 'Dive Instructor' (about $2,500).

The hierarchy does not end there. A diver can become a 'Master Dive Instructor' for $2,000, and on, all the way up to a 'Course Director' for $3,000 or more. A Course Director has spent about $10,000 on his diving education. The more money a diver invests in his or her education the more they can earn from teaching. Once a person has become a Dive Master (which I am) it is possible to work at diving schools or on diving boats. To be a diving instructor or a head diving instructor (which Johanna is) means that one is allowed to teach everything from Open Water to Dive Master level. To teach five beginners, for example, an instructor earns 5 x $500 = $2,500 for five days' work. A Course Director, who teaches five diving instructors, can bring in 5 x $2,500 = $12,500 for ten days' work.

A diving instructor can work anywhere in the world, either as an employee or on their own (Johanna taught countless guests to dive on board *Jennifer*). Of course, instructors do have costs for rooms to teach in, boats and diving equipment, as well as their fees to PADI. The really big money in the diving business lies in all of the equipment and accessories. PADI is very active in this area too, providing its member businesses with profiles of the diving market and other market research assistance. It is all very commercial, but also very professional. It is fair to say that PADI is an excellent benchmark example for other companies to study, in terms of its marketing, teaching, quality and follow-up.

In the 1980s a new aid for divers was developed – the 'diving computer'. The biggest risk in diving is getting the diving sickness called 'the bends'. When a person is underwater – that is to say, under pressure – nitrogen is transferred from the air they breathe into their blood. The nitrogen, now in the form of small bubbles, must disappear from the diver's blood before he or she comes to the surface. If this doesn't happen the bubbles can plug up the body's blood vessels, and this can be life threatening. To prevent this, divers have used diving tables to provide information about how deep they can stay underwater and for how long. But today diving computers take care of all of this.

A diving computer can be carried around in your hand or in a console connected to the oxygen tank. Every second the computer gives information about your depth, the greatest depth that can be reached during the dive, how many minutes the dive has been, how much air is left and how long you can stay at the current depth.

Furthermore, the data of all previous dives is stored on the computer. The diving computer can then be connected to a regular computer and all the information can be transferred. The profiles of all the dives can be studied and stored. The latest diving computers are very user-friendly and safe, but of course they aren't free – they cost between $400 and $700. I would never consider diving without one.

THE FOREIGN AID DILEMMA

THE REPUGNANT WELFARE STATE SYNDROME

The Federated States of Micronesia (FSM) is made up of four small island nations: Kosrae, Pohnpei, Chuuk and Yap. The whole of Micronesia – that is to say the Marianas, Carolines and Marshall Islands – first belonged to Spain and then, until the First World War, to Germany. From the end of the First World War until the end of Second World War they belonged to Japan. After the Second World War they were turned over to the United States as a strategic mandate area under the UN's supervision. The right of the US to have military bases in the area was included in the administrative mandate.

The plan was that the whole of Micronesia would eventually become a single, self-governing nation. However, Palau, the Marianas and the Marshall Islands didn't want to share the revenues generated by the American military bases with the smaller islands and thus chose to become separate independent states. It was only Kosrae, Pohnpei, Chuuk and Yap that came to form the FSM.

The Marianas were totally sold on the 'American way of life' and chose a quasi-colonial status, which made them American citizens with access to the US welfare system. Guam was already an American colony and military base from the Spanish-American War of 1898. The remaining three states: the Marshall Islands, the FSM and Palau, were ambivalent toward the United States. The following expression is indicative of how they thought: 'The best thing about the United States is the opportunity for us to go there; the worst is that they come to us.'

The islands strove for independence but needed American money to make a western consumer lifestyle possible. They chose a compromise – a 'Compact of Free Association' with the US, which made them independent states on paper, and allowed them to become members of the United Nations. The drawback was that they were forced to allow American military bases onto their territory.

In return, the islands got billions of dollars, a practice that was supposed to cease in 2001 but has been prolonged. The US has never demanded any accounting for how the money is spent. On top of this, these islands also receive support/aid money from Japan and Europe. So where has all the money gone? It has disappeared in private consumption rather than being invested for the benefit of all. There is virtually no private sector, mostly due to the fact that the public sector's wages are so high that the private sector cannot compete. Most of the foreign money is spent on salaries and benefits for civil servants who are not given any specific responsibilities, or it disappears deep into the pockets of the politicians themselves.

Consider the following: These small island states import 12 to 15 times more than they export. Junk food and canned food (mainly corned beef and similar items), cigarettes, beer and Coca-Cola make up 60 per cent of all imports. The remaining 40 per cent is made up of consumer goods such as VCRs, outboard motors and generators as well as gas and diesel. This means that American (and to a certain extent Japanese and European) taxpayers are paying for the people of Micronesia's new lifestyle. With all that money rolling in every year, no one is really concerned about the future or has any desire to work. When the agreement and its money were supposed to expire in 2001, the party should have been over. Those who lived on the outer islands might have been able to manage on what nature gave them, as they did in earlier times. But the majority that lives on the main islands and in the small cities would have a tough time as nearly everything – food, drink, fuel and so on – has to be imported.

The result could have been a loss of their independence – they might have had to ask the United States for colonial status, which would give the population the right to American welfare benefits. The problem is whether or not the US would want to have the island states as colonies. Now that the Cold War is over the strategic value of the islands of the South Pacific has disappeared (and in any case, the Americans already have the Marianas and Guam) and these new colonies could be a real economic burden. What could save them, however, is the military build up of the Chinese armed forces, especially its naval forces. For the strategic planners in the Pentagon, it is of paramount interest to control the whole of the Pacific Ocean. Memories from the Second World War, and the battles both at land and at sea, will never be forgotten by the American military. At any rate, the agreements with most of the island states have been extended until 2014 and will probably be prolonged into eternity.

With one of the highest birthrates in the world, nearly nothing to export (note the export/import ratio of 1:15), and the western countries' lessening support, the future looks bleak. To make things even worse, there is also a brain drain taking place. The smartest and most ambitious young people leave the islands to study in the United States and almost never come back – except for holidays.

A QUESTION OF RESPONSIBILITY

The question of foreign aid can be expressed like this: Is it realistic to have small, independent nations with a few thousand inhabitants who cannot support themselves? Is it the responsibility of western countries' taxpayers to give the people of these nations money for things that they don't need on their tiny coral islands? Is the purpose of foreign aid programs to finance the Third World's budgets, enrich politicians and civil servants and support the spread of western junk culture?

One of the most grotesque foreign aid projects I can think of is the new boastful, oversized government building on the Marshall Islands. The capital city of Majuro is really just a glorified village inhabited by over 25,000 people – almost half of the country's population. The EU has paid for the building of a gigantic, air-conditioned, ultra-modern glass and concrete creation that is totally out of place among the palm trees, huts and low buildings.

We had a bizarre experience in this building. When we went to the customs and immigration authorities (which are now in the new government building) they wouldn't let us come in. Their reason was that we didn't have ties on. No one was allowed into the building without a tie and full-length trousers. The guards were totally inflexible on this point, not to mention unfriendly and condescending. This had never happened to us before and has never happened anywhere else afterwards, either. All we could do was to go back to the boat and find something that could pass for a tie. We soon learned that on Fridays it was possible to go in to the office without a tie. This was the day the fishermen from the outlying atolls came in to get their support payments and demanding that fishermen wore ties just didn't work.

It is absurd that a coconut economy with 60,000 inhabitants has received an ultra-modern office building as a gift from Europe's industrialized

countries that would be more suited to Manhattan than to a little strip of coral. The small nation's political leaders had then become megalomaniacs and decided to refuse to allow most of the population to even set foot inside of the symbol of their power – except on Fridays, of course.

Australia and New Zealand have now taken responsibility for many of the countries of the region, partly because they used to administer them on behalf of the United Kingdom. They are fed up with the way money is wasted, and they have the guts to say so. They have told the small Pacific island states that they have to reduce the size of their public sectors, cut politicians' and civil servants' salaries and balance their budgets. The islands' governments have protested and said that Australia and New Zealand have no right to interfere in their internal affairs.

This is despite the fact that Australia has provided them with an extraordinary aid project – the patrol boat project. Australia has given one or two new patrol boats each to most of the Pacific island states. Maintenance, spare parts and equipment are included in the project, which is administered by the Australians themselves. If they had given the support in the form of money it would have simply disappeared. If they had given only the boats they would soon have broken down and fallen apart.

During our sail through the South Pacific we saw many of these effective patrol boats. The main purpose of them is to enable the countries to patrol their large economic zones stretching 200nm out around their coastlines. There has been a large amount of illegal foreign fishing that the island nations have not been able to do anything about before, but nearly all of them have now increased their incomes from the fish licences the foreign fish fleets must buy to fish legally. Many fishing boats that have been operating in the region without licences have been caught and forced to pay high fines. This Australian project is an excellent way to help these countries help themselves.

I know from experience that island schools never have enough supplies, which is why we always sailed around with plenty of pencils, erasers, pencil cases and notebooks that we gave out to grateful teachers and chiefs. When you think about the millions of dollars that these states receive every year from western countries it is scandalous how little of it gets down to the grassroots level.

DOES PARADISE EXIST?

We had spent two years among the South Pacific's islands – was this really a paradise on Earth? There is a common perception that we are fed from childhood and which is later reinforced through seductive tourist brochures that there is indeed a South Seas paradise. The palm-covered, small coral islands with their glistening white sand beaches, beautiful lagoons shifting between all imaginable shades of blue and green, warm water, exciting snorkelling and diving and the friendly, exotic people are all supposedly part of this paradise.

It is difficult for westerners to spend long periods of time on these islands. I now know that I would never be able to live there permanently, at least not in the way that the islanders do: without electricity, books, newspapers, cinemas, TV or restaurants. I could not tolerate for long the dull, unhealthy, fatty, low-fibre food or live without the distinction between breakfast, lunch and dinner. With little or no education, there would be no other way of supporting oneself then fishing or farming plant roots. Even members of the Peace Corps get worn out before long.

There is also very little contact with the outside world. Once a person has become a western consumer, I think it is impossible to turn back. There is a big difference between living in the South Pacific and sailing around the South Pacific on your own boat, bringing along parts of your western lifestyle. On board *Jennifer* we had a variety of foods, books, films on video, CDs, a computer with an internet connection, e-mail and a short-wave radio (to listen to the BBC and Voice of America). Most of all, we were able to come and go from place to place as we pleased.

I believe paradise does exist, but not in the South Pacific or any other geographic place – I think it exists in a person's mind. If you are secure in yourself and happy with your life you can be almost anywhere. If you aren't secure and happy, the South Pacific's palm trees and beaches won't help you become so. The contrast between being happy or not in paradise is illustrated best by the comparison between the chief (Ersin) and the finance minister of the Marshall Islands. The former was completely content to live and work on his little atoll island, whereas the latter couldn't wait to fly back to the capital city's modern civilization.

That it might not really be paradise is also suggested by all the young people who are leaving the outlying islands, and they don't return – except on their holidays. Would I go back to the South Pacific? Yes, absolutely – but only on my own boat.

PAPUA NEW GUINEA – 10,000 YEARS IN A LIFETIME

Leaving 'paradise', we travel 'back' 10,000 years in time, down the huge Sepik River in a dugout canoe, and end up in the middle of a tribal war. We witness the damage of a volcanic eruption at Rabaul, discover sharks on a reef, go down into a gold mine and face a travel prohibition.

PALAU TO PAPUA NEW GUINEA

THE SAILFISH

At the beginning of April 1995 Johanna and I sailed 1,000nm from Palau to New Guinea. This was one of the longest passages we had done in quite a while. Not since the trip from Australia to Tonga in June 1993 (2,700nm) had we travelled so far. It was a good voyage with a variety of winds. At the start we had beam winds of up to 20 knots and *Jennifer*'s speed was 8 knots. Soon the usual routines kicked in; three hours on watch and three hours of rest. During the day, we didn't keep any real watches and our autopilot Arnold did the steering day and night. During the night we were on three hour shifts, but sometimes we cheated. The sea traffic here is almost nonexistent, so the night watch mainly consisted of taking a light sleep in the cockpit and looking out every 10 to 15 minutes.

One day we succeeded in catching a big sailfish. It weighed 20–25kg and fought hard against capture. After a 30-minute struggle, the fish was finally landed aboard *Jennifer*'s stern platform. That's when we realized how big it was – almost 2m long! It felt wrong to kill such a large fish, especially as it was impossible for just the two of us to eat it all. The problem was now how to get it off the hook and return it to the sea. Considering the fish's long spear and sharp teeth, it was impossible to simply loosen it. I attached a rope around its fin so that we could hang the fish up. I then managed to get the hook out. It was with a sense of relief that we watched the big fish return to its freedom.

We crossed the Equator for the third time. We got changing winds; sometimes it was calm, sometimes we had heavy rain and strong winds. We frequently had to put out or take in the genoa or raise and take in the mainsail. The rain at the Equator is very heavy – in just half an hour, as much rain fell as during an entire summer in Sweden! We motored when it was calm. During the week-long voyage, we each had a lot of time to ourselves. I read two books, did the book-keeping for the last couple of months, cleaned the engine, changed its oil and filter and sent faxes about future bookings to a number of agents as well as to the new crewmembers who we were going to meet in New Guinea. I even finished an article about our visit to Bikini atoll, which was later published in a Swedish sailing magazine. Because of the warnings we had received about crime on New Guinea, I practised my skills with the shotgun. On the passage down to New Guinea, we started to take malaria pills, and we continued to do so during our whole stay there.

10,000 YEARS IN A LIFETIME

New Guinea is the second largest island in the world; only the island of Greenland is bigger. The inhabitants of New Guinea speak more than 700 different languages, which represent almost half of all the known languages in the world. The country was one of the last to be fully mapped and some tribes on the highlands were unknown to the outside world until the 1930s. New tribes are still being discovered. They are still living in the equivalent of the Stone Age and have never seen a white man. The European colonists showed little interest in New Guinea until the early 19th century, when Germany colonized the eastern part of the country. Holland later took over the western part – mostly to protect its profitable colonies in the Dutch East Indies (later Indonesia), while Britain took over the southern part to protect their Australian colony. When Australia became independent in 1901, it inherited the British part of New Guinea. After the First World War, Australia also inherited the German part of the island. After the Second World War, the UN demanded independence for all the colonies and in 1975 New Guinea became an independent state. The country was extremely unprepared for this step. New Guinea did not have enough skilled manpower, administrators or politicians – and they had the economical and social structure of a primitive village. Even today, New Guinea has big problems despite being rich in natural resources such as copper, oil, and gold (we visited a gold mine on the island of Misimi) as well as large areas of rainforest.

When we arrived, the country was nearly bankrupt and corruption and unemployment were thriving. To make things even worse, a civil war had been going on for several years during the 1990s, as the island of Bougainville

(which has one of the world's richest copper mines) fought to become independent. This war was draining the majority of the country's few resources. Natural disasters, such as the volcanic eruption in Rabaul (1994) and the flooding of the Sepik River have only served to make the situation worse. Because of economic problems and the sudden exposure to the western consumer-driven lifestyle, a serious gang problem has arisen. The gangs are composed of ruthless unemployed young men who rob people and banks and attack, rape and torture their victims. The capital Port Moresby is particularly affected by this phenomenon. A more detailed analysis of this violent mentality can be found in the first foreign minister's autobiography *10,000 Years in a Lifetime*.

MADANG AND THE ARCHIPELAGO

We arrived in the picturesque town of Madang, which is on the north side of New Guinea. After clearing in with the customs and immigration authorities we anchored in a bay close to the city. We met an Australian called George, who lived in a house by the beach, and he allowed us to anchor by his land at the seafront. This was perfect for us as we were worried about break-ins; we thankfully accepted his hospitality.

A few days later, our new crew arrived: Håkan from Stockholm, who had crossed the Atlantic twice aboard *Jennifer*; his friend Manfred who works in the video industry; Clark, an avocado farmer from California who found us through my agent in San Francisco; and Christian, a newly graduated economist from Lund, in Sweden, who found us through my agent at home.

We planned to sail up the Sepik River with *Jennifer* for a week and then continue among the outer islands of New Guinea. The river was quite flooded at this time and we were advised against taking our own boat, especially as large trees and trunks were floating down the river at speed. We had to change our plans. It seemed that a canoe might work. After some research, we found a guide who could take us along the Sepik River in a hollowed-out tree trunk with an outboard motor.

In the few days before our journey we sailed in the archipelago of Madang. We were close to the Equator and the winds are very light and unreliable, so we explored the area mostly under motor. After just two days, Christian had had enough. He thought that it was too hot, the locals were too hostile and there was not enough wind. But this was not the whole story. The first evening, he had started to cry. He missed his girlfriend and did not want to be away from her. Possibly he was worried or jealous, as she was still in Lund and perhaps having the time of her life. I felt sorry for Christian and offered him the chance to come back for a month at some other time, or perhaps return for two weeks together with his girlfriend.

During this time, we visited a research station on an island outside of Madang. The work at the station focused on the nearby coral reefs, which are some of the richest in the world. The researchers were looking for compounds that could be of interest in finding a cure for cancer. It was here that the Canadian physician Terri, who had sailed with us between Panama and Tahiti, had been doing her research.

EXPLORING THE SEPIK RIVER

Finally, the day for our river tour arrived. We left *Jennifer* in George's hands, having arranged for a bright light to illuminate the boat at night.

At over 1,100km long the Sepik River is one of the great river systems in the world, carrying a huge volume of water, especially when in flood. We had arrived in New Guinea at the end of the rainy season. The river was approaching full flood, and the water level increased every day during our tour. The flood was so extreme that it was thought that it might not return to its normal level for several months. Because of the high water levels and the poor road network we were forced to fly in a small aeroplane to the river and then go by jeep for half a day to reach the village of Pagwi, our starting point. They dropped us off just before we reached the village and we had to wade the final distance with water up to our waists and our luggage on our heads. In Pagwi, with help from our guide Peter, we negotiated the rental of a canoe with an outboard motor. The canoe was a simple hollowed-out tree trunk with a very low freeboard and not much stability, which made us worry that it was going to capsize. The solution was easy, though. After trying it out for a few unsteady minutes, one of the older women instructed the guides, in no uncertain terms, to take out the biggest canoe in the village instead. At 12m long, this canoe was a beauty, carved out of a huge trunk. It was big and comfortable and had seats for ten people. Other than the five of us from *Jennifer* (Johanna, Håkan, Manfred, Clark and myself), there was only our guide Peter, the two canoe 'drivers' and our food and luggage. It was with much excitement that we finally started our river tour.

Because of the flooding, there were plenty of crocodiles in the river, many of whom had escaped from their cages at the crocodile farm close by. A few days earlier, a giant crocodile (reputed to be 10m long) had caught a 14-year-old boy – and before that, 12 other victims – in front of the whole village. Both the army and the police were chasing this highly dangerous crocodile.

For five days we floated, or sometimes motored, down the river in very

pleasant weather. Sometime huge floating piles of reeds and sea grass passed us at speeds of 3–4 knots. In the evenings, we stopped at small villages where we could stay the night at one of the guides' many relatives. Those overnight stays were the highlights of our river tour.

The houses were built on poles and were surprisingly large. The first night, we stayed with Peter's sister, in a big building that measured 30 x 12m. We were introduced to the three members of the family – who each had their space in one corner of the building – and we slept in the fourth corner. We cooked our own food over an open fire and slept on the floor with a mosquito net wrapped around us. Because of the huge flood, the gardens were underwater and the food was short. Despite that, everybody we met was friendly and hospitable and shared their limited food supplies. The biggest problem was going to the bathroom. Normally the homes had outhouses, but these were now flooded. Instead, we were taken out in small canoes and had to sit on one edge of the canoe and go. Each stay-over cost about $5 per person, but we also gave our hosts some of our supplies: rice, jars of food, tobacco and medicines.

One afternoon we got lost on the river. Maybe the tidal stream was stronger than they had expected and we had missed the little tributary we were supposed to take, but the guides didn't know where we were. After a while, the motor stopped. It soon became dark, and we had to paddle upstream. For several hours we kept a lookout in the dark for escaped crocodiles. Finally, we landed in a small bay where we woke up a family in their hut; they let us stay the night. We were so tired that we just wrapped ourselves up in the mosquito net and fell asleep on the floor. The Sepik River is famous around the world for its beautiful wooden craft. Every village has a 'spirit house', called a Tambaran, which is tall and elaborately decorated, like a beautiful piece of art. This house is where all the local crafts are collected, and only men are allowed inside. The art impressed us; there were masks of different shapes, sizes and colours and even some crocodile heads. Everything was very inexpensive. Big masks had a price of $20 and the smaller ones only $4–5. What limited us was storage space, rather than the small cost of the items. Of course we bought many of the beautiful things, and some of them are still hanging on *Jennifer*'s bulkhead. On the fifth day, we reached the mouth of the river, our final destination. We hitchhiked back to Madang on a truck platform, together with 25 farmers and agricultural products that were going to the market there. The trip took seven hours, and along the way, we passed through several plantations with tall palm trees in straight lines and small cacao trees planted between the rows.

LONG ISLAND AND THE REEFS

After the Sepik River adventure we sailed around in the archipelago of New Guinea for over five weeks. Our first stop was the volcanic Long Island, approximately 100nm east of Madang, a nearly perfectly round island with a crater lake in the middle. After anchoring with the bow out towards the sea and ropes from the stern attached to a palm tree, we went ashore and greeted the chief. One of the young people that spoke English translated for us. We got permission to stay the night at Long Island. The younger ones were curious about the boat, and us, and many paddled out to visit. When it got dark, we brought the video player out in the cockpit, and with 20 young people as the audience we played *Mr Bean* – because most of them didn't speak English, we thought that they would understand an almost-silent actor. A sad thing happened during the film. Because not all the youth in the village could fit in the cockpit, a resentful feeling arose among those who couldn't see the film. Suddenly, rocks began to rain down on the boat. Of course I got angry and some of the older youths rowed ashore and caught the guilty parties. We don't know what they did, but we heard a lot of screaming. Later in the evening, Håkan took out his guitar. To our surprise, some of the young men came out to the boat with their own guitars. The repertoire was a mix of native and western songs and music, including many Swedish drinking songs.

When we saw a reef, especially if it was far offshore, we usually anchored and did some snorkelling and diving. The coral reefs in New Guinea are some of the best places in the world to dive, with excellent views. On every dive we saw turtles, barracudas, many small fish – and sharks. We also found several walls to dive on. To dive on a wall is like flying very slowly down an apartment building with windows. You take a peek here and there, and there is always someone home: for example a lobster or an eel. We saw plenty of dolphins but never succeeded in diving together with them; perhaps they had had bad experiences with people. However, they often showed up around the boat when we sailed, jumping and playing and seemingly curious about us.

TRIBAL WAR

One morning, a potentially dangerous yet slightly comical situation presented itself. We had heard that tribal wars were still ongoing, and suddenly we were in the middle of one. We had stopped in Kimbe, a port on the island of New Britain, where we had planned to buy provisions. When we went ashore, we noticed that there were lots of people on the move, most of them headed out of the town. It was strange, considering that it was early morning. There were also police cars driving around. Only when a man advised us to leave the town as soon as possible did we understand that there was a tribal war. Several hundred men with machetes and guns were just outside the town. Unemployment, flooding of the Sepik River and the catastrophic volcanic eruption in Rabaul had combined to ignite the fight between the tribes moving in to the town and the ones already there. The day before, a man had been killed and a woman had been raped in one of the tribes outside the town, and now a vendetta had started; they wanted revenge on the tribe in the town. The few policemen had little means of stopping it. At first we found shelter in a small travel agency that had bars on the windows and the door. After a while, a shopkeeper offered to drive us back to the harbour. Safely there, we got ready and sailed away in a hurry. Later, on the BBC, we heard that three people had been killed and several wounded in the riots.

VOLCANIC ERUPTION

Rabaul was once a beautiful town with the best natural harbour in the Pacific. This provincial capital is surrounded by at least five extremely active volcanoes, and the harbour itself is an enormous crater from a big volcano. After an eruption in 1937, the city was totally destroyed. Rabaul was built up again, and during the Second World War the Japanese had a big navy base in the township. General MacArthur's aircraft sank a large number of ships in Rabaul harbour and today the wreck diving here is among the best in the world. In September 1994, two of the volcanoes had huge eruptions and again the city was destroyed. Six months later, when we sailed into the harbour, people were still looting and plundering and a curfew was in place. Since we could not go ashore, we decided to observe the damage of the eruptions from the safety of the boat. It was a terrible sight. There was still smoke coming out from one volcano, thousands of burned trees stood naked on one of the volcano's sides, while the other volcano had totally lost all its vegetation. Rabaul itself was partly buried in ashes and mud, and people were digging where their homes once stood. The town resembled a bombed-out city. The eruption prompted the movement of the capital from Rabaul to Kokopo, while the slow rebuilding work took place.

THE ISLAND OF NEW IRELAND

KAVIENG

After Rabaul, we sailed north for a day to Kavieng on the island of New Ireland. We had weak tailwinds and flew two foresails with the spinnaker booms on each side of the mast. We had a big banana stock bought in Madang, but they ripened almost simultaneously and we had to eat them all within a few days. By the time we reached Kavieng we were all tired of bananas. It was unusually hot, and there was little wind because we were still close to the Equator. The heat below decks made it hard to sleep and the sheets were soaked with sweat during the nights. We sometimes slept on the cushions on deck, but as it often rained during the night this was not a practical solution either.

SHARK!

On our way to Kavieng, we stopped at a reef that looked exciting to explore. Johanna jumped in the water with a snorkel to check if it was worth diving there, while we floated nearby in the boat and waited. Soon we heard a scream: 'Shark!' I reversed quickly, and Johanna literally flew back up onto the platform. Five sharks had closed in at high speed to inspect her, stopping just half a metre in front of her. She had never been so scared in her whole life. Diving is totally different from snorkelling. If you are diving, you can move more freely, you can swim up and down or hide behind a reef. When you are snorkelling on the surface, you really have no way to defend yourself. In the shark's view you are a struggling creature out of its element, who is probably stressed and scared. And like the rest of us, sharks are a little lazy. If they see an easy prey, they bite. To the shark, a snorkeller is like a seal and a surfer who is paddling with arms and legs on the board is like a turtle. Turtles are the natural prey of the sharks. No one was interested in diving after Johanna's confrontation with the sharks, so we continued our trip to Kavieng.

AEROBICS IN PARADISE

We stayed for a couple of days in this little place, far from civilization, and sailed around its archipelago. At the Kavieng Club, the hub for high society and foreigners, we quickly met new people. The Kavieng Club even had an aerobics club, and when they heard that I was an instructor they asked me to lead the female class on the island. Before I knew it, I was leading an aerobics class for the local women.

Outside Kavieng, we visited an island paradise where a man called Boston had built a simple but pleasant enough hotel consisting of a few small huts, a restaurant and a bar. The inhabitants on the island had made fun of him at first – how could he think that anyone would pay money to just sit in the sun and look at the sea? But when the tourists started to come, they changed their minds and were happy to be hired by this entrepreneur.

In Kavieng, Clark, Håkan and Manfred signed off after a month of sailing and Lorraine signed on. She was American and had taught English in South Korea. Lorraine was on her way home to the USA and sailed with us all the way to Australia.

THE TROBRIAND ISLANDS

FREE LOVE

The Trobriand Islands (or Kiriwina islands as they are now officially known) are a small group of islands in south-east New Guinea. They became famous after the First World War, when the Polish anthropologist Bronislaw Malinowski wrote his book *The Sexual Life of Savages in North-Western Melanesia* (1929). This was an account of courtship, marriage and family life among the people of the Trobriand Islands.

On these islands, the young people are encouraged to have as many sexual partners as they want – without guilty feelings – before they get married. The young men move into the village's 'bachelor hotel', the Bukamatula, where they can bring their women. This custom has always been a nightmare for visiting missionaries.

SHARK CALLERS

When we anchored by the island of Kiriwina in southern New Guinea, many small canoes came to meet us. They were out to hunt sharks, and were known as 'shark callers'. A thick rope with a lot of coconut shells attached to it was shaken underwater to call the sharks to the surface. The hunters then tied a rope around the sharks and clubbed them to death. After that, they dragged the shark, sometimes as big as the canoe, up into it and paddled to the beach. The whole village then feasted on shark meat.

EXPATS

In New Guinea, we met many expatriates still living there. Almost all of them had arrived in New Guinea before the country became independent in 1975. If you read James A Michener's novel *Return to Paradise* (1951), you can understand that this was a wild time. The men were adventuring Crocodile Dundee-types who came to New Guinea to try their luck as crocodile hunters, ranchers and, most of all, gold-diggers.

Lately, entrepreneurs and big forestry and mining companies have also found their way to Papua New Guinea. All the white men we met were married to local women, some young enough to be their daughters (or sometimes granddaughters). George, for example, had met his wife when she was

14 years old and he was 50. She was now 19 and he 55, and they had two children. They were planning to move to Australia where the children could receive a better education. One could not help but wonder how she found herself in this situation. Perhaps she had made a wise choice. The Guinean husbands can be violent when they are drunk. As with other native peoples we had witnessed, they can't seem to handle their liquor.

Papau New Guinea is now making it harder for foreign newcomers to live there. Through new laws, the government tries to reserve as many jobs as possible for its own countrymen. The problem is that the local inhabitants often lack the skills that foreigners have. The IMF (International Monetary Fund) has put a condition on new loans that these new rules have to be taken away. In Papau New Guinea, as in many other developing countries, the work ethic is totally different from that in the west. We met a young Australian couple that had tried to run a hotel in Kavieng. After only a couple of months, they were so embittered that they gave in and they couldn't wait to go back home. Foreign people often go back to their land of origin and one of the last colonial periods is ending.

TRAVEL PROHIBITION IN THE LOUISIADES

We spent the final part of our sailing tour in Papau New Guinea in the south-east archipelago. This area is called the Louisiades and contains several unoccupied islands. On the main island of Misimi, we planned to clear out of the country and sail to Australia. However, they gave us a travel prohibition, ie the authorities refused to clear us out. When we had arrived in New Guinea six weeks earlier, the immigration authorities had made a mistake and did not issue us with a visa, which is technically required to enter the country. In other words, we were in the country illegally and an overambitious clerk had discovered this oversight in Kavieng. Our passports were then sent to Port Moresby to get a visa stamp in them, and we were supposed to pick them up in Misimi. I was not too surprised to hear that the passports hadn't arrived when we reached Misimi, but I became irritated when I heard that we had to pay a fine of $1,500 for our 'crime' against the visa law. Despite the fact that it was the clerk's fault in Madang, the decision remained unchanged, and our passports would stay in the capital until we paid the fine. I immediately sent a fax to the Swedish embassy in Canberra through the satellite unit on the boat. The embassy got in contact with the Swedish general consul in Port Moresby, who contacted the official at the immigration authority. When I called him the next day, there was a different tone to his voice. He had suddenly understood that it wasn't my fault. The passports

were to be sent to Misimi and there was no longer any fine to be paid. I understood that he was impressed that I had connections in the diplomatic world. It was with a strong feeling of relief that we were able to leave New Guinea and sail towards Australia.

While we were waiting to get our passport problem sorted out, we visited the gold mine. An Australian multinational mining company runs it, and the deposit contains a lot of gold. People from nearby islands come here to work, and most of the island supports itself through this activity.

Did we meet any violence and gang problems? No. On the contrary, we only met friendly people in Papua New Guinea. But in the local papers we read almost every day about robberies and murders in Port Moresby. I could now put away the shotgun with ease.

BACK TO AUSTRALIA

We made the passage of 550nm to Cairns in northern Australia at the beginning of June 1995. We had a gale blowing on the beam, and did a record fast crossing, with more than two days at the average speed of 8 knots. It felt good to be back in the 'real' world again. Since we had passed through the Panama Canal in February 1993, we had spent almost two and a half years in the Pacific. Apart from visits to New Zealand and Australia, 80 per cent of our time had been among the Pacific islands.

RETURN TO AUSTRALIA – PANDORA'S BOX

Our return to northern Australia is also time to overhaul *Jennifer.* We then sail to the Great Barrier Reef, pass over the Pandora's Box, encounter crocodiles, visit aborigines and find five new crewmembers in Darwin for a rally-race to Indonesia.

NORTHERN AUSTRALIA

In June 1995 we arrived in Cairns, in northern Australia. Yet again we had to go through an extended process of clearing in. It was time for a full overhaul of *Jennifer* and she was taken to the boatyard. The usual struggle with 'the list' began: paint the hull, install new electrical connections and belts for the generator, look over the fuel pumps for the diesel engine and repair the gennaker and spray hood. The propeller had to be changed as electrical charges had started to corrode it and bigger zinc anodes had to be mounted (we had to buy a new propeller in Singapore). The inflatable dinghy was in such bad shape that when we were going to take it into the city one morning, we found that it had already sunk with the outboard motor attached. Luckily, the painter was still attached to *Jennifer* and we could pull the whole thing up. I had to buy a new motor, but at least the dinghy could be repaired. It was time to get a chart for Indonesia, and I also bought a depth sounder that could 'see' forward. Its purpose was to discover reefs before we ran aground. We discovered pretty soon that the sounder didn't really work; the depths were not shown in real time, ie there was a delay on the screen. It is true that it might be interesting to know that you had 'sailed' on land, but not for $1,000. I later returned the depth sounder for a refund.

OSMOSIS

The overhaul was expensive. The cost of $7,000 was the same as the income earned from the paying crew in New Guinea and Australia. It was also clear

that *Jennifer* had osmosis (the boat equivalent of bubonic plague), a GRP 'sickness' where water slowly seeps into the gel coat and creates small bubbles in the hull. Osmosis takes a long time to repair and is expensive, costing anywhere from $5,000 to $15,000. The boat also has to be put in the boatyard for 4–6 months. First the gel coat has to be planed down, the hull dried out and finally a new layer of epoxy has to be applied. If the osmosis is serious, you have to go deeper into the plastic and it becomes even more expensive. I decided to take care of the problem later in the Caribbean, where we planned to go during 1997.

PANDORA'S BOX

After two weeks in Cairns we sailed towards Darwin on the northern coast of Australia, a distance of 1,200nm. The paying crew was made up of Lorraine, who had been sailing with us from New Guinea; her boyfriend Justin, who flew in from the USA; Chris, a Polish photographer who lives in Australia; Terri, an accountant from Australia (and also girlfriend to Anders who had sailed aboard *Jennifer* from Cairns to Tonga in 1994). We spent a week on Lizard Island waiting for a gale to blow over. Lizard Island is a beautiful island close to the Great Barrier Reef, with its own lagoon, small luxury hotel and a research station. There was a warning for heavy gales (with wind speeds of at least 29 knots) day in and day out, between our island and Darwin. Because of that, we couldn't do many dives at the world famous Barrier Reef this time either.

We passed over the wreck of the warship HMS *Pandora*, the ship that Britain sent out to capture the mutineers from HMS *Bounty*. Even though *Pandora* never found the *Bounty* (whose crew had found their way to Pitcairn Island in the Pacific where they burned the ship), *Pandora*'s crew succeeded in capturing the few mutineers who had stayed on Tahiti. The cruel captain of the *Pandora* built a cage on deck, where the captives were kept: Pandora's box. When the ship headed back to Britain, it sank on the reef that we had just passed. Many of the captive mutineers drowned in this horrible cage.

JUMPING CROCODILES

North of Cooktown, we sailed up the Escape River, hoping to see the crocodiles that Queensland is known for. We caught sight of a 5m-long crocodile, on a warm beach by the mangrove trees. We admired the flexibility of the reptile as it went into the water. Despite its large size, we did not see a single ripple where it dived. Crocodiles can move with unpredictable speed so a human has no chance if one attacks. They can also jump up in the air from the water with help from their strong tail. One sailboat with a dog on board had experienced a scary incident. A crocodile, which had probably picked up the scent of the dog, had been swimming close to the boat. It jumped up, grabbed the dog off the boat and disappeared down in the water. The dog didn't have time to bark and the owners, who were aboard, heard only a splashing sound. After hearing this story, we learned to be careful and every evening we pulled up the platform and secured the cockpit doors very carefully.

On the tip of Australia we stopped at Thursday Island in Torres Strait, between Australia and New Guinea. We had reached the northern tip of the continent, and continued west from there, again with a heavy gale warning and the mainsail down. We sailed across the Gulf of Carpentaria, past Arnhem Land and in between Thursday Island and Darwin to Gove. Gove, a remote island, has a friendly yacht club where sailors are welcomed. We rested there for a couple of days before we began the last leg to Darwin. On the way there, we passed through a hole in the wall – a narrow canal between two islands – where strong tidal streams converge and become even stronger and faster. We sailed at full speed through the 1km-long canal at low tide. The knot meter showed 6 knots, while the GPS showed 14 knots, meaning that the tidal stream had a speed of 8 knots. On both sides of the canal, the water looked as if it was boiling and literally falling down into the middle of the channel; it was exiting and scary, but *Jennifer* made a great passage.

THE DARWIN TO AMBON RALLY

As a circumnavigator there are several rallies you don't want to miss: the Atlantic Rally for Cruisers (ARC) from the Canaries to the Caribbean in November; Antigua Sailing Week in the Caribbean in April; Muscot Cove on Fiji to Vila in Vanuatu in September, and Darwin to Ambon in Indonesia in July (nowadays Darwin to Bali). The races are planned so that circumnavigators can take part in most of them. They are mainly social arrangements, with plenty of festivities, happy hours and wet T-shirt parties. The participants in the Darwin to Ambon race cover a distance of 600nm and are given permission to sail in the Indonesian archipelago, which normally takes a lot of time and effort to obtain. We took part in 1995, the year when Indonesia was celebrating the 50th anniversary of its independence. Two races were hosted: the Darwin to Ambon race and the Darwin to Bali race, with a continuing race from Bali to Jakarta.

Darwin Yacht Club has a big, beautifully situated clubhouse, which can easily host all the parties and happy hours for 150 boats and their crews. We were looking for new paying crewmembers – Terri signed off and we were now down to three: Johanna, Chris and myself. At various parties at the yacht club, we found five more people: Judith, an artist who lived in Darwin; Meena, who had been born in India but held a British passport and taught English in Darwin; Ian, a chief judge in Darwin; Caroline, a British backpacker who had just signed off another boat, the *Ombak Penari*; and Christine, a journalist from New Zealand who lived in Phuket and was planning to write about sailing for different magazines.

KAKADU NATIONAL PARK

While we were in Darwin, the capital of Australia's Northern Territory, we made the three hour drive to Kakadu National Park. The park is in an impressive mountain range, with thick, original green rainforest. We took a river and saw some of the rich bird life and a large number of crocodiles. We also saw ancient cave paintings and dwelling places. In the Northern Territory, the aborigines try to live in the same traditional way as they did before the Europeans immigrated to Australia. They are a nomadic and hunting people whose culture has existed for 40,000–50,000 years. The adaptation to western civilization has been complicated, and alcoholism and crime have spread rampantly through the tribes. Still, the situation is improving. The Australian government and authorities have accepted that the aborigines once dominated the continent. In one of the most important present day trials for aborigines, in 1985, the highest court of justice decided that Ayers Rock – in the middle of Australia – would be returned to the aborigines and leased back to the National Parks and Wildlife Agency.

INDONESIA – DRAGONS AND SPICES

Leaving Darwin, we sail through the Indonesian archipelago, meet the boat from hell, visit the fabulous Spice Islands, and encounter the Bugis tribe – the traditional pirates of South-east Asia . . .

DARWIN TO AMBON

The July 1995 rally from Darwin to Ambon took place in beautiful weather but we had little wind for sailing. The first days were almost dead calm and the tide actually carried us back towards Darwin. We actually pushed *Jennifer,* swimming in the direction of Ambon. With only light winds we could eat our meals at a properly laid table in the cockpit, even with all the sails up. Every day, the organizers made an announcement on the SSB-radio, and it was exciting to see how much the tide had affected the different boats. The race was divided into different categories: Racing (with spinnaker), Cruising (without spinnaker) and Rally (engine allowed). We sailed in the Cruising category, but when the wind still hadn't appeared after some days, we announced over the SSB-radio that we had changed to the Rally category and started the motor. No one in the crew was unhappy about this as we had the same goal – a relaxing voyage to Indonesia, whether sailing or not. Of course, the wind came up a couple of hours after our change of category. We finished on the night of the fifth day and to our surprise came in third place in the Rally division (you had to tell the organizers how many hours you had used the engine). In Ambon the authorities had prepared a party with flags, tents, and tourist information. The tents were needed because it was the rainy season and the sky opened up every day.

THE BOAT FROM HELL

In Ambon, we anchored next to *Ombak Penari*, a 98ft (30m) schooner. Peter, the owner, was a handsome and outgoing Australian who had had his yacht built in Indonesia. He sailed her with paying crew, mostly made up of backpackers. However, Peter sailed too cheaply for his own good. He required hard work from his crew but made the mistake of not serving enough food on board – maybe just one chicken and some rice to feed 12 people at a meal. Most of the crew had been aboard since Cairns, where we first met them. They were now tired of Peter – *Ombak Penari* was called the Boat from Hell – and many quit. And where did they go? They came to *Jennifer*, who was paradise in comparison: double cabins with heads (*Ombak* did not even have heads), a video and CD-player, candlelit dinners, home-style meals, scuba diving and only moderate work. Not everybody who wanted to leave *Ombak* could do so. Some had paid the fare for whole trip to Jakarta, including one young girl who had no money left. Since many from our racing crew were leaving to return to Darwin by plane, after a few days in Ambon we had a few vacant places. Marcus, a diving instructor from Zurich who had taken a year off, signed in, as well as a Dutch aircraft engineer called Hans. And Caroline, who in Darwin had already made the decision to leave *Ombak Penari*, stayed aboard *Jennifer*.

Peter never understood why his crew left the boat. But that was the least of his problems. Another more serious problem had already come up in Darwin, where he was arrested for his unpaid bills (his judge was actually our crew member, Ian). Peter managed to get out of this situation, but in Ambon he did not bother to clear in his firearm with customs, which I always do despite the extra bureaucratic procedures. To smuggle drugs or weapons is a serious crime, and Peter was arrested again, but released after only a few days. However, when customs later found a whole box of rifles – probably on its way to Timor where a revolt had been ongoing for some time – he was again arrested for gunrunning, and the police impounded his boat. Indonesia was a military dictatorship in 1995, and gun smuggling was a serious crime. At the time I was convinced that they were going to give him the death penalty. Many years later, we heard that Peter had escaped prison, cut the chain on his boat and single-handedly sailed *Ombak Penari* 1,400nm through rough waters back to Cairns. It was a pretty impressive story. When we later arrived in Bira in Indonesia, where his boat had been built, we learned that he had not even paid for it.

The problem with Peter was that he was living in the wrong century. If he had lived hundreds of years ago, he would have made an excellent pirate. But modern-day 'pirates' such as Peter make it harder for honest long-distance cruisers like us. To sail long distances was not a problem until the end of the 1960s. Then, hippies and poorer sailors started to sail to warmer places, grew marijuana on the islands and lived off the poor inhabitants. Of course, this upset the authorities and they came up with new rules for long-distance cruisers. Now we have to clear in and out at every harbour, sometimes in up to five different places: immigration, customs, the harbour captain, the navy and the health care authorities.

FISHING

Indonesia is the world's fourth most populated nation after China, India and the USA, with over 200 million people. We sailed around the world's biggest archipelago in Indonesia for seven weeks and visited some of its most remote places. We stopped at uninhabited small islands (found through reading *National Geographic*, diving magazines and various travel stories) mostly to find new places to dive and snorkel. Indonesia, Papau New Guinea and the Philippines have some of the richest coral reefs in the world and we made many fantastic dives. Even though the visibility and the corals were impressive, we saw hardly any fish. The long-distance fishing trawlers from Korea, Japan, Russia and Taiwan plunder the waters and the local fishermen catch the rest for food. Both day and night we could see up to 50 – and sometimes even 100 – Indonesian fishing boats. All of them were small, with two or three people aboard and sails made from simple plastic sheets. During the night, the fishermen use strong lanterns, and during the days they use dynamite. One day when we were sailing through a small archipelago, we heard a dull explosion and then saw a big cascade of water. Seconds after the explosion three men jumped into the water to pick up the fish. It is a totally irresponsible way to fish on coral reefs. In the long term, the fishermen lose more than they gain and ruin the precious coral.

SUHARTO AND THE COMMUNISTS

From the early 1800s Indonesia had been a Dutch colony. It was occupied by Japan during the Second World War, and after the war ended, Sukarno (Indonesia's first president), proclaimed the country to be an independent state. Holland – as well as France with its colony Vietnam – wanted to keep their lucrative colonies and sent troops to stop the revolt. After long and bitter fighting, in 1949 Holland finally had to accept Indonesia's independence (with the exception of the Dutch territory of West Papua New Guinea). For many Indonesians who lived outside the main island of Java, not much changed after independence. The Javanese took over the role as oppressors and revolts blazed against the Javan leaders. The Javanese placed military governors on the outer islands. They were only stationed there for six months at a time as the central government did everything they could to prevent them from identifying with the local people.

In 1962 Indonesian troops took West Papau New Guinea from Holland by force. In 1965 the communists tried to grab power in Indonesia. They failed but six generals of high rank were killed and their deaths were attributed to the communists. General Suharto then stepped in with the army and took power, becoming the second Indonesian president in 1967. After this, a brutal hunt for communists began and one million people were killed or imprisoned. Suharto and his family systematically plundered the whole country until 1998, when he was overthrown by a student revolt and went into hiding.

In a developing country like Indonesia it is noticeable that manpower is cheap. The big grocery stores have plenty of assistance. Despite the cheap labour, big multinational companies are moving from Indonesia to Vietnam and Burma, where the price of labour is even lower.

THE BANDA ARCHIPELAGO – THE FABULOUS SPICE ISLANDS (MOLUKU)

When Vasco da Gama sailed east and found the sea route to Asia via Africa and Columbus sailed west over the Atlantic and stumbled over America, they had a purpose for their voyages. This purpose was to find the fabulous Spice Islands (today known as the Moluku Islands).

Centuries ago, spices were in high demand and the prices were high. Spices were important because they not only made it possible to flavour food but also to conserve it and make medicines. In medieval times, Arabian merchants controlled the spice business. After the fall of Constantinople in 1453, the Muslims gained a monopoly on the market. The Europeans realized that the spices came from the east, but the Muslims refused to unveil the secret of their location. So it was the search for these spices that brought the European seafarers out into the world. The Portuguese were the first to find the islands, by sailing east – but soon even the Spaniards found them – by sailing west. This is how it would be for many centuries. The Pope had divided the world between the two competing Catholic Great Powers. Later the English and the Dutch arrived and the European colonial period began.

On *Jennifer* we also succeeded in finding the Banda Islands, a small archipelago with seven islands centred on a large volcanic island, 1,080nm east of Java. The islands' rich soil is perfect for the nutmeg tree and large scale plundering has been going on here for centuries. The Dutch succeeded in creating a spice monopoly – with the Dutch East India Company established in 1602 – and made enormous fortunes. A ship filled with spices used to earn at least triple its value when the cargo was sold in Amsterdam, and it is estimated that the Dutch East India Company shipped nutmeg for a total value of $500 million. The company, which can be compared to the Exxon or Microsoft of today, was one of the biggest, most influential and lucrative companies in the history of the world. These successes didn't come without sacrifice and cost, however. Holland and England were fighting over control of the spice business. Finally, England traded one of the small Banda Islands for one of Holland's smaller islands in America – Manhattan.

The inhabitants on Banda were not sitting idle while the Dutch company practically stole their spices. They revolted. The Dutch responded with terrible cruelty and brutality against the inhabitants. The Governor General chained the men, tortured them and had Japanese mercenaries not only cut their heads off, but first cut them into pieces. Even the Dutch soldiers were terrified. There is a little wall painting in the Banda Museum that retells this cruel scene.

In 1799 the Dutch East India Company went bankrupt and was dissolved. They hadn't managed to keep their monopoly as nutmeg seeds were smuggled out of Grenada in the West Indies and Zanzibar. However, the most deciding factor came from within the company itself; corruption, smuggling and theft had blossomed, from the Governor General at the top to the lowest ranked clerk at the bottom.

Our stay at the Banda Islands was the highlight of our Indonesian voyage. The sail from Ambon, which covered 150nm, was spectacular. The Banda Sea is well known and for good reason. At night the whole sea was fluorescent and shone like a lit pool. We had perfect winds, good weather and enjoyed the sailing immensely. When we finally arrived in Banda we anchored opposite the volcano, by the little city of Bandaneria, a worn-out but picturesque colonial city with small streets and almost no cars. The island still has a big fort from the Dutch era. We climbed the 650m-high volcano and got a bird's eye view over the archipelago.

A local family taught us how to harvest the nutmeg flower and nut. Their garden had a cinnamon tree, and we could cut the cinnamon bark from the trees ourselves. The production of nutmeg is still the most important industry on the Banda Islands, but the old plantations only produce 5 per cent of what they once did. Indonesia, who controls 75 per cent of the production in the world (to which Banda only contributes a small part) and Grenada, who controls 23 per cent, have started an export cartel. If Banda had been allowed to keep its income from the nutmeg business, they would have been as rich as the oil-producing Gulf States. But today, Banda is an isolated outpost with few visitors – forgotten by the world, even by Indonesia.

SULAWESI ISLAND AND THE BUGIS TRIBE

Halfway between Borneo and New Guinea is the island of Sulawesi (known as Celebes before its independence in 1949). On the south-east side of the island lives the Bugis tribe, a group of people known for their pirate business. With jewel-decorated swords and silk turbans, they look like the arch pirates of South-east Asia. In reality, the opposite may be true. From Indonesia's point of view, the European adventurer was the plunderer and colonial conqueror, and the Bugis tribesman the defending seafarer. Anyhow, the European businessmen and explorers feared them.

We arrived in the village of Bira in the south, where big boats, including prahu (meaning 'boat') are built. We met the boatbuilder who had constructed *Ombak Penari* and he told us how Peter stole his boat. He had asked to take her out on a test voyage, and sailed away to Australia. In Bira, up to 30 ships of different sizes were under construction along the beautiful white beach. The ships are built practically without modern tools, just as the canoes in Micronesia. The longest boat was 131ft (40m) long.

We met a German who had just had his prahu finished. He planned to sail with paying surfers in the Indonesian archipelago. A 131ft (40m) prahu, ketch- or schooner-rigged with engine and sails cost only $200,000 when we visited. You get a lot of boat for your money.

During our stay in Bira, we were invited to a Muslim Bugis wedding. Johanna and I had passed a house where they were preparing for some kind of party, Johanna started to talk to the women and soon we were invited to the big event that was going to take place the next day. We were the only western people at the wedding, which took place in the bride's parents' home, a small two-storey hut. It was an unusual experience for us. The young teenage bride didn't look happy, while the groom, a middle-aged man, seemed much more content. The only time the girl smiled was when she said goodbye to us; hopefully it was an act that the bride should appear so serious. Men and women were hosted in different rooms and Johanna and I split up. All the guests passed through a room where the bride's parents sat. In another room sat a priest, surrounded by flowers and the smell of incense. The guests were supposed to pass through here too. The couple received plenty of gifts and even money – big bundles of cash were left lying on the table. We were the only ones who had cameras and everybody wanted to have their photo taken. I was soon out of film, but I didn't tell anyone – I just kept on taking photos of anyone who wanted me to.

KOMODO ISLAND

DRAGONS

The island of Komodo, just west of Flores in the southern part of the Indonesian island chain, is one of the few places in the world where there are real dragons. The biggest ones can be up to 5m long. They kill their prey in the same way as you see in the movie *Jurassic Park*, tearing them apart with their claws. They have a reddish forked tongue that flickers around like a flame. This might be where the myth about dragons breathing fire came from. The dragons live on wild goats and buffalos, but don't hesitate to attack people if they get the chance. A couple of years ago, a Frenchman walked off a trail, even though the guide had forbidden him to do so. He was immediately attacked, torn apart and eaten. We saw six of the historic reptiles when we, guarded by two local guides with wooden cudgels, hiked around the island.

SURVIVAL OF THE FITTEST

Biologically-speaking we were in one of the most interesting parts of the Earth. A zoological border cuts through the Indonesian archipelago. This border runs between Borneo and Sulawesi in the north and continues down between Bali and Lombok in the south. Nowhere east of this line will you find the tigers, elephants or other big predators that you can find in Asia, and nowhere west of the line will you find the Birds of Paradise or tracks from the traditional animals found in Australasia.

The dividing line is called the Wallace line. Alfred Russel Wallace spent eight years travelling around in the Indonesian archipelago during the 1850s, sometimes together with the Bugis pirates. He was looking for the answer to why different species developed as they did. One day, during a bad malaria attack with high fever, he had his vision about the survival of the fittest. He wrote down his thesis and sent it to the already well-known Charles Darwin and asked for his comment.

Darwin, who had been sailing aboard the *Beagle* in the Pacific in the 1830s, had come to the same conclusion. Darwin faced a tough decision. The theory that human beings were not created by God but descended from the apes went against what the church taught, and Darwin risked being sued for blasphemy in Victorian England if he published his thesis. He had wanted to publish it after his death, but because Darwin didn't want to lose the honour, Wallace's article forced him to publish during his own lifetime. In 1858, he published his theory of evolution, but without mentioning Wallace's contribution – so perhaps Darwinism should be called Wallaceism. As sailors, we could partly see the reason for the Wallace line. The tide and the currents around the line are very strong around the islands and it must have been difficult, at least for animals that swim, to cross over. Unfortunately, these same currents limited where we could safely dive. Even though we had four diving pros aboard, we felt that it was just too risky.

BALI

THE RING OF FIRE

You can find a third of all the active volcanoes in the world in Indonesia. Along the Sumatra-Java-Bali island chain is situated the Indonesian Ring of Fire, with many active and some extinct volcanoes. Between Sumatra and Java is the island of Krakatoa. In 1883 Krakatoa experienced one of the most violent volcanic eruptions in the history of the world. The explosion created shock waves that travelled seven times around the world, and changed the local climate for many years.

We visited Bali for just over a week. It is an enchantingly beautiful island with long white beaches, green terraced rice fields, old Buddhist temples and a big volcano in the middle of the island. Southern Bali is the area of Indonesia most exploited by tourists but the rest of the islands lead a pretty undisturbed existence.

The small town of Ubud in central Bali is found up in the mountains and is Bali's cultural and artistic centre. Ubud is on its way to becoming commercialized, but not as extensively as the southern part of the island. Here we experienced a big cremation ceremony: 40 corpses were going to be burned at the stake on the same day. Before noon, a long funeral train walked through the city, as relatives dressed in black pushed a very colourful wagon decorated with dragons. The train, accompanied by interested tourists, walked at a slow pace to a field on the outside of the city. Each body was placed on its special spot on small platforms. Then the fire was lit and soon there were huge flames, accompanied by a lot of smoke. We had just witnessed a bizarre but fascinating Buddhist ceremony. In Ubud we met Dr Lawrence Blair, the author of the book and the documentary *The Ring of Fire,* produced by the American TV-company PBS. Lawrence and his brother Lorne left civilization behind in the 1970s to follow in Wallace's footsteps, financed by the ex-Beatle Ringo Starr. For ten years they filmed a documentary about the rare Bird of Paradise, the headhunters, cannibals, Bugis pirates, dragons, volcanic eruptions, pearl divers and wizards. Those unique films are now collected on four videos and in a book of the same name. Lawrence lives in Ubud in an old teak house on stilts, with pleasant open rooms without glass windows.

With a view over the rice fields and the volcano, Lawrence is connected to the modern world by fax and computers and he has an air-conditioned studio where he is working on new film and video productions. His next project was to find the giant octopii that are reported to be 29m long, living thousands of metres underwater. Today Lawrence is still living in Bali and working on projects to do with the natural world in Indonesia.

TO SINGAPORE

We left Bali at the end of August 1995 to sail to Singapore, 750nm west of Bali. The crew signed off in Bali, and now Johanna and I were alone again until the beginning of October. Because we were so close to the Equator, we did not have much wind, so we motored most of the way. This was another occasion I was glad we had the big diesel tanks, which gave us the chance to motor up to 1,200nm. On the way from Indonesia, we stopped by the Thousand Islands, just outside of Jakarta, the finish for the Jubilee Race from Darwin. On the SSB-radio, we had heard that the harbour was dirty, but the authorities had really tried to make the visit memorable for the participants.

Indonesia's Thousand Islands are small and beautiful and are often visited by wealthy people and tourists from nearby Jakarta. From here we continued on to Singapore – and civilization – at a relaxing pace. On the way we crossed the Equator once more, for the fourth time. Just before we arrived at our destination we met a tropical downpour and strong winds. We looked for shelter on Batan in the Philippines, just across from Singapore, about 10nm away. There is a new luxury marina with a hotel on Batan, totally different from what we have seen in other parts of Indonesia. There were few boats in the marina and even fewer guests at the hotel. Even if many people from Singapore came over during the weekends, someone must have lost a fortune on this establishment. We could choose between staying here (the harbourmaster offered good prices to long-distance cruisers) and take the ferry to Singapore every day, or else sail ourselves. We chose to sail to Singapore Island ourselves.

Singapore, the tiny but successful city-state, is probably the only place on Earth where you have to pay a fine for spitting on the street or walking against a red light. And you might remember the 18-year-old American who was whipped after vandalizing cars in 1994, when the then US President Clinton tried to intervene on the young boy's behalf. I noticed a similarity with Sweden on the subway; everybody seemed a little quiet, maybe subjugated by the state – the power of Big Brother. We anchored on the northern side of the island by NatSteel Marina, which was the least expensive marina available to us at a cost of $20 per day. The new Raffles Marina on the west coast cost four times as much per day, so it was not hard to choose where to go. Either location meant that we had to take the subway (or a rental car) approximately 45 minutes to the city centre. A third, even less expensive option would have been to anchor in Malaysia and take the ferry to Singapore every day.

When I first visited Singapore in 1980, there was a great deal of construction work going on in the city. Now, 15 years later, it was still going on. The entire city seemed to be a huge shopping centre. We took the chance to visit Singapore's land station for the Inmarsat satellite communication system. Singapore's land station is an impressive construction, with huge antennae angled towards the satellites.

HO CHI MINH – FIRST BOAT IN VIETNAM

We arrive at Ho Chi Minh (Saigon) – by sailing the notorious South China Sea and up the Saigon River – as the very first sailboat to visit since the Vietnam War. Here we have a good welcome and come face to face with Vietnamese bureaucracy. We go into the Mekong delta and down into the impressive Cu Chi tunnels where 16,000 Vietnamese soldiers lived during the war – and we leave the country with a giant bill.

THE SOUTH CHINA SEA

We were given a warm welcome when, in September, we arrived in Ho Chi Minh (formerly Saigon). The road there had been a long one. Vietnam was not a part of the route when I had originally planned the circumnavigation in the beginning of 1990 – the possibility of receiving permission to visit the country wasn't very likely. But the fall of communism and the market economy's rapid growth might have changed the attitude of the leaders in Hanoi and in 1995 I thought it might be possible to sail there. Six months before we arrived in Vietnam, I had met the American Bob Bullock in Guam. He travelled widely in Vietnam for his work and had a lot of contacts there. Through Bob, I got in contact with Ho Thai Binh in Ho Chi Minh and a long correspondence started between us. Binh's first task was to get us a written boat invitation. This meant that someone in Vietnam would undertake to sponsor us during our visit there. With such an invitation, you can then apply for a visa (by comparison, visiting the country by plane is much easier). Neither Binh nor I realized how much work we had ahead of us in negotiations with the Vietnamese bureaucracy.

Everything seemed ready by September. The authorities gave us notice that we had to pick our visas up in Singapore. You can understand our surprise then, when at the embassy in Singapore, we were informed that it was impossible to sail to the country. After several days of sending faxes to Hanoi and

Ho Chi Minh, we finally got our eagerly awaited visas – we could start sailing. Between Singapore and Ho Chi Minh is the South China Sea, a distance of 600nm. It is one of the most feared seas on Earth. Pirates are known to be active in the Malacca Sound, so it was with some trepidation that we sailed away. Again we prepared the shotgun and the tear gas. Johanna's plan was to hide her hair in a hat so it would look like we were two men aboard. If anybody came aboard, she would hide in one of the big closets with the rifle ready. Whoever opened the closet would get his head blown off.

The first part of the sailing went well – we had steady winds and good speed. The weather ranged between sun, haze, clouds, rain and torrential rain. Just as in Indonesia there were countless fishing boats out on the South China Sea. In contrast to Indonesia, most of the fishing boats here were powered by motor. During the day, many of the boats came up to us and waved. Sometimes the fishermen wanted water or cigarettes, some came out of curiosity and some came to sell fish. No one was menacing or stubborn. We waved back and kindly said no to all the invitations. It was harder through the night. All the boats used lights to fool the fish up to the surface, and some boats moved while others were anchored. There was a confusion of lights around us. It was difficult to make out exactly what the ships were doing.

Johanna had to wake me up several times during my free time to ask for help in understanding all the lights; sometimes we were only 10m from a roaring fishing boat – it was scary. We had help from the radar, but with this many boats there were too many contacts to keep track of. It was easier to understand the surroundings visually. We never felt threatened and no pirates tried to board us. Our autopilot broke on the last day and later I noticed that our middle shroud, the wire between the two-shroud divider was broken. We had to steer manually for the rest of the day. The middle shroud could wait to be repaired, and a change of wind relieved the pressure on it.

During the five-day voyage, we read about Vietnam. The most interesting book was *A Bright Shining Lie: John Paul Vann and America in Vietnam* (1988) by Neil Sheehan. Neil worked at the *New York Times* when the paper publicized the Pentagon Papers, which Daniel Ellsberg had copied without permission and given to the newspaper (something that Nixon sued him for) in 1971. Vann was a general in Vietnam and early in the war had enthusiastically fought for an American victory. After a while, he was frustrated by the hopelessly corrupt South Vietnamese presidents and generals, as well as the American government's way of handling the war – with lies, betrayal, secret warfare and the indiscriminate bombing of civilians. Because of his honesty and courage, he was controversial within the American military. Vann died during the war in Vietnam, the country he loved despite everything that was happening. Another unveiling story about the war is David Halberstam's Pulitzer-winning book *The Best and The Brightest* (1972).

UPSTREAM IN THE SAIGON RIVER

We made landfall in Vietnam by Vung Tao, a town by the Saigon River's outflow. Again we faced the same attitude as at the embassy in Singapore. We could not possibly get permission to stay in the country on a sailing boat. We were forbidden to land. Binh's mission now was to get us cleared into the country and up the Saigon River. Now Binh realized the difficulty. He had been more occupied with arranging publicity on television and in the papers than to make our entrance to Vietnam easier. His main task had been getting us there in time for the press conference. I realized that I had ignored an important factor. Vietnam is still a communist state, obsessed with security and suspicion. After two days – with countless faxes, calls via the VHF and visits to the police, customs and coastguard officials – we got permission to sail up the Saigon River with a policeman and a pilot aboard. Finally, we started to experience Vietnam. The river is the main fairway to Ho Chi Minh and on the river is a motley collection of boats. Different types of sampans travel up and down the river. These are canoe-like boats, which are powered by one person who either stands in the stern with a long oar, or sits down in the boat and pedals with his feet, as on a bike. There are also boats with outboard motors with 4–5m propeller shafts as well as cargo ships.

For the first time in decades, the river was travelled by a sailboat – *Jennifer*. The Vietnamese did not know anything about yachting or long distance sailing; the concept doesn't even exist in their language. *Jennifer* was categorized as a cargo boat, as private boats didn't exist. After six hours, we reached Ho Chi Minh and a big towboat met us and helped us to moor between two big buoys. The buoys were laid in long rows along the river and cargo ships were moored on each side of our giant buoys. *Jennifer*, who was tiny in comparison to these commercial ships, took up only a little part of the allotted space.

On the riverbank opposite Ho Chi Minh there was a little village of small, unpainted wooden houses. The whole village was very active. For the villagers the river was their livelihood. As soon as we were moored a woman came by in a small sampan loaded with beer and vegetables. The sampan was a floating store. Mini villages of floating sampans offering different kinds of

services surrounded the cargo ships around us. This is where we were moored throughout our entire visit and we always had a policeman aboard.

THE WELCOME

Just as we moored in the Saigon River, our friend Binh met us with a boat and drove us into one of Ho Chi Minh's best restaurants. A large crowd of journalists was waiting for us with flashing cameras and there were girls with roses. Binh's happiness was obvious and there was a lot of shaking hands and hugging. He was proud that we were visiting and we were happy to be his guests. On the walls in the restaurant, big streamers with *Jennifer*'s logo hung with the text 'Welcome to Vietnam Lars and Johanna' as well as a copy of our around-the-world route. They also held a press conference and a banquet for us. The friendly Swedish consul Nils Sundvik was also invited. During the conference several journalists interviewed us while four young beautiful women – in deep blue silk dresses – played traditional Vietnamese instruments in the background. We were photographed on the platform with these beauties. For days after the banquet, we read about ourselves in many newspapers and one of them even had a picture of us on the front page. Whenever we were in a store and the employees recognized us there was a big commotion and they did not let us pay for our goods. The Vietnamese are not used to celebrities, other than communist party bigwigs.

One day we were out sailing on the Saigon River, with both the pilot and the policeman aboard. By following our boat, television and press could, for the first time, see a sailing boat with full sails. When we started to tack between the merchant vessels, which were moving up and down the river, the pilot was noticeably nervous and asked us to take down the sails and start the engine. The whole show was aired on television the next evening. During our stay, the Swedish film institute and the Vietnamese culture department jointly arranged a Swedish film festival, and we were invited. The Swedish consul Nils introduced both the film and us. We were asked to come up on the stage and we received enthusiastic applause. After that they showed the movies. The Swedish film *Sailing Yacht Glädjen* (meaning 'Joy') was shown – it was a sailing movie where two Swedish families face a number of unpleasant things. It was hard for us to understand the movie. It was dubbed into Vietnamese, had French subtitles and a few Swedish voices in the background.

THE VIETNAMESE BUREAUCRACY

To be welcomed as heroes and to obtain permission to sail along the Vietnamese coast are two totally different things. After three days of meetings with Binh and ourselves on one side and various authorities on the other, it became clear that we were not going to be allowed to sail north along the coast. One reason was the question of our boat insurance. Obtaining insurance for a circumnavigation at a good price is not easy, but it is normally negotiable. But unusual routes, such as visiting a communist country, were too much for the insurance companies. It was also difficult to explain the purpose for our stay to the Vietnamese. People in the west, including bureaucrats as well as border and immigration clerks, understand the meaning of a circumnavigation. But in Vietnam, who had been at war for the longest part of the century – against France, Japan, USA, China and Cambodia – it was unbelievable that anyone would sail around without actually 'doing' anything. We changed our plans and decided to travel around Vietnam on land. The travel agency Viet Tour, who sponsored our stay, offered to pay for our accommodation. We now had to decide what to do with the boat. At a meeting with the police, the officer offered to look after *Jennifer* for a cost of $1,000, which I refused. The police were not going to take responsibility for the boat's safety, but there was nowhere else to moor it. Again we had to change our plans; it was now to be day trips around Ho Chi Minh. The different between east and west – between open and closed communities – is enormous. In the west, everything that is not illegal is legal. In the east, everything that is not legal, according to the law, is illegal. There was no law about sailing as a leisure activity in Vietnam and therefore it was illegal to simply sail around for pleasure.

Outside Ho Chi Minh we took a trip in a small sampan on the delta of the Mekong River. The Mekong River originates in Tibet and passes through China, Laos, Cambodia and Vietnam where it creates a rich delta before it runs out into the South China Sea. The river is rich with fish and we saw some Vietnamese people in typical Asian cone hats swimming in the brown cloudy water with their fishing nets.

THE CU CHI TUNNELS

One of the most impressive attractions in Vietnam is the Cu Chi tunnel system that is located about two hours north-west of Ho Chi Minh. The building of the tunnels started in the 1940s and they were used for military campaigns during the Vietnam War. Some 16,000 Viet-Cong soldiers lived and fought here against the Americans in the late 1960s. The tunnels are dug in a 200km-long network, with ingeniously constructed ventilation and light systems. The tunnels are three storeys deep and divided into dormitories, field hospitals, kitchens, command centres and weapons factories. Everything is very simply built. The tunnels are only 1.2m high and 0.8m wide, which makes them

very uncomfortable to move around in. Soldiers would have had to crouch in the darkness and the heat.

Some of the visiting tourists could not go down into the tunnels because of claustrophobia, while others came up soon because of the heat or because they were too narrow. Having completed military duty on a submarine I was one of the few who dared to go down to the third level. Here it is only crawling height, dark and even hotter than before. I tried to imagine how it must have been to sleep, eat, work and above all fight a war under these difficult conditions. The Americans had a hard time finding the tunnels among the mines and bamboo spears hidden in the ground. The USA started to use scent dogs and the Vietnamese responded by putting out pepper to mislead them. When too many dogs had been injured or killed by the bamboo spears and mines, the dog leaders refused to send down any more. Then the army decided to send down soldiers, with the same tragic results. Finally, the USA sent in bombers and devastated the entire Cu Chi province, partly with bombs, partly with poisonous defoliants that stripped the leaves off the trees over large areas. It was the most bombed, gassed, burnt, defoliated and destroyed area in the history of warfare. But it came too late; the USA was already losing the war and had started to pull their troops back. Today, the tunnels are a tourist attraction run by the Vietnamese army, with souvenir shops, video presentations and guides. It was surreal to see these men and women working in the tunnels in communist army uniforms, a relic from the past.

NEVER FORGET THE PAST

In Ho Chi Minh we visited the old Presidential Palace that is today a museum. It is maintained in the same condition as when the North Vietnamese tanks broke the gates and the regime collapsed in the April of 1975, when the last remaining American soldiers escaped by helicopter from the American embassy's roof. When the North Vietnamese stormed the palace, they met the last South Vietnamese president. 'I have been waiting all day to pass on the power,' he said. 'It will not happen,' was the answer. 'You cannot give away something you do not have.'

Another well-known museum is the War Crimes Museum, with terrible photos of the American bombings and tortures. That the Viet Cong and the North Vietnamese side also committed huge war crimes is not mentioned at all.

In Ho Chi Minh we spent time with Binh and his family. Binh and his wife had totally different backgrounds. They are both from North Vietnam, but while Binh's father was a capitalist and his property was confiscated after the Second World War, his wife's father was a member of the FNL (Forces

Nationales de Libération) and fought against the USA. Today Binh is an entrepreneur and has a company that imports sea safety products. His wife is a journalist and author and has written many books. The best-known book is *Never Forget the Past* in which she proudly poses in a photo with Jane Fonda, who visited Hanoi during the middle of the war in the 1970s. Fonda was harshly criticized for the visit and regretted it later.

DOI MOI

An aspect that of Ho Chi Minh that took us by surprise was the heavy traffic. Everybody seemed to be working day and night, weekday and weekend. Bikes, mopeds, motorbikes and heavy Russian-manufactured trucks were on the go all the time. Other than taxis and police cars there were not many ordinary cars.

The Vietnamese economic reforms of the 1980s are called Doi Moi ('renovation') and Vietnam has used China as a model to base her economy on. The goal was twofold: to create a relatively free market economy but at the same time keep the communist party's monopoly on power. In the quest to improve the standard of living and regain lost time, work goes on until late at night and the social life partly takes part on the sidewalks, so work time and leisure time seem to mix together. The future is represented in the need to collect, take apart, repair and reuse most of the products, even garbage. Nothing goes to waste.

We were amazed that all kinds of consumer goods could be found in Vietnam; many were smuggled in. The markets were full of food, fruit and vegetables, probably because the farmers could now sell their products themselves. A lot of a family's meat comes from keeping live animals. With a lack of refrigerators and freezers, keeping live animals is the most effective way to keep food fresh. Vietnam is one of the world's leading rice exporters and we saw thousands of sacks of rice in the harbour that were taken as cargo on the commercial ships. With a persistent, patient population of 75 million, an iron will to succeed and plenty of cheap manpower, Vietnam might become one of the new tiger economies during this century.

A GIANT BILL

The cost for our stay in Ho Chi Minh was high. The clearing-out took place aboard *Jennifer*, with representatives from the harbour office, customs, police, the pilot and the agent. They presented us with a bill for $1,200 for the pilot, towboat, harbour fee, police and agent. I protested and a violent discussion started, mostly between the police officer and myself. I explained that in the rest of the world it would not be reasonable to demand such a high fee from sailors in this way. I refused to pay the police bill of $500 out of the total $1,200 and a tense feeling arose in the boat. After that, a discussion in Vietnamese between the different officials started and I tried to figure out who had the highest status, which wasn't easy considering all the stars and marks of different sizes and styles on their uniforms and hats. Since they obviously didn't want us to leave the country with a bad experience, most of them tried to persuade the police officer to drop his demand, which he did after a while. It must have been a loss of prestige for the police officer and he looked displeased. The police usually have the last word in a dictatorship. Eventually, I paid $700. When the formalities were complete, we had a general discussion. It emerged that the authorities had learned a lot from our visit. Two French boats had just been given permission to visit the country and were already on their way to Ho Chi Minh. For them and future boats, it would be easier to sail to Vietnam.

SOUTH-EAST ASIA – PIRATE DANGER

We sailed one of our hardest passages, without the autopilot, to Thailand, continued to the Ko Samui Islands and south along the east coasts of Thailand and Malaysia. We then headed back to Singapore and up through the Malacca Strait with its notorious pirates. We visited Phuket, which became one of our favourite islands. And I reached a landmark birthday.

THAILAND

In early October 1995, we sailed from Ho Chi Minh to Pattaya on the east coast of Thailand, a distance of 600nm on a journey that took five days. It was one of the hardest passages of the whole circumnavigation. Our autopilot had broken the day before we reached Ho Chi Minh, and when we reached the city we sent the autopilot to the USA for repair. It wouldn't be returned until a month later in Singapore.

The weather was poor, with lots of rain and variable winds, which meant that we had to motor half of the time. Because we were missing the autopilot we had to steer manually day and night – three hours on the helm and three hours off. The difference between having an autopilot and steering manually was such that we could not really do anything except sit by the steering wheel during our shifts on the helm. There was no chance of making a sandwich, going to the bathroom or reading. All these things had to be done during our three-hour break. This was tough at night, especially as many fishing boats were out in the darkness. This meant we had to be extra careful.

We were very tired when we arrived in Pattaya and went directly to bed without clearing-in. Pattaya is about two hours away from Bangkok by car, and is a dull place with lots of hotels and a narrow beach. It has a bad reputation because of vice; the whole city is like a huge brothel and many men from Europe travel here just for sex. We rested here for a week waiting for

our next crew. In the meantime, we rented the latest videos. You might think that when you are out sailing you don't need this kind of entertainment. But after being out at sea for a while, you get cravings for a taste of civilization. For example, I always buy *Time* magazine or *Newsweek* whenever I can.

THE KO SAMUI ISLANDS

In the middle of October we started our journey south along the east coast of Thailand and Malaysia down towards Singapore, a distance of 700nm. We stopped by several islands, including the beautiful Ko Samui Islands in the Bay of Thailand. The small islands used to be the backpacker's favourites in the 1970s and 1980s. After travel agents discovered the islands and an airport and luxurious hotel were built, Ko Samui lost its charm for the back-packing youths. The smallest and most northern of the islands, Ko Tao, was still relatively unexploited. Only backpackers stayed here and the main activity was diving; almost every second store in the little street was a diving store. The middle island, Ko Phangan, had a poorer reputation. The island was not exploited in the same way as Ko Samui and not as basic as the northerly island Ko Tao but had turned into a place where some young people searched for drugs.

One day we sailed into a Thai fishing village on the mainland. When we motored up the canal it almost ended in catastrophe. There was a big power line crossing the canal. People were standing, pointing up in the air and yelling, but at first we didn't understand what they meant. Just a couple of metres before we reached the power line, we understood the serious situation we were in. Before I managed to reverse the boat, the forestay touched the power line. What saved us from getting an electric shock through the boat was that the genoa was rolled on the forestay, so a metal-to-metal connection did not occur. We were offered a place by one of the fishing docks and the whole village came to look at us – and we at them. Only one of the villagers could speak English and none had seen a western sailing boat before.

SINGAPORE AGAIN

Back in Singapore it was time for repairs again. During the span of a week, two of the shrouds had broken and had to be supported by ropes. Luckily Singapore has chandleries with the correct size shrouds and shroud screws. The propeller that had been sanded in Australia was now so thin that it had to be replaced.

We anchored by the NatSteel Marina on the northern side of Singapore. Although the water wasn't clean and the visibility less then 1m, we had to dive down to change the propeller. We used several ropes: one between us so we would not lose each other in the heavy currents, one to the heavy new propeller, one that was going to be attached to the old one, and a number of ropes attached to all the tools. After half an hour, the change was done. The old anchor chain was rusty and replaced with a new one at a cost of $1,200.

Singapore was full of Christmas decorations in October, and the shopping hysteria was worse than the month before Christmas at home. This is despite the fact that Singapore is a multicultural society that does not have any Christmas traditions of its own. It's only the foreigners who have brought Christmas to Singapore.

THE MALACCA STRAIT

In the middle of October we sailed from Singapore through the challenging Malacca Strait towards Phuket in Thailand. We covered a distance of 550nm. For most of October and November there was not much wind, but there was a lot of rain and we had to motor between the hard rain squalls that often suddenly appeared in the area around the Equator. Autumn is a transition period between the south-west monsoons that blow between June and September and the north-east monsoons that occur between November and March. The monsoons dictate whether it is best to sail on the east or the west coast of Thailand. The west side (Phuket) is best during the north-east monsoon season. There is also the best wind for long-distance cruisers to continue to the Indian Ocean. During the south-west monsoon season it is rainy and windy in Phuket, but perfect on the east side of Thailand, for example the Ko Samui Islands.

In the Malacca Strait we stopped in Port Klang, Malaysia's largest port, and went on a day trip by train into the capital of Malaysia, Kuala Lumpur. Here they were building two of the tallest skyscrapers in the world, the Petronas Towers, completed in 1998. It seemed an insane project for a poor developing country and an expression of the leading politician's megalomania, or maybe his inferiority complex.

Another stop was at Penang, a charming island that is a state in the Malaysian Federation. Part of our crew was changed here. Many yachts were gathered in Penang to take part in the Phuket King's Cup Regatta, Asia's annual sailing event. The beautiful Langkawi Islands, between Malaysia and Thailand, was the last stop in Malaysia. These islands are a popular destination for long-distance sailors. Because Thailand gives different lengths of permission to stay, many long-distance sailors have to leave Thailand regularly just to clear in again and apply for new visas. As a free port Langkawi is the perfect place for them to sail to and is just a day's trip from Phuket. It is also the perfect place to stock up on provisions because you can buy food and drink at low prices. We finally arrived in Phuket in the beginning of December and stayed for two months.

PIRATES

Besides hurricanes there is nothing else that scares a seafarer more than pirates. There are countless stories about how these fearsome marauders of the oceans have plundered merchant vessels around the world. The best-known historical area for pirates is probably the Caribbean. There has been an ongoing battle between Spain (the traditional sea power in the new world) and later arrivals such as Britain, France and Holland, over the wealth of the Americas. The pirates or 'privateers', were adventurers and opportunists, many of them sanctioned by the European royal houses in exchange for parts of their plunders. This was looked upon as a legitimate part of warfare, and the pirates became an extended arm of the state.

Sir Francis Drake is an excellent example of such a privateer. He raised a fortune, both for himself and for the English Queen Elizabeth I, and was given a peerage as thanks for his success. Possibly the most dangerous of all privateers was Sir Henry Morgan, who continuously plundered, burned and tortured people in Panama and other Spanish fortified cities. He was also given a peerage and later in life became the governor of Jamaica, with the main task of rooting out the pirate business in the West Indies (Britain had now taken over the role as the most important colonial power in the area).

Other historic pirate areas that still exist include the Mediterranean (especially outside Morocco and Nigeria), and in Asia: the South China Sea and the Malacca Strait. The Caribbean Sea used to be notorious for pirate attacks. Until the 1980s the drug dealers needed yachts in order to sail unnoticed with their cargo to the USA. Many sailboats were captured, their crew shot and thrown overboard. The boats might be used only once to smuggle a load of drugs and then be sunk. Traditionally pirates wanted to rob the boats of their valuables, bind the crew and sink the boat to get rid of the evidence.

Knowing the possibility of pirate attacks I had bought a shotgun for $200 in Martinique in 1992. To buy a firearm legally in this part of the world is simple; if you have the money you can buy anything. The seller almost succeeded in selling me a high-powered rifle with a huge firepower for $1,000. Sometimes out at sea, I practised with my shotgun.

We had the five tear gas guns that we had bought in Guam strategically placed on the boat, for use in case of pirates boarding. The only time I tried

Top Pilot whales in the South Seas. We frequently encountered dolphins, but whales were rare. A few times, we saw large humpback whales, which were exciting to watch.

Left At anchor in the tropics, with two large banana stocks hanging on the stern. Bananas can keep for about ten days, after which they mature almost simultaneously and the crew have to eat them all.

Bottom *Jennifer* running with the Trade winds on the longest non-stop stretch of our circumnavigation (between the Galapagos and Marquesas islands – 3,100 nautical miles). Note the fishing line on the starbourd side.

Top *Jennifer* anchored at Fatu Hiva in the Marquesas Islands of French Polynesia. This island is one of the most spectacular and beautiful in the Marquesas, and is where Thor Heyerdahl of Kon-Tiki fame spent a full year with his wife trying to live off the island and writing a book about it.

Right Jan and I prepare a newly caught dorado.

Left We found these ancient stone tikis deep in the jungle on the Marquesas island of Hiva Oa. Similar statues are found in South America – one reason why Thor Heyerdahl claims the Polynesians might have arrived from there.

Bottom In a lava-lava skirt in *Jennifer's* galley.

Top Fruit and perishables were stored in the saloon in nets, which each held up to 20kg. The saloon was airy and dry, and food stayed fresh for a long time.

Bottom *Jennifer's* navigation station. This was also my office where I handled bookkeeping, kept in touch with agents and guests and planned the routes.

Top Tobago Cays in the Grenadines. The four uninhabited islands and their delightful lagoon is the most popular anchorage in the Caribbean. The snorkelling is great.

Bottom Spinnaker flying in spectacular Phuket to the south of Thailand. The wind needs to be just the right strength, ideally about 10 knots.

Top *Jennifer* at anchor between two large buoys on the Saigon River in 1995. We were the first yacht to be granted permission to visit Vietnam after the war, and we got a great reception: a welcome party, flowers and coverage in the press and TV.

Right Johanna climbs out of the deep, hot and narrow Cu Chi tunnels in Vietnam. The Vietnamese army lived and hid here during the Vietnam War, and the tunnels contained hospitals, ammunition factories and food stores, and served as communications and supply routes. In an attempt to destroy the tunnel system, the American B-52s bombed the region heavily, but with little success.

Left As we found in communist Vietnam, clearance procedures in Cuba were time consuming. Here are customs, immigration, health, army, police and security officials. But everyone was polite and helpful.

Bottom A burial ceremony in the city of Ubud, in the mountains of Bali. Forty corpses were burnt this day, according to Buddhist tradition. A spectacular scene for us westerners.

Top The Rock Islands of Palau, Micronesia – one of the most beautiful places on earth and one of the best dive sites. This island nation and its many outstanding anchorages are surrounded, and protected, by an enormous reef.

Right *Jennifer* anchored amongst the Rock Islands. The foliage reaches all the way to the water, making it impossible to go ashore.

Bottom In the 'stone bank' on the island of Yap, part of the Federated States of Micronesia. The 'money' usually stays in the same place, as everyone knows who owns what. In this bank there are 50 large 'coins'.

Left A number plate on Yap.

Bottom Lorraine and Johanna in front of two Jam Houses, where jam – the most important food – is stored, in the Trobriand Islands of Papua New Guinea.

Top A boy in a wooden canoe made from a single tree on the Sepik River in Papua New Guinea. We went down the river in a larger canoe for five days; an exciting adventure.

Right A young girl at a market by the Sepik River. She is holding a small ape.

Top *Jennifer* anchored in the large Bikini lagoon. We entered the lagoon without proper permission, to dive around the aircraft carrier *Saratoga*, sunk during a nuclear explosion in 1946.

Bottom Me and Johanna on Bikini atoll. America tested numerous atom and hydrogen bombs here during the 1940s and 50s. The inhabitants were forcibly removed, and because of the radiation they haven't been able to return. We had our best dives ever in the lagoon, around *Saratoga*.

Top Johanna and I repairing the mainsail after a rain squall ripped it apart overnight. The sewing machine is heavy, and the repair took two days.

Bottom The Royal Palace in Tonga's capital, Nuku'alofa. The palace was built in the 19th century but today the king lives in a more modern mansion.

Top Every autumn, humpback whales return to Tonga's Vava'u archipelago to mate and feed their young. Sailors can swim with them but have to be careful not to go between mother and child.

Bottom The male crew with Ylva, who joined us from Tonga to Fiji, New Caledonia and New Zealand. Here in Fijian waters, *Jennifer* is in the background with the wind generator working.

Top On the 180° meridian cutting through the island of Taveuni in Fiji. Bo, Johanna and Maria are standing in tomorrow while Ulf is standing in yesterday. The international date line, however, passes east of Tonga, due to the fact that during the 19th century a British governor wanted both Fiji and Tonga on the same time.

Bottom The wooden sign for Malololailai's airport – Malololailai is situated among the islands off the west coast of Fiji. Here, at Musket Cove Yacht Club and its $3 bar, circumnavigators meet and socialize.

Left Johanna and I on the diving platform, ready for a dive in the South Seas. We have wetsuits, cylinders and dive computers, and I carry a knife – just in case.

Bottom Diving at the Great Barrier Reef in Australia, being confronted by a large 'Potato Cod'. He was used to divers and didn't mind being patted.

Top *Jennifer* in downtown Auckland, New Zealand, in 1993/94. Many circumnavigators stop in New Zealand during the hurricane season (December to April) and drive or hitchhike round the North and South islands.

Right The crew taking a refreshing swim, hanging on to the boat by a rope. This was one of the most popular activities when we were under sail in good weather. In the foreground you can see the platform, perfect for swimming and diving.

one of these guns – it is really a spray type gun, small and handy – Johanna and I were down in the boat while a crewmember, Urban (without me knowing) was sitting in the cockpit. I pulled the trigger, aimed for the cockpit and then heard a whimper from Urban, who almost lost his breath. I apologized, but was also pretty satisfied – the tear gas spray worked effectively.

The pirate situation for long-distance sailors is better today. These days, drug smuggling is often carried out using small airplanes. The pirates of today are no longer interested in the sailors' meager possessions. Most people sail with credit cards and bring only a few hundred US dollars in cash between each harbour. Other than cameras, portable GPS units, VHF radios and laptops, there is not much of value on board. These consumables can certainly be attractive, but pirates are mostly interested in cash. Pirates therefore aim for merchant vessels instead. They always have a lot of cash to be able to pay the harbour fees, fuel, etc. These days, pirates have modern weapons and fast boats. They approach the boats at high speed from behind, and get aboard with ropes. Usually they lock the crew up and empty the safe. A couple of years ago, three fast pirate boats attacked a big ship in the Malacca Strait. It was a dark and rainy night, and the ship they were boarding was a big Russian aircraft carrier! A warship full of armed elite soldiers does not hesitate to open fire and the pirates had to flee the ship and escape out into darkness.

In the South Pacific, we got to know some of the biggest private yachts in the world. The skipper on one of them told me that when they were going to pass through the Malacca Strait, they hired Gurkha soldiers to sail with them as an armed escort.

During our voyage over the South China Sea, we heard on the radio about a merchant vessel with a cargo of sugar that had been boarded by pirates, who stole both the boat and the cargo and brought it to China. The USA had satellite photos of the incident but Chinese authorities denied any knowledge of it. Sometimes it is a renegade unit from a country's own defence forces that wants to earn some extra money. It can be the navy, coastguard or a customs unit with uniforms. To help straighten out the problem that piracy causes in the shipping business, the International Maritime Bureau (IMB) Piracy Reporting Centre has been established in Kuala Lumpur. This centre is manned day and night and maintains continuous contact with coastguards and navy units in many of the countries of the world. With the development of communications, it is becoming harder for the pirates to act. I had the Piracy Reporting Centre's fax programmed on my Inmarsat C unit and could reach them in a matter of seconds in an emergency, something that thankfully we didn't have to do.

To make it even harder for the pirates, the International Maritime Organization (IMO), the Piracy Reporting Centre and ship-owners have an electronic payment system for the merchant ships. In that way, the ships do not need to carry a lot of cash aboard. From 1999, it became mandatory for all commercial ships in the whole world to have at least one Inmarsat C unit aboard. This means that the merchant vessels can be in continuous fax or e-mail connection with the Piracy Reporting Centre, and attacks against ships can be mailed/faxed out to other ships in the area in a matter of seconds. This was previously done via the radio, a much slower medium.

PHUKET

Phuket's archipelago, with its many islands, was a pleasant surprise. Phuket itself is an island, almost the same size as Singapore, with many hotels, youth hostels, good beaches and a large number of tourists. Patong on the western side of Phuket is seen as a bit of a tourist trap. Sailors anchor in one of the many tranquil bays, such as the southern Nai Harn Bay, where the exclusive Royal Phuket Yacht Club is based in a luxurious hotel. It is not really a yacht club apart from once a year in December when it hosts the annual Phuket King's Cup Regatta. The main harbour for sailors is Ao Chalong, on the south-east side of Phuket. Here several hundred boats are anchored and there are restaurants, bars, laundry facilities, food shops and sailmakers. The sail-maker, Rolly Tasker, an older, successful competitive sailor from Australia, recently built a large sail loft. In the loft work only beautiful young Thai women, which made it very pleasant to visit. When I asked why no men worked for him, he answered, 'Women have better work ethics. Men take more breaks and go out and smoke marijuana and hit on girls. This is more efficient for the company.'

The most beautiful archipelago I have ever seen is situated between Phuket and Krabi on the mainland. It is perfect for day sailing, with few dangerous reefs and plenty of protected harbours, but in somewhat shallow water. The islands are tall, wild and green with lovely white beaches. There are caves and tunnels perfect for snorkelling and diving and easy to explore with a dinghy. If you want to sail for longer, you can go south to the Langkawi Islands in Malaysia. Alternatively you can go to the Similan Islands north-west of Phuket in the Andaman Sea, where the water is fantastically clear. I could easily spend a year in Thailand – during the north-east monsoon season I would be based in Phuket and during the south-west monsoon season I would be based among the Ko Samui islands.

After our visit to Vietnam, *Jennifer* had several paying crews. Even though

Thailand is far away from Sweden, the flight there was cheap and many friends came to sail with us in Phuket's archipelago. They brought with them Swedish fish roe, newspapers from Sweden and post. These reminders of home are always appreciated. We've had many people on board who had taken a long break from home – either quitting their job or taking a long vacation from school or work. Elisabeth, a friend from Sweden who signed on in Singapore, and Michelle, who came through the agent in California and signed on in Penang, had the same background. Both were in their 30s, had university degrees in marketing and good jobs, but had decided to take a break to get a different perspective on life. On top of that, independently of each other, both of them had been hiking in Nepal just before they came to the boat. Percy and Magnus, who worked for Skanska, a construction firm in Saudi Arabia, had both read the article 'Adventure for sale' in January 1995, contacted my agent in Stockholm, and come down with their girlfriends for a two-week diving and sailing holiday. During the same period, we also had an American computer programmer from California through the San Francisco agent. Another group included friends from Malaysia, Curt and Björn, who had their own company there. They sailed on board with their families for a week. A Swedish family came over Christmas and New Year: Örjan, a business consultant and Karin, a jazz dance instructor who came with their four children. Two of the children took their diving certificates.

Two other crewmembers who had taken a long time off and signed on in Pattaya were Douglas and Evan. They were a father and son from California. Douglas was an entrepreneur who is now the owner of the biggest consultancy company in the world specializing in risk assessment: natural catastrophes, earthquakes, hurricanes, volcanic eruptions etc, with offices on all continents of the world. Douglas took almost a whole month off work and sailed with us from Pattaya to Singapore, partly to do something different, but mainly to spend time with his son Evan, who had taken a year off from school. Evan was not tired of school – he was intelligent and one of the top students in his class – but the family had taken the decision together, agreeing that he should see the world and also spend some time travelling on his own. Since Evan was interested in sailing, he chose to sail on *Jennifer* as one of the activities during his year off. Douglas and Evan had hired an education consultant in California, who had made contact through my agent in San Francisco. From the same agent, John, who was 18 years old, also signed on in Singapore. Below I have inserted extracts from Evan's logbook, which he wrote during the two months he was aboard. His conclusions and comprehension are impressive – he was only 14 years old when he wrote them.

'I have had the most fantastic opportunity to travel the world for a year. This is a report of my travels; my observations, feelings and my view of the world at the age of 14 years old. I travelled to Japan, the start of my journey, and then via Bangkok to Pattaya in Thailand. Here I met the boat Jennifer. *During the two months I have spent on board we have been sailing to many islands in Thailand and Malaysia.*

At Christmas this year I will have a break of two weeks at home in California. After that I will go to Switzerland, where I will go to school five hours a day, six days a week and ski the rest of the time. As one part of the program I will go to France and Italy to learn about the local history and geography. After that I am open for any new adventures.

Lars is Swedish. He quit his job to live his dream to sail around the world. He was born in Stockholm and started to sail when he was ten years old. He backpacked around the world for three years after finishing his studies at Stockholm University. When he returned he started to work at a law firm. After two days, he realized that he hated law and quit after three months and got a new job as an international trader. In 1988 he resigned, sold everything he owned and built a sailing boat. This 49ft (15m) Beneteau sailing boat is named after his goddaughter, Jennifer.

Johanna was born in Holland. At the age of seven she moved to Canada with her family, where she studied botany. She loves diving and moved to Belize in 1985 and started a diving business on an island near the coast of Yucatan, Mexico. She is a Master Dive Instructor, the highest rank within diving. They are both fit and live healthily. They eat vegetarian food several times a week. Lars hosts aerobics on the beach whenever he can, which is quite hard exercise.

The second evening on the boat, after a supper of burgers, something pretty funny came up. We understood that it is not usual for Lars and Johanna to eat meat every day. They thought that because we were American we would want to eat meat on a daily basis. We explained to them that this was not the case. Vegetarian food was fine for us, as we had planned to eat healthily anyway. During my journey I have faced similar situations, because I am an American. At many restaurants the 'American Breakfast' is an ordeal – with eggs, bacon, toast, coffee and pancakes. I actually never eat anything for breakfast except muesli and juice.

I discovered that America has a great influence around the world. This influence creates a stereotypical American. Every country that I have visited so far had a McDonald's and almost all of them had a Kentucky Fried Chicken and Burger King too. One of my goals is to get to a country without a McDonald's! In Thailand, we saw many people who watched

American movies. Even when you have your supper in a remote fishing village, everyone in the restaurant watches the movie Forrest Gump, *with the highest volume on. What people see of America in movies is a perfect world. They think that what they see is the real America. Americans protest that the Japanese cars take over the car production. It is a wonder that other countries do not protest against American food, products, cultures and ideas that we export over the whole world.*

We did a number of night sailings. To sail during the night is very relaxing and gives you time to think. I use the time to write about the journey in my diary.'

'It is 2215 hours and I am on my watch. We are divided into three-hour watches. This watch is from 2100–2400 hours. It is very calm on the ocean. I have learned some new things about navigation. I can position us on the chart, plot our position on the GPS, take the course and calculate the speed and distance. I have got more experience now and am more aware of what I can do.

We have not sailed as much as I would have liked to yet, because the winds have not been very strong. I have started to read the book Maiden Voyage *about Tania Aebi's solo sailing around the world at the age of 18 years old. She was the first American woman, and one of the youngest overall, to sail around the world solo.*

I have also finished the book Dove *about Robin Lee Graham's solo sailing trip around the world, which he started when he was 16 years old. I have also been thinking about sailing around the world. But I want to finish school first.*

On board we have almost reached the first waypoint, which means that we are getting close to an island and will soon have to change course (I know this because I was the one who plotted the course). When you sail at night you hold a certain course and keep an eye out for ships on the horizon. I had done night sailing before and I think it is one of the best parts of sailing. There is not much to do or see, so you can relax most of the time. The stars are clearly visible in the sky with no city lights to interfere with the sight. This is what space travel would be like. You float through the darkness and the only thing you see is the stars and the moon. The groups of fishing boats that we saw during the nights were like galaxies. When you pass one fishing boat there is another one further on. Every light is like a little star.

The most important thing I have gained from sailing is my new-found self-confidence. Even if that was all that I got out of this trip it still would

have been worthwhile to do it. I feel much more self-assured. More than anything I have had new experiences. I have sailed through rough weather and travelled around in a foreign country on my own, without knowing the language. I have also learned a lot about Asian cultures and have a much better understanding of their geography. I have become a traveller instead of a tourist. I have also learned many new things, particularly about sailing. I have learned to dive with air tanks and have taken my PADI Open Water Diving certification. I have learned that things might not turn out as planned. It is OK. I feel secure enough to fly anywhere in the world and do anything – I did not feel that before.'

TURNING 50

While we were in Phuket, I turned 50. It was without doubt a milestone in my life. Many people know about 40-year-old crises, but to turn 50 is a bigger milestone, I think. I can clearly remember my father's 50th birthday. I was 14 years old and made a short speech at my mother's request. Other than my siblings there were only older people at the party, probably in their 50s. I did not see a big difference then between old and really old. Everybody over 25–30 was old. And now had I reached that age myself. It's not that I felt old, but the number 50 could simply not be escaped.

Being 50 is like driving across the huge North American continent. At 20, 30, and 40, you only drive west – and there is nothing on the horizon. At 50, you suddenly see the Rocky Mountains. At that moment, you realize that life ends at some point. For the rest of your life, you travel slowly towards the mountains – towards the end and what inescapably happens: death. At 50 you realize that you will not live forever. However, if I had the opportunity to be 20 or 30 again, I would not choose to do so. The life experience I have earned will not be traded away easily, even if a little extra hair on my head wouldn't hurt.

Overall, I was satisfied with my situation. I had my own boat on a circumnavigation and was living my dream – much earlier in life than I had dared to hope for. On top of that, I was healthy, something that one values more and more highly as you get older.

On my 50th birthday, 4 February 1996, we changed crew again. We had a new crewmember to come with us to Sri Lanka. Richard from the USA had taken a month-long vacation from his work at the World Bank's Global Environment Facility. In a beautiful bay outside of Phuket Johanna, Richard and I celebrated my big day with a good dinner and champagne, and philosophized over life.

THE INDIAN OCEAN – THE OTHER SOUTH PACIFIC

We sail from Phuket to the rarely visited Andaman Islands, where there is a tribe that has escaped civilization; then on to Sri Lanka with its civil war and to the Maldives where we dive with hammerheads. We sail to one of the last paradises on Earth, to the Seychelles and the Aldabra atoll with 150,000 giant turtles. We then start making our way to Africa.

ANDAMAN ISLANDS

In February 1996 we sailed to the Andaman Islands in the Bay of Bengal. The islands, which belong to India, are 400nm north-west of Phuket. Sailboats that visit must have a visa for India with a special permit for the Andaman Islands. This permission is complicated and time-consuming to obtain so only about ten boats visit the islands every year. We had obtained our Indian visa in Phuket, but not the special permit. Our guest Richard, who had obtained the necessary permit in the USA via the World Bank, had the stamp in his passport. I was surprised by its simple design when I saw it, and decided to copy it. When we cleared in at Port Blair – the capital and main city in the Andaman Islands – they looked extra-carefully at my stamp and asked where I had got it. I told them over and over again that I had got the stamp in Phuket and eventually we cleared in.

MAN IN SEARCH OF MAN

On the Andaman Islands are four original tribes of aboriginal people. One of these is the Great Andamanese, which may be one of the oldest tribes in the world. Unfortunately, their contact with civilization has given them health problems and changed their traditional lifestyle. Because of this the Andamanese tribe is hostile towards outsiders and prefers to live an isolated existence. The number of people in the tribe today is fewer than 600, out of a previous population of 250,000. When India became independent from Britain in 1947 it became responsible for the Andamanese tribe. The Indian Prime Minister Nehru, said: 'There is no reason to try to make them into bad copies of ourselves. This is a group of people that sing and dance and try to enjoy life; it is not people who are active in the stock market, yell to each other and think that they are civilized. We should not interrupt in their lifestyle, but help them live according to their wishes and traditions'. Today, however, many of these people have become 'civilized', which generally means that they are marginalized and mixed up with Indian immigrants.

North Sentinel to the west is a little island with only 150 inhabitants. It still says no to all connection with the rest of the world. As soon as an authority figure and/or an anthropologist tries to come ashore, they face a rain of arrows and rocks and this has so far kept people from the island. In the July 1975 issue of *National Geographic,* there is an article called 'The Last Andaman Islanders' about a failed attempt by modern humans to make contact with the aboriginal tribe. Hopefully, the people on the island will continue to succeed in resisting contacts with civilization, as this would surely lead to their destruction. Only an armed attempt to get ashore would be possible with this stubborn tribe, which is determined to avoid the temptations of 'civilization'.

THE NOTORIOUS PRISON

The British were the first outsiders to settle on the Andaman Islands in the 18th century. The British colonial government in India started to send political prisoners (whom they believed were dangerous for India) there, and during the many riots in India in the 19th century, the stream of political prisoners sent to the Andaman Islands increased. They were called mutineers by the British and freedom fighters by the Indians. The Cellular Jail that housed them was completed at Port Blair in 1906. It was unique as a jail because for the first time each prisoner was kept in a cell in solitary confinement. The prison was a three-storey building with seven long wings stretching out from a central tower, like a starfish. The irony was that the majority of the prisoners were the most competent and intelligent minds in India. They were the ones who had studied at the universities of Oxford and Cambridge in England and become educated and 'civilized'. The 'mutineers' were treated extremely brutally, forced to do hard labour and subjected to daily torture. They tried to break down the prisoner's will to resist, mostly without success.

Today parts of the prison still remain, including four of the wings and the tower. It is currently an Indian national monument. I walked along one of the silent corridors and stopped for a few moments in one of the cells.

It was a creepy feeling. There was an Indian film being made about the freedom fighters when we visited. This would become a documentary about the terrible prison for the outside world to see.

WORKING ELEPHANTS

The most important raw material on the Andaman Islands is timber. From Port Blair, we sailed to Havelock Island, one of the few islands we got a permit to visit. Here the elephants are still used to do the hard work in the rainforest. We even got to ride one of them, to my great pleasure – I felt like a five-year-old, even though I had just turned 50. It was fascinating to see the elephants, often in pairs, lift the big tree trunks out of the rainforest and up onto the old-fashioned trucks. The elephants even helped start the trucks by pushing them forward. On the other hand, it was sad to hear and see those giant trees crack and rumble, falling to the ground. When we left the rainforest, Johanna and I were silent, as we realized that we had seen something that was going to disappear – the elephants in the rainforest, and eventually the rainforest itself.

SRI LANKA

CIVIL WAR

We covered a distance of 800nm in six days of easy sailing between the Andaman Islands and Sri Lanka, and stopped on the south coast of Sri Lanka at Galle, an attractive city dominated by a big fort built by the Portuguese and Dutch in the 17th and 18th centuries. Here Johanna researched the Dutch influence, which is visible in the old fort. The anchorage for visiting sailboats was in a naval base, and the navy regularly detonates bombs underwater to scare away possible Tamil Tiger saboteurs. If one of our crew wanted to clean the water line or even take a swim, we had to give notice to the naval base – otherwise, there was a risk that the dynamite could go off when we were in the water. The civil war was mostly going on in the north and eastern parts of Sri Lanka. But even in the capital, Colombo, a bomb had destroyed big parts of the city centre only days before we arrived. The reason for the war is that the majority of the people (the Singhalese Buddhists) oppress the minority (the Tamil Hindus). The minority protests by requesting independence, or at least a local government. The majority refuses, and continues with the oppression; the minority revolts. After a number of years of a bloody and brutal civil war, the majority is beginning to accept a local government, which most of the Tamils also accept. Unfortunately, the extreme sect (the Tamil Tigers) refuses and asks for independence. The majority refuses and the violence continues.

THE OLD CEYLON

We did a four-day trip up into the mountains and visited old Buddhist temples and ruins. Adams Peak is a 2,224m-high mountain with a Buddhist temple on the summit. We started our hike to the top at 0200 hours in total darkness and arrived in time to see the sunrise, the main reason for our climb. We were almost the only westerners there; all the others were Singhalese Pilgrims. The sunrise was an extraordinary, solemn experience of beauty.

A visit to Sri Lanka – or Ceylon as the British once called the island – is not complete without a visit to a tea factory. I thought, in my ignorance, that tea production was simply to pick the tea leaves from the bush, dry, pack them and export the tea. We learned that it is so much more. It can be compared to vine production, with different characteristics and qualities depending on how high up the slope the tea bush grows, how much sun it gets, when the tea is picked and how it is dried, fermented and roasted. Ceylon tea is famous over the world for its high quality.

THE MALDIVES

THE GREENHOUSE EFFECT

At the beginning of March, we sailed a distance of 400nm from Sri Lanka to the Maldives. The journey took three days, accompanied by a warm north-east monsoon. The Maldives is a huge archipelago south-west of Sri Lanka. The archipelago is almost 500nm long with 26 big atolls. Each atoll has an azure blue and green lagoon and countless small islands with palm trees and white beaches. There are over 1,000 islands, none of which has an elevation of more than 3m above sea level.

Because of this the population of 225,000 people who live on these islands is always concerned that the whole chain of atolls will get flooded and disappear in the next 30 years, because of the rising sea level – perhaps caused by the greenhouse effect. The Maldives' government – together with other small coral island states – are energetically working with the UN to decrease the pollution from the industrial world.

Not surprisingly, tourism is the biggest source of income. The Maldives has been very successful with its tourist industry, started by an Italian entrepreneur on uninhabited islands in the 1970s. There were some 325,000 visitors every year in the 1990s, mostly interested in diving. This can be compared to the South Pacific's most popular destination, Fiji, which had 280,000 visitors in the mid-1990s and Tahiti with 125,000 visitors each year. In 2000 there were nearly 500,000 visitors but the tsunami in 2004 created huge damage to low-lying atolls and the destruction subsequently decreased the numbers of visitors.

The government tries to stop the western civilization from affecting the Muslim people. Out of the 26 atolls, only ten are open for tourism. This should be enough, as every atoll consists of 30–40 islands. Furthermore, there are no hotel areas close to the villages on the tourist atolls. Every little island has a hotel establishment and the local employees at the hotels live on a nearby island and commute to work by boat. This means that most of the tourists never get to see a real village. All they see, other than their own hotel island, is the capital city of Malé (on the island of the same name). Despite the pictures of paradise in the brochures, the country has had its share of political violence. After becoming a British protectorate in 1887 the Maldives became independent in 1965. In 1988, the country was threatened by a coup d'état. A group of disappointed businessmen had hired 400 Tamil mercenary soldiers from Sri Lanka to overthrow the president. In response the Indian Prime minister, Rajiv Gandhi, flew in 1,600 paratroopers. The mercenaries fled in boats and within hours the popularly elected president was reinstated to power.

THOR HEYERDAHL'S THEORY

Norwegian adventurer Thor Heyerdahl is best known for sailing on reed rafts across the three major oceans of the world: *Kon-Tiki* over the Pacific in 1947, *Ra* over the Atlantic in 1969 and *Tigris* over the Indian Ocean in 1978. Heyerdahl also carried out excavations on Easter Island and the Maldives in the 1980s, which are not as well known. The Maldives has been Muslim since 1153, but its history is even older. The people of the Maldives prefer not to talk about the era before the islands became Islamic, but after hard background work, Heyerdahl succeeded in getting permission to excavate in the Maldives at the beginning of the 1980s.

What had caught his attention was a statue with the same appearance as the ones he found on Easter Island on the opposite side of the globe. The statues had, among other features, long ears like a Buddha but also resembled an Incan statue from Peru. Heyerdahl's theory is that the Maldives, as early as 2,000 years before Christ, was a part of an old seafaring and trading route. Furthermore, according to a local traditional story, a race with white skin, blue eyes and long ears had built these statues and worshipped the sun.

There are also some legendary stories from Peru, Easter Island and Mexico, about a group of people who were seafarers, with a similar appearance to the traditional Maldives stories. They came from the east and followed the sun's track. It is not impossible that this race of people, who were not Europeans, were the earliest seafarers – long before the Polynesians, the Vikings or Columbus – who with an astounding knowledge of navigation sailed across the oceans between the old main cultures: from Mexico and Peru to Easter Island, to the Indus Valley in today's Pakistan to the Maldives, Mesopotamia and Egypt. They sailed back to Mexico before they disappeared from history and only left statues and legends to amaze us. It's an exciting, if controversial theory.

THE CREW AND OTHER SAILORS

At this time, we had many paying crews on board. Most of them were divers, while others took the chance to take a diving certification course with Johanna. Three Swedish couples signed on in Sri Lanka – all engineers who worked in Kashmir in India on a hydroelectrical project for a Swedish company. Along with Percy and Magnus from Saudi Arabia they had come through my agent in Sweden after reading an article about *Jennifer* in a Swedish boat magazine. It is interesting to think that Swedes who work out in remote and inaccessible areas are reading Swedish boat magazines and deciding to live their dream to sail and dive in tropical waters. Geoff, an American friend and financier from my time in Switzerland, came and sailed for a third time with his new Polish wife Basha. For three weeks we had four happy surfers from California aboard. It was exciting to watch them surf below the big waves that rolled in from the Indian Ocean.

In Sri Lanka, Lori, who we met in Palau in Micronesia the year before, signed on. She was a Canadian teacher and diving instructor who had been teaching English in Japan for four years, and could both speak and write in Japanese. Lori and later Sue were two of our guests who stayed on board the longest – five months. In the Maldives, also through my agent, Björn, an economist, and Kajsa, a laboratory chief, came aboard and sailed with us to the Seychelles. Bill, a 75-year-old American, also signed on but signed off again after a week. He had came for a month of sailing; the Maldives-Chagos-Seychelles route is approximately 1,800nm (or two weeks) of sailing if you do it in one stretch. But naturally, the rest of us wanted to stop to see a little of the Maldives and Chagos, something that Bill wasn't interested in.

During the little more than two months that we spent in the Maldives, we met many other long-distance sailors. Almost all were headed west, either to the Red Sea or South Africa. One boat had come from the Red Sea on its way to Australia. The Australian surfer, Steve, had taken four paying crewmembers on board his 38ft (12m) yacht *Capricone* in Phuket. They were all diving instructors and had paid in advance to sail to England. The whole idea of their sailing trip was to dive in the Maldives. Steve preferred to surf and the mood on board was low. Sometimes his crewmembers would dive with us. When Steve changed his mind and wanted to go back to Indonesia to surf, a breaking point was reached. The crew went to the police, and since according to international laws the captain is responsible for his crew, Steve had to pay for the crewmembers' tickets to their respective home countries. *Atlanta* was another boat that we met, a wooden ketch with a very low freeboard. The skipper Laurie had his hands full with his motley crew of nine people. His very independent 14-year-old daughter was not happy when Laurie took aboard a woman who was supposed to be her teacher, and the daughter did not have any wish to study. Later, when Laurie had a short relationship with this woman, his daughter exploded. We had to comfort many of *Atlanta*'s and *Capricone*'s crewmembers as they often came over to *Jennifer* for an easy and relaxing time.

We had a wonderful time in the Maldives, doing plenty of sailing and interesting diving. Sometimes, with only Johanna, Lori and myself on board, we sailed to our favourite atoll, the Aria atoll. We anchored inside the lagoon close to the opening. Every morning at six o'clock we took the dinghy, went out to the opening and down into the crystal clear water. At a depth of 30–40m we met what we had hoped to see – hammerhead sharks. They arrived right on time every morning, as if they were going to work, and almost didn't care about us. Sometimes one of them came up closer to check us out, but kept on going. These were exciting dives. We also did some lovely stream dives. The tide makes the water move at a speed of four knots in the narrow passages of the atolls. You move fast, almost too fast to see everything that is happening in the water.

THE CHAGOS ISLANDS – THE LAST PARADISE

The Chagos Islands are situated in the middle of the Indian Ocean, between South Africa and Asia, 600nm south of Malé, the capital of the Maldives. It is the last remaining British/Indian ocean colony, out of an Empire that once stretched around the Indian Ocean. In 1970 England agreed to lease the Diego Garcia atoll, a part of the Chagos group, to the defence forces of the USA. Part of the agreement included not having any of the inhabitants living permanently on the rest of the islands. This explains the overgrown ruins on Boddam Island in the Salomon Atoll. The previous inhabitants were moved to Mauritius, south-west of the Maldives. Long-distance sailors are allowed to visit the island, because they are only temporary visitors.

Our arrival at the Chagos atoll group was spectacular. When the sun rose, the Salomon atoll, which is 3nm wide, showed up on the horizon. We could see the 11 islands more and more clearly as the day became brighter. With the binoculars we could see how the morning sun's beams were reflecting in the hulls of the anchored sailboats. Around seven o'clock, the sun was high enough in the sky for us to dare to go over the reef. When we slowly sailed through the only opening in the atoll, we could clearly see the coral and the fish that were swimming under the boat. There were two places to anchor.

We had heard on the short-wave radio that a number of boats had arrived here several months ago, and we wondered what they had been doing here for such a long period of time. Once we had arrived, it was easy to understand that the Chagos Islands are the paradise everybody is looking for. The uninhabited islands radiate a feeling of peace. We steered slowly up between the other boats and anchored on the shallow sandy bottom. The water was incredibly clear. Eleven boats were anchored by Takana Island; we knew many of them already. *Argonauta*, with Sally and John aboard, we had met in Fiji in 1994, and again in Thailand and the Maldives. The British boat *Jolly Jumper*, with Claire and John, had been in the Maldives when we were visiting, and we had met another British boat, *Omuramba*, in Sri Lanka. *Escargo*, a Swedish homemade wooden boat that we first saw in Phuket had taken 56 days to sail from Thailand to the Chagos Islands. They had brought with them a large amount of beer and rum and had been drinking it during the passage. The first day we spent re-establishing old connections and getting detailed information about the atoll and the other boats.

Most sailors stay here between 2–3 months and some sail to Chagos every year (with most boats alternating between the two anchorages). On our first visit we anchored off the little island of Takanaka. By the full moon, the strong tides attracted giant rays to come and look for food in the narrow passage between the islands. We snorkelled and swam with two big rays that weren't at all frightened by us. They swam upside down underneath us to get a better look at us and sometimes swam straight at us with their big mouths wide open to catch plankton. In the same place we saw 15 stingrays swimming in formation. All this activity attracted three sharks. As there was not much space between the sharks and us, we let ourselves drift with the strong tide back to *Jennifer*. We went ashore to take photos and tried to catch some of the big coconut crabs, which live almost exclusively on land. They have claws bigger than a male hand, which makes it possible for them to open coconuts. We caught five of them and invited some of the other boats to a feast on Johanna's birthday.

There were about a dozen boats anchored near the island of Boddam. Most of them had come from South Africa – the western Indian Ocean is the most popular sailing area for the South Africans. *Airborn* had three teenage boys aboard. Except for a couple of hours of schoolwork every day, they had a really adventurous life. Some boats, such as *Glee Plus Two*, had small children on board who really loved their Robinson Crusoe lifestyle. A great deal of time was spent ashore in Boddam, which now had the social life of a village. Among the ruins on the island was the yacht club, whose walls were painted with names and logos from the visiting boats. Around the corner from the yacht club was the bakery where you could bake bread in a wood oven. Along the path to the yacht club was an old church with its colourful glass windows. There was also an old well where you could fill up with fresh water and there were places to do your laundry. The most popular spot was the place where you went ashore; here you could find a building, used as workshop, where many sailors worked on different projects. Beside the workshop was the volleyball court, where most of the crews came to play. The afternoon was the social time of the day. After being out at sea for a long time it is good to meet other long-distance sailors to exchange charts and information. Many of the boats had been in places where we were going and others were going to places where we had been.

Apart from meeting the other boats, exploring the islands, walking on the untouched white beaches, fishing and working on the boat, we spent a lot of time diving. We found an interesting area to dive outside of the reef. We first had to swim through a 50m-deep tunnel on the reef to get to it. The current around the tunnel, which was going in the direction of the deep blue sea, attracted a lot of fishes; big rays, barracudas and the biggest tuna I have ever seen. When we finally left the Chagos Islands to sail on to the Seychelles we felt that this stay would feel like the climax of our six-year long circumnavigation. Chagos is the last paradise – a long distance sailor's dream, although the British have recently implemented restrictions on visiting yachts.

The Chagos Islands are still uninhabited, but the islanders' plight has been told by Australian investigative journalist John Pilger, in his 2004 book and documentary *Stealing a Nation*. In 2000, the English High Court ruled that exiling the islanders was unlawful but in 2008 the Law Lords upheld the UK Government's bid to stop Chagossians from returning to their homeland. The Chagossians may now take their legal battle to the European Court of Human Rights.

CROSSING THE INDIAN OCEAN

Sailing between the Maldives and the Chagos Islands meant that we crossed the Equator again, for the fifth time. I had always wanted to dive near the Equator.

The other crossings of the Equator had been during night or in bad weather. But now the conditions looked good. We watched the GPS with cameras ready for the classic photo of the zero-latitude. It was calm and we prepared to dive. We tied a long rope in the stern and dived to 30m. The water was so clear that we could see the whole boat, with mast, sail and even the name on the hull. The only living things we saw were giant, shiny rainbow creatures – perhaps sharks – up to 2m long. It was as if we had been shrunk and were floating around in a water drop, while someone was looking at us down a microscope.

The distance from the Maldives to Chagos is 250nm from the southernmost atoll; from Chagos to the Seychelles is 1,200nm. Several times during the voyage we took a bath by jumping into the water from the stern, holding on to a long rope behind the boat. The faster we sailed the harder it was to hold the rope. One day I was up the mast enjoying the view when I saw a fin break through the water. We approached slowly and saw that it wasn't a shark but a blue marlin. We sailed several times around the huge fish, with its beautiful blue dorsal fin.

Halfway to the Seychelles we met the south-east Trade wind. We did an average speed of 7 knots and could therefore gain some lost time. Life aboard wasn't as pleasant any more, but it was possible to lie on the foredeck if you didn't object to getting a cold shower every now and then from the waves that splashed over the bow. The routine was to sleep, stand watch, eat, read and sleep. Dolphins often visited during the day at a distance, but at night they liked to swim next to the boat. We would suddenly hear a sizzling sound from their breathing, and sometimes we could even smell their breaths of air. When we were 100nm from the Seychelles the birds came to meet us. At night they tried to land on the top of the mast, something that I wanted to discourage. I was not only concerned because of the Windex on the top of the mast, but also because they make the boat dirty.

In case of a storm or hurricane, *Jennifer* has both a sea anchor that you put behind the boat and a drogue that you put out in front. I decided to try out the sea anchor on our way to the Seychelles. It looks like a little parachute, 1.5m in diameter. You drag it behind the boat with 75m of rope to help decrease the speed during a storm or big waves. It was a valuable practice as we made a lot of mistakes when we put it out. When it finally worked it was like using a brake; our speed decreased from 7 to 3 knots. The drogue is enormous, 6m in diameter, placed in the water with 200m of rope in front of the boat when the sails are down and the boat is drifting with the wind. The drogue will then hold the boat's bow to the wind, so that the waves come in from the front instead from side. It feels rather like being anchored. Tests have shown that a boat drifts only 20nm per day with the drogue. The main purpose is to prevent the boat from capsizing, to wait out a storm or hurricane and to let the crew rest. Hopefully we will never have to use it.

After eight days of sailing we reached the Seychelles; a new country, a group of islands that are totally different from the Maldives and Chagos.

THE SEYCHELLES

The Seychelles is made up of 115 islands with 80,000 inhabitants and is situated in the southern Indian Ocean. The main islands in the inner groups of islands are high and hilly, and the outer islands are coral islands. The Seychelles was a British colony before it became independent in 1975. The first president, the dissipated James Mancham (1976–7) aimed to develop the country into a tourist paradise. He succeeded; the jetsetters of the world, movie stars and celebrities flew in to party. The rich businessman Adnan Khashoggi bought large pieces of land in the 1970s. The soft erotica film *Goodbye Emanuelle* was filmed on the Seychelles, but it was too much for the political radical inhabitants on the island. In 1977 they executed a bloody coup.

President Rene took power and created a socialist, one-party state. Rene hired North Korean bodyguards, creating a terrorizing regime as a result. 'The grands blancs' (the rich whites) were either deported or left the country voluntarily. In 1982, South African mercenaries invaded the country disguised as rugby players. They were discovered in the airport and shooting started. The mercenaries fled by hijacking a plane. In the beginning of the 1990s, Rene allowed a multi-party system, pressed by international demands to get foreign aid to the country. During the Cold War the Seychelles was a spy centre. The USA had a satellite station on the island. Russian advisers, North Korean soldiers, mercenaries, American Marines, diplomats, and the CIA, KGB and MI6 were all represented on the Seychelles.

Despite the fact that tourism was (and still is) the only industry of importance, the socialist regime started to work against the tourism industry, immediately after taking over power. Foreign boats had to pay $100 per day, which stopped yachts coming to visit. With no tourism the economy collapsed, resulting in social turbulence. Meanwhile, the president realized that the Seychelles's major resource was the blue water and the white beaches (and a small fishing industry) and that tourism was necessary. The regime started to support tourism and the country was looked upon again as a tropical paradise. Today visiting sailboats pay $10 a day. The country tries to avoid mass tourism, first by making everything expensive and second by being

engaged in its environment and nature. The country has several nature reserves. In one of their beautiful forests, Vallée de Mai, you can find the biggest coconuts in the world, Coco de Mer, with fruits that can weigh up to 20kg. Bird Island is a bird reserve, where one million birds breed. Many areas are now marine national parks where you can see whale sharks, the biggest fish in the world. A whale shark can be up to 15m long and it is a diver's biggest dream to see one. Whale sharks eat plankton and are not dangerous to people; sometimes divers can even touch them.

We spent a little more than two months in the Seychelles. Unfortunately the weather was not very good; the south-east Trade wind was blowing most of the time and we got a lot of rain. In the Seychelles we had a visit from friends from Stockholm: Eva, Thomas, Caroline and Jan came to sail with us for the fourth time.

THE ALDABRA ISLANDS

The highlight of our stay at the Seychelles was the visit to the Aldabra Islands. At 20nm in length, it is one of the biggest atolls in the world and 600nm from the capital, Victoria. Johanna, Lori and I sailed the 1,200nm to Aldabra and back to Victoria in bad weather: gales and headwinds with huge waves and rain. It was days of hard sailing. When we came back to Victoria, Lori had had enough of sailing and took a week's holiday on land. One year later when she was back in Canada to start a new life she wrote about the time on *Jennifer* as the best in her life. She said that she wished she was back on the boat – even to sail to Aldabra.

It was worth the experience. The atoll is the most well known, remote and interesting of the outer island atolls. There are no airports and it can only be reached by boat. No one lives there permanently except for the 12 people who work at the research station with extra space for visiting researchers.

Aldabra is a unique atoll and can be found on UNESCO's World Heritage List. About 100,000 giant land turtles (or tortoises) live on Aldabra. It is comparable with the Galápagos Islands, which now has only 200 giant land turtles. The oldest turtle in the world is called Esmeralda and she lives in the Seychelles. She is almost 200 years old and is mentioned in *Guinness Book of Records*. One night we were lucky enough to see a sea turtle crawling up on the beach to lay her eggs. First she dug a hole, laid 100–150 eggs and camouflaged them while her tears were rolling. She didn't really cry, but the tears helped keep her eyes free of sand. After the procedure she was almost exhausted and crawled back to the sea in the moonlight.

We spent a lot of our time doing exciting dives. The tide here is strong and it makes the Aldabra Islands a perfect place for drift dives in or out of the lagoons. One day a group of hammerhead sharks swam close to the boat where we were anchored. Immediately we took our neighbour's dinghy and slowly followed them. When we were close, Johanna and I put on our masks and fins and jumped into the water, but we didn't dare let go of the boat. Watching them was both nerve-wracking and exciting at the same time.

MADAGASCAR

Other than New Guinea, Madagascar was the first truly poor country that we visited. A clear sign for us of the wealth of a country was the number of outboard engines. In almost all the places we have visited, local people have had enough money to buy their own outboard engine. Even the inhabitants of remote islands of the Southern Pacific and the Indian Ocean – at least the ones with American or French foreign aid – have outboard engines. But the people of Madagascar paddle and sail their small shallow canoes, which are cut out of wooden trunks.

In Madagascar most of the people live outside the regular economy. They are not interested in getting paid with money for their lobsters and bananas. They would rather exchange it for T-shirts, fishing equipment, pots and other things. We spent most of our time in the islands around Nosy Be ('big island'), which is the largest of the islands to the north-west of Madagascar. The island's main city, Hell-Ville, is a worn-down community that stagnated when the French gave Madagascar its independence in the 1950s. The large, old, rundown colonial houses on Main Street are still standing as historical monuments.

We didn't get a warm welcome when we cleared into Hell-Ville; something that I had been warned about by other sailors. The custom clerks wanted to take a fee that I had heard we didn't have to pay. We refused to pay and we didn't get permission to stay. The result was that I cleared in and out at the same time and told them we were going to sail away. We stayed three weeks in the country without permission. Meanwhile, I heard that an irritated sailor had contacted the Madagascar embassy in South Africa to complain about their fees. In just a few days the intractable clerk got a reprimand from the capital and the harassment stopped. Unfortunately we did not visit the island of Madagascar, the fourth biggest island in the world, because it was impossible to leave the boat in a safe place in Nosy Be. We spent two lazy weeks in perfect weather without guests, climbing up on the high islands, watching lemurs, the monkey-like primates that live up in the trees and can only be found on Madagascar.

Stefano, an Italian, became an interesting acquaintance. Half of the year he lived on the small islands on Nosy Comba, where he distributed and prescribed medicines for people on the islands (although he is not a doctor), taught them healthcare and helped them build water and sewer systems for the village. The rest of the year he spent in Italy where he coached a water polo team and collected free medicine from charity organizations. He had been doing this for seven years and the satisfied inhabitants of the islands had given him a stone house on the beach, which he had renovated into a very charming home. Many long-distance sailors visit the sociable Italian. Stefano told us about the extensive corruption in the country, and how the foreign aid from the western world pays for four-wheel drive cars for the politicians in the capital instead of healthcare and education for the people.

MAYOTTE AND COMOROS

At the end of August we sailed from Madagascar to the island of Mayotte, a little more than a day's sail from Nosy Be. Mayotte is one of the remaining French colonies in the Indian Ocean. When the nearby Comoros Islands became independent in 1975, Mayotte chose to stay under French power. This proved to be a wise decision, even though the Comoros regime didn't accept Mayotte's independence. A strong left-wing radical group quickly took power and ruined the country. An ex-president hired the notorious French mercenary Bob Dernard, who was made famous by his activities in the Belgian Congo and Frederick Forsyth's book, *The Dogs of War*. Comoros was invaded by Denard with help from 29 French mercenaries, who killed the dictator. The ex-president then seized control of the country. After that there were a number of coups and political assassinations involving Denard. He travelled back home to France in 1993 and was arrested for murder, but the accusations against him were later dropped. The French Foreign Legion is stationed on Mayotte. This force makes it possible for France to quickly step in against the rebellious regimes in Africa and Comoros.

The best part of the French colonies is – whether they are positioned in the West Indies, Pacific Ocean or the Indian Ocean – it is always easy to clear in and out and there is always plenty of food and wine. Since we had heard of the immigration authorities' corruption in Comoros and the big sum of money they requested for clearing in visiting sailboats, we snuck in a day in Comoros after Mayotte. We had almost reached a new continent – Africa.

AFRICA – THE THIRD WORLD'S THIRD WORLD

We travel on to Africa, the poorest continent in the world, sailing to Tanzania, Zanzibar, Kenya, Mozambique, South Africa and around the Cape of Good Hope. Hurricane winds hit us outside of Mozambique, tearing our mainsail apart and injuring Johanna during an unintentional gybe. We visit Durban and Johannesburg, explore beautiful Cape Town and look for a new crew for our Atlantic crossing to Brazil in South America.

THE AFRICAN CONTINENT

At its worst Africa signifies civil war, starvation, corruption, dictators and AIDS. It is not only the last century's unexplored continent, but also the lost continent of the future. It is the third world of the third world. The American journalist, Robert D Kaplan, gives a terrifying analysis: 'There will be collapses of several municipalities in parts of Africa where the government is losing control over the areas where they can not terrorize with the army or the police; groups of unemployed young men will plunder tourists, destroy forests, erode soil and people will die from AIDS.' Another author, military historian Martin van Creveld, sees a future of chaos and ethnic conflicts. Van Crevald's books are mandatory reading for American diplomats and the military. Not even the newspaper the *Economist* can find much hope for Africa. Many of the dictators in Africa are the richest men in the world. The late Mobutu (Zaire's overthrown president) and Moi (Kenya's former president) could, together with family and friends, pay off their respective countries' foreign debts with their Swiss bank accounts. They have stolen money from their own people and also from the western foreign aid. The Organization for Economic Co-operation and Development (OECD) has criticized Sweden for giving Tanzania foreign aid without requiring statements of accounts, and a big American bank has admitted that foreign aid money meant for a certain

country sometimes never leaves the bank, but has instead been transferred directly to the dictator's/president's private accounts.

A nostalgic person associates Africa with known and exciting places like Timbuktu, Zanzibar, Kilimanjaro, Kalahari, The Victoria Falls, Serengeti, Masai Mara the Pyramids and the Nile. They remember people such as Livingstone, Stanley, Kitchener, Rhodes and Karen Blixen (*Out of Africa*). I too prefer to forget about many aspects of the Africa of today and be a nostalgic traveller of yesterday.

THE NATIONAL PARKS

We arrived in Dar es Salaam in Tanzania at the beginning of September in 1996. After clearing in to Tanzania we continued a short distance to Dar es Salaam's yacht club where we anchored. The club is a typical third world country club – well equipped and beautifully situated – but only open to white visitors and local servants; an oasis in a society that isn't working very well. For a dollar per night, the club provides 'boat boys' who live aboard in the cockpit to prevent break-ins. We rented a boat boy for a week and went on tent safari. With a jeep – along with two Swiss youths and a guide – we visited the Serengeti and Ngorongoro National Parks. On the way we passed Kilimanjaro, which I had climbed in 1986. When the first European explorer passed the beautiful snow covered mountain in the 19th century and went back home to Berlin to report the snow on the top, they laughed at him; it was considered impossible to find snow that close to the Equator.

Serengeti is one of the biggest national parks in the world, known for the annual migration of millions of animals between Serengeti in Tanzania and the Masai Mara Park in Kenya. The Ngorongoro Park in Tanzania is situated in a big crater, approximately 20km in diameter. In this miniature world you can see almost all the big African animals. We camped on the edge of the crater and watched a fabulous sunset over the mountain. During the cold nights we could hear the sounds of Africa's animals. Early the next morning we drove the 700 vertical metres down to the bottom of the crater. We spent the whole day watching the animals, especially the few remaining rhinoceroses. It is extremely exciting to watch the animals in their natural environment. Twice we saw animals that were victims of other animals: a hyena that took a gnu and a jackal that killed a gazelle. Both of the hunts were slow and cruel processes where the victim escaped several times in despair before it finally died. We saw all of the 'big five' animals: elephant, buffalo, lion, leopard and rhinoceros. During the safari we read Karen Blixen's book, *Out of Africa*, which gives an understanding of the Africa that existed only 60 years ago.

ZANZIBAR – LIVINGSTONE AND STANLEY

Few places on Earth have such an exotic feeling as Zanzibar, a little island off Africa's east coast. The place has been as notorious for its slavery as for its spices. During the 19th century Zanzibar was eastern Africa's most important business centre and can be compared to 20th century Hong Kong with its laissez-faire market economy. Both the slave trade and the production of cloves, smuggled from Banda in Indonesia, were once the biggest industries in the world. Muslim Sultans reigned for centuries on Zanzibar, until the British stopped their reign by making slavery illegal. Most of the slave expeditions to Africa – with up to hundreds of carriers and traders – started and ended in Zanzibar.

Many 19th century missionaries and explorers such as David Livingstone and Henry Stanley also started out in Zanzibar. In the early 1870s, Stanley, who was a reporter, had been sent out by an American paper to find Livingstone, who was thought to be missing. Stanley wanted to embrace Livingstone when he finally found him. However, Livingstone was considerably older, with a saint-like reputation around the world, and Stanley only dared use the formal and now well-known greeting: 'Dr Livingstone I presume?' Stanley, who had made several expeditions in Africa and was well known in his own right, forever after had to suffer for this greeting, even when he was conferred an honorary doctorate.

Today's Zanzibar has big problems. Immediately after the island-nation became independent from England in 1963, a bloody coup against the Arab-Islam rulers began on the island. A revolutionary, Stalin-inspired junta seized power and the Arabs were killed and deported. The perpetrators of the coup were worried about a counter-attack, so they formed a union with the then-named Tanganyika on the mainland. The United Republic of Tanzania was so formed.

Zanzibar has only 3 per cent of Tanzania's population but gets 20 per cent of the national budget. The radical regime that has run the country down was demanding 50 per cent per cent of the budget, risking the dissolution of the union. We could clearly see this conflict. Although we had cleared in at Dar es Salaam in Tanzania, we also had to clear in to Zanzibar. Our Tanzanian visas were not considered valid, and I argued for hours with the customs and immigration authorities. Reluctantly, I realized that it was futile fighting against the authorities in this hopeless regime, and I paid the fees they asked for.

We anchored outside the Sultan's old palace in Zanzibar and explored the narrow streets and historical monuments. Spice production has not been encouraged by the government and has decreased catastrophically. Today the farmers no longer consider it profitable to grow spices. Instead, many earn their living by guiding tours around the spice fields. One of their tours was a highlight of our stay in Zanzibar, mostly thanks to the guide's strong personality. In Zanzibar we met three young Norwegians, and we gave them a ride to the rarely visited neighbouring island of Pemba, 80nm north of Zanzibar. We discovered that one of their parents was building a luxurious hotel in Pemba, a combined diving and sport fishing hotel of the highest international standards with prices of up to $1,500 per day. We stayed a week and explored Pemba's incredible reefs in some the fantastic diving.

KENYA

BRUSHES WITH DEATH

From Pemba we sailed 250nm further north to Kenya. We had planned to clear into the little town of Kilifi, north of Mombassa. At the entrance to Kilifi there are three high power lines, crossing the sound to the bay where the city is situated. The listed passable height during low tide was 22m. However, no one had informed us that we should pass on one side of the sound, where the wires were higher. Since there were rocks and reefs in the water on both sides of the sound, it was not obvious that we should do so. *Jennifer* has a mast that is 19m tall, plus a lightning rod made of stainless steel that is 1m tall. I was steering and Johanna and Kea (an American teenager who had signed on in Dar es Salaam) were on the bow. We went slowly towards the power lines and passed under the first two. Just as we were going under the third one Johanna screamed: 'Reverse!' A second later, the lightning rod hit the power line. The 30,000 volts of electricity came down through the mast, through the engine and keelbolt and out into the water. One of my hands was holding on to the reverse gear, which had a direct connection with the engine and I was thrown back against the stainless steel stern railing. I was stuck against the railing as the electricity went up and down through my body. I had ended up with my arms stretched over, with my back against the railing. The electricity must have rushed in through one arm, along my body and out through the other arm again.

After a few seconds, when the boat started to reverse, we came loose from the power line and the electricity let go of me. I could hardly breathe. My back muscles were cramped and I couldn't move. Johanna and Kea – who both had been standing on the teak deck – had only felt a tickle in their feet and were not hurt. Johanna was quick to get to the cockpit and put me on a bench. Later she told me that I was deathly pale and my hair was standing straight up. Through the VHF-radio Johanna got in touch with another sailor who helped us in under the power lines and to an anchorage. I had problems breathing and couldn't be moved. Soon the local village doctor came aboard. While I was conscious and could breathe with difficulty, he checked to see if my spinal cord was injured and if I had become paralyzed. When he was sure that everything was okay, he gave me a shot and pills against cramps. I couldn't move and had to stay in the cockpit for a week. I could breathe pretty well when I was totally still, but as soon as I became stressed, my back muscles cramped and I had difficulty breathing. If I tried to move, my back cramped again. When the little antenna to the transistor radio fell on my back unexpectedly, my back muscles reacted by cramping immediately. For a week, Johanna took care of me in the cockpit, gave me food, books and helped me with my personal hygiene. Slowly I got better and after one week I could take care of myself again.

A short distance from where I had been stuck on the railing, a wire had burned a hole in a 25mm thick stainless pipe. Earlier I had tried to drill a hole through the pipe but given up. It was unbelievable that I was still alive. Witnesses of the accident told us that they had seen a bright stream of light go from the forestay into the water. Most of the electrical equipment was burned out: the radar, GPS, CD-player and the satellite telex were all dead. I sent the instruments to England and got the same answer from all the manufacturers: There is no use repairing them. It was an expensive story. Understandably, Kea soon left the boat and his parents wanted their money back, even for the two weeks before the accident. My agent thought that it was best to pay, so yet more money disappeared. But I was still alive, without any permanent injuries, and the boat was only lightly damaged.

During my recuperation Johanna took the opportunity to travel to Uganda to see the big mountain gorillas. She was lucky and saw big male silverbacks, and several females with young. The book and the film *Gorillas in the Mist* describe how Dian Fossey studied the gorillas and tried to protect them before she herself was killed by a poacher. The gorillas are now under threat of extermination because of the civil wars that have been fought in Uganda, Rwanda and Zaire/Congo.

Another serious incident happened in the Maldives. We were lowering the outboard motor to the dinghy when a hook broke. The motor fell into the water and disappeared to a depth of 30m. I was stressed and asked Johanna to quickly prepare a diving tank. Full bottles normally have a small cap on the top of the tank. Johanna, who apparently was also stressed, took an empty bottle and, without checking out how much air was in the bottle, gave it to me. I jumped into the water with it and started to dive to the bottom. After 10m it became hard to breathe and only then did I look at the air meter and discover that it was empty. I came up quickly and very irritated, and I asked for a new diving tank. Unfortunately the same thing happened again; Johanna took an empty tank and I did not check the amount of air before I dived. This time I made it to 20m before I found it hard to breathe. Again I discovered that I was low on air. Another complication was poor visibility. I had brought a long rope to attach to the motor. The rope had fallen down to the bottom and was running up to the surface but I couldn't see it clearly because of the bad visibility. I then thought that the surface was in the direction of the rope. I started to swim with it but a check with the depth meter made me realize that I was going in the wrong direction. The air had practically run out and I was over 20m down. In my despair I thought: 'Is this really the end; the circumnavigation and my life too?'

I struggled out of the diving equipment and started a free rising. This means that the diver continuously expels air out of the lungs, which expand due to the decreased pressure at shallower depths. Thanks to the fact that I have done a lot of snorkelling over the years – and free diving down to 20m with only a mask, snorkel and fins – I had the confidence to try to surface. After countless free dives I knew my normal limit and, strangely enough, I also knew that I could go beyond it. Despite a couple of fateful seconds when I was frantically swimming upwards and my lungs felt like they were going to burst, I reached the surface. I was ready to faint. Terrified, Johanna helped me up on to the big sun mattress on the cabin roof, where with fast breaths, I eventually managed to calm down. Both of us had learned a lesson. Even though we are experienced divers we now know that if you stress out and panic, it can be fatal. Besides, the fault was mine. Even if it was reckless of Johanna to give me empty tanks it is always the diver who should check the equipment; it is, after all, his life that is at stake.

A third brush with death happened in the Mozambique Channel between Madagascar and Mozambique during our sail from Kenya to South Africa. We had three young people on board: a British couple, Ben and Sarah, and the Norwegian named Jon that we picked up in Lamu, Kenya. None of them had done much sailing before. The 1,700nm of sailing took 16 days and was enjoyable for most of the time. Again we passed Zanzibar and continued south along the coasts of Tanzania and Mozambique. We avoided clearing into Mozambique because we had heard that it was a hassle and expensive, but stopped several times by the beautiful islands outside the coast. One afternoon, dark clouds appeared in the sky and we temporarily reefed down the mainsail and the genoa, even though the wind was still light. Later that night the storm came, all of a sudden. In no time, the wind increased from only 10 knots to hurricane strength (more than 58 knots). Ben, Johanna and I took in the genoa fast and managed it without it breaking. Then we had to deal with the mainsail. To avoid a gybe I asked Johanna to move the traveller (a track on the cabin roof where the main sheet is attached) out of the wind. The rope had tangled itself while Johanna was sorting it out and the unexpected gybe came. Johanna was thrown down on the lee side with terrible force and tossed against the lifelines. All of us had harnesses on but it was the lifelines that caught Johanna. We got Johanna below deck where Sarah and Jon (neither of whom wanted to go up on deck) took care of her. Ben and I now had to take down the mainsail. We attached our harnesses to the jackstay, and started to crawl to the mast. Before we left the cockpit I looked at the wind meter – it said 62 knots. Lightning flashes lit up the night, the rain was whipping us on our backs and it felt like a water cannon. The rain was not falling straight down but came from the side with great strength. The mainsail had started to break and it fell apart fast. Even though we didn't have a sail up *Jennifer* heeled, maybe 30°, on bare poles!

The bad weather was deafening. Ben was calm and totally relied on me: 'Just tell me what to do'. Tangled in our harnesses (you always get tangled when you can least afford to), we eventually furled the broken sail and crawled back to the relative safety of the cockpit. Johanna was badly hurt; she had pain in her leg and her back after hitting the lifelines. After one hour the wind disappeared and it was quiet again. We continued to Durban by motor and put up the genoa. Johanna's leg healed but her back gave her a lot of problems. During most of our stay in Durban she was confined to bed and had to go to a physiotherapist several times. In a short space of time both Johanna and I had got back injuries, but thankfully not at the same time. In the meantime Johanna recovered. Our crew, with this new experience, decided that they would never sail again. Ben's diplomatic comment from the guest book: 'The hurricane-boat-clinging lesson was very educational, if only to remind me I feel safer on land,' and Sara's comment: 'Truly don't know how you yachties keep it up – but you have all my admiration and sympathy.'

LAMU

3,000 DONKEYS

One month after the electrical accident, Johanna and I sailed from Kilifi north along Kenya's coast to the beautiful island of Lamu, a distance of 90nm. The island, with its small town of the same name, was once an important place for business under Zanzibar's sultans. Today Lamu's islanders make a living through fishing and tourism. Just outside the town, in the little village of Shela, we anchored near the Peponi Hotel. Shela had largely been taken over by Europeans, who have rebuilt the houses into charming private guesthouses. The narrow streets are even smaller than Zanzibar's; you cannot get through with a car, which explains why there are no cars on the island. Instead there are up to 3,000 working donkeys. During a walk in the city we saw a sign on a house: *The International Donkey Protection Trust.* At first I thought that it was a joke. After entering the building and talking to the manager we discovered something very interesting. The foundation, which is a British charity organization, is a sanctuary for donkeys in need of free care and rest. In the third world, donkeys are often abused and overloaded. The foundation's main task is animal protection, but it also has another task. As many of the owners are among the poorest and least educated in society, the foundation teaches them how to take care of the donkeys properly. Their donkey might be their main, and sometimes only, asset. In this way the foundation is engaged in the best kind of aid project: to help the islanders help themselves. The manager told us that the owners learned a lot. They realized that the longer the donkeys live and work, the better it is for the owner.

SOUTH AFRICA

AN UNCERTAIN FUTURE

South Africa is perhaps the only country in Africa that has a somewhat promising future: infrastructure, educated workforce and natural resources. But it will probably not happen. There are many frustrated and downhearted people, scared by the high crime rate and depressed by the politics. Black South Africans had expected much improved living conditions when the ANC won power, but there is still a long way to go. The black ANC government is working with programs that will give jobs to as many black people as possible, often jobs previously out of their reach, but at the same time their school and university standards have to improve in time to allow them to take better jobs. Both black and white South Africans think about leaving the country and some South Africans are fortunate enough to have European passports allowing them to do this. According to the BBC, 1,000 people left South Africa every day during the 1990s, many unofficially.

Incompetence and corruption are commonplace in South Africa. The Orange Free State, a state in the South African union, has in reality already gone bankrupt, their resources stolen by the local politicians. This fact forced the central government to dismiss the state government and take direct control. Another state, the Natal State, is also headed in the same direction.

CECIL RHODES

One of the most powerful men in Africa's history is Cecil Rhodes. He was an Englishman who moved to the Cape colony in 1870, when it belonged to England and the gold and diamond rich areas in the north belonged to the independent Boer Republic. Rhodes gave the mining business a try, looking for gold and diamonds, and he soon succeeded (with help of hostile captures, bribes and secret affairs) in uniting all the diamond mines into one company, De Beers. He became the executive director, with control over the diamond business across the world. In addition to De Beers he also owned gold mines. But Rhodes was not yet satisfied; he wanted to have more power and estates. To conquer the areas that would later become Zimbabwe and Zambia, Rhodes hired mercenaries that easily overpowered the strong Matabele (Zulu) nation. These enormous areas (that later split up into the two nations) were named Rhodesia in 1895, in memory of Rhodes. The British government, which hesitantly gave its permission to Rhodes' conquest of Rhodesia, was happy to include it in the British Empire. A British prime minister told him: 'Take what you can – and ask for permission later'. When Rhodes was at the peak of his career as the boss of De Beers, he also owned several gold mines and the Rhodesia Company and was the prime minister in the Cape colony. Rhodes had become 'an African Colossus'. With all those titles you can only wonder if Rhodes had any conflict of interest.

Rhodes was a typical capitalist and imperialist. His vision was to create a British Africa from Egypt in the north to the Cape Province in the south by fighting the Portuguese, French and Germans who also wanted to have their own colonies there. Rhodes started the apartheid system in South Africa when, as a mine owner, it was in his interest to maintain cheap and essentially captive manpower. The cruel Boer war (1899–1902) was run with his private mercenaries, where Rhodes and the Englishmen occupied the diamond- and gold-rich Boer republics and included them in the new South Africa. Rhodes realized that rich men were not going to be remembered for their wealth but for their visions. Apart from the fact that he increased the British power in Africa with huge areas of land and united South Africa's states (albeit by force), Rhodes is remembered as the founder of the Rhodes scholarship. In his will he stipulated that a fund was to be created to make it possible for students from the British colonies, USA and Germany to study at Oxford. Two well-known holders of a Rhodes scholarship are former US President Clinton and the former UN's Secretary General Kofi Annan. We visited the

Rhodes monument in Cape Town – a huge bombastic statue with walls at the foot of the Table Mountain – and also his little house by the ocean where Rhodes died in 1902, at the age of 49.

INSPECTION OF *JENNIFER*

Durban is Africa's biggest harbour. With its long beaches and good surfing it was the most popular holiday location in the country, both for South African and foreign tourists, until rising crime rates scared most of them away. We anchored by the international dock in the middle of Durban. For visiting sailboats it is a very pleasant harbour with all the facilities within walking distance. Everything seemed inexpensive to us, thanks to the low value of the South African rand. When we provisioned for our Atlantic sailing it felt like we were being paid to buy things. *Jennifer* was now eight years old and had sailed 83,000nm (almost three times around the world); so it was time to inspect her hull and equipment. In Durban we took *Jennifer* out on land, painted the bottom, polished the hull and varnished below deck. We bought a new spray-hood, dinghy, outboard motor and anchor winch and all the sails were repaired after the storm in the Mozambique Canal. Sixty per cent of the stainless rigging was replaced. My motivation to replace the major parts of the rig increased when a 43ft (13m) Norwegian sailboat came in with a broken mast. A screw had broken 400nm out in the Indian Ocean and the whole rig had fallen down within a few seconds. The cost to replace the rig and sails was £60,000.

THE CAPE OF GOOD HOPE

The first seafarer to sail around the Cape of Good Hope was the Portuguese Bartolomeo Diaz, in 1487. He hit a big storm when he rounded the Cape and had to return to Lisbon when the crew threatened mutiny. When Diaz told the Portuguese king about the journey he called the cape the 'cape of storms'. The king, who was keen to encourage more seafarers to find the seaway to the Spice Islands and India, decided instead that the cape's name was going to be the Cape of Good Hope. The second seafarer that rounded the Cape of Good Hope was Vasco da Gama. He was also surprised by a big storm before he managed to sail around it in 1497. He continued to India and became the first European to discover the seaway to Asia. Sailors often discuss what route is the safest during a circumnavigation: the Red Sea and the Suez Canal, or the Cape of Good Hope. Because of the strong winds (often 40 knots or more for several weeks) and unstable activity in the Red Sea (pirates, for example), and the numerous reefs, many insurance companies recommend taking the route around the Cape of Good Hope.

I have met many circumnavigators that found the Red Sea very hard going with a head wind and gale for long periods. The irony is that the Norwegian boat in Durban that lost its mast in the Indian Ocean had been persuaded by its insurance company to sail via the Cape of Good Hope. But the 800nm of sailing along the coast between Durban and Cape Town is also one of the most dangerous stretches in the world. The strong Agulhas current runs south along the coast at up to 6 knots per hour. When there are strong south-west winds, the wind and water meet and enormous waves are created. It is marked 'abnormal waves' on the chart. The waves can be up to 15m high and can destroy big ships. A 10,000-ton ship sank off Durban in just a few minutes, without any survivors, when we were there. Sailors are always extra cautious here and continuously check the weather and the barometer, and always plan different emergency harbours on the way.

We waited a whole week for good weather before we sailed to Cape Town. We were lucky and sailed directly to Cape Town in five days. We had two South African couples aboard: Chris and Kathy, Tim and Laurin. Chris, 35, was a happy, outgoing Afrikaner (a white person with Dutch origin) and former police officer, who was burned out because of all the violence on the streets and was now on disability pension. He did not want to talk about his past, but you had an idea that he hadn't stood up to the brutality in the police force during Apartheid. Tim and Laurin, both in their 30s, had graduated as number one in their sailing course and wanted more practice. Both wanted to leave the country and try their luck abroad and had applied for jobs in the West Indies as charter skipper and crew/chef, respectively. They were friendly and efficient and later we heard that they had found jobs on a catamaran in the Virgin Islands.

On 24 December 1996 we rounded the Cape of Good Hope. My advice to potential circumnavigators that must choose between the Red Sea and the Cape of Good Hope is to choose the second option if you have enough time. Apart from the fact that South Africa is a fantastic country to visit, it is possible, with good planning, to handle the sailing between Durban and Cape Town. By contrast, you do not have any influence over the reefs, hard winds and few secure emergency harbours in the Red Sea.

CAPE TOWN

Many people look upon Cape Town, with its characteristic flat mountain, Table Mountain, as the most spectacular city in the world. It is surrounded

by many beautiful vineyards that let you taste and buy their excellent wines. The curving and narrow road south to the Cape of Good Hope runs along the coast with amazing views. Cape Town has the fewest racial problems in South Africa and its vitality and nightlife are bubbling. The contrast with Johannesburg is huge. We took the train from Durban to Jo-burg, as it is called, and visited Jarl and Viveka, our Swedish friends who had been living there for 20 years. I had expected that Johanna and I would explore Johannesburg on our own and then go out to the suburb where our friends lived. Viveka was horrified by my suggestion and asked us to take a taxi directly from the station out to their home. After meeting the Swedish colony there, during the Lucia-celebration in the Swedish church, and hearing horror stories about armed robberies, break-ins, rapes, tortures and car thefts, I realized the kind of pressure that people are living under in South Africa. Children and young people can't travel alone due to the risk of robbery or kidnapping and have to be driven to school, friends' houses and sports events. To simply ride a bike over to a friend's house is impossible.

We spent two weeks in Cape Town, visited the Royal Cape Yacht Club, sampled South African wines, hiked up the 1,000m-high Table Mountain and interviewed new potential crewmembers. We also had an unusual charter. A Norwegian clothing company had flown out photographers and models into the country and we all went out on *Jennifer* for the photoshoot.

SOUTH AMERICA – CARNIVAL AND A TRIP ON THE AMAZON

We cross the South Atlantic, via the island of St Helena, to Salvador in Brazil where we arrive in the middle of the Carnival. We spend two months in South America, sail up the huge Amazon River and stop at Papillon's Devil's Island in Suriname, before arriving at Trinidad in the West Indies in April, a total distance of 6,500nm.

THE SOUTH ATLANTIC CROSSING

We crossed the South Atlantic from Cape Town to the island of St Helena (1,700nm) and on to Brazil (1,900nm). From the first day to the last, we had the south-east Trade wind on our backs. At the beginning of the trip the wind was strong, the weather was poor and most of the crew that we had picked up in Cape Town became seasick – none of them had been sailing before. The Royal Cape Yacht Club has a noticeboard where skippers and crewmembers can advertise for opportunities to go to different destinations. There were many who wanted to sail to Brazil and the Caribbean. Most were South Africans with no money who hoped to find work on a boat; others were backpackers from Europe, the USA, Australia and New Zealand who were going travelling.

Because we needed paying crews, the South Africans were not of interest to us. I interviewed several young people and finally we assembled a mixed international crew. Aside from Johanna and myself, our crew was made up of: Sue, an elegant, recently divorced British woman who decided to sail in the West Indies and stayed aboard for five months; Jeff, an intellectual American geologist who had been working in Russia for several years and was now on his way back to the USA to finish his master's degree; Wolfgang, a friendly German diving instructor and 'party animal' who had been travelling for several years and now had his base in Thailand; Joseph, a young spoiled American 'university drop-out', who had been travelling to discover the meaning of life and was on his way back to university to study philosophy; Marten, a British metalworker with a sense of humour; and Lennie, a young egocentric South African computer expert who managed to work two months per year as a highly paid internet consultant and travelled the rest of the time. In Salvador, Lennie, Jeff and Joseph signed off while Louise, a young blond Danish artist we met during the Carnival, signed on. In Belém, by the Amazon River's estuary, one of Johanna's friends Judy signed on; she was a former diving instructor who lived in Hawaii running an aquaculture project.

ST HELENA

In the middle of the South Atlantic Ocean is the little island of St Helena, which has 5,000 inhabitants. Like Pitcairn Island in the South Pacific, St Helena is a British colony. Both are exceptionally isolated and neither yet has an airport, so the only way to get there is by boat. It can be very difficult to get ashore. The swells from the Atlantic are sometimes so big that it is impossible to get on the pier from the dinghy without capsizing or getting soaked. When we arrived in the capital, Jamestown, early one morning there were heavy rain clouds over the mountain and the island didn't feel very welcoming. However, our five-day visit was a pleasant surprise. The island is beautifully green with plenty of valleys and friendly people, despite a lot of rain.

The island's most famous visitor (when he was banished after the defeat at Waterloo) was Napoleon. We visited his former house, now a museum, where he lived with his favourite generals and servants and we even visited his grave. There is no name on the gravestone. The French asked for 'Napoleon Bonaparte – the emperor of France' on the inscription, but the English only allowed 'Napoleon Bonaparte'. The French then decided not to have a name at all. Napoleon's remains were later moved to the dome of Les Invalides in Paris in the 1840s, but the gravestone still remains on St Helena. Both the house and the gravestone are maintained by the French state as national monuments, and the French tricolor hangs outside the house – a memory of France's last era of greatness. On St Helena we met several other sailing boats, including *Moonlight*, with three lighthearted South Africans on board. We sailed with them over the next six months. A replica of James Cook's ship, *Endeavour*, sailed into Jamestown while we were there. The sight of this three-masted sailing ship with an enormous British flag almost made us believe that a new Napoleon was being deported to the island.

BRAZIL

'THE POPE'S MISTAKE'

Brazil is the world's fifth largest country in overall area and has a population of nearly 192 million people. Brazil's history is special in two ways. First of all, the country should not exist at all. By the Pope's decree in Tordesillas in 1494, the world was divided between the historical superpowers, Spain and Portugal. The New World, which Columbus had just 'discovered', was given to Spain, and the Old World – Africa and Asia – was the lucky draw of the Portuguese. The Pope drew the line at 50° west without knowing that what was going to be Brazil was situated much further east. Thanks to this mistake, this made it possible for Portugal to take Brazil, which is situated in the New World. Secondly, Brazil is one of the few countries that became independent without a war against its former colonial power, while the rest of North and South America fought violent wars for freedom against Spain and England. When Napoleon invaded Portugal in 1809, the crown prince fled to Brazil. After Napoleon's fall, the prince, who was now a king, refused to return to Portugal – he had fallen in love with Brazil. He decided that Rio was going to be Portugal and Brazil's common capital, which meant that Portugal would become a colony of Brazil. After pressure from Portugal the King finally returned to Portugal, but his son Pedro stayed and declared Brazil independent in 1822, without spilling any blood. One problem with visiting Brazil is that almost nobody speaks English, and barely any Spanish or French either. In a way, Brazil is rather like the USA; the countries are so big that they tend to think that they are the whole world.

CARNIVAL!

Our first harbour in Brazil was in the old city of Salvador in the state of Bahia, once the capital of Brazil and the richest city in the New World. They had just built a modern marina in the middle of the city centre, where many long-distance sailors moored their boats. We arrived in Salvador in time for the Carnival festival – an explosion of dancing, music and crowds. Clearing into a developing country can be hard work under normal circumstances, and doing it during Carnival in Brazil is an ordeal. Not until the carnival was over did I succeed in finding all the authorities – and by then it was time to clear out. Salvador is a centre for the country's Afro-Brazilian culture, where people are a mix of races and the women are not as beautiful as in Rio. The best part of the carnival took place in the old part of the city, where spontaneous mini-carnivals were staged. The main carnival parade was built on huge, richly decorated trucks, with orchestras and artists on the platforms.

We joined the crowd on the move towards the centre, but the closer to the centre we went, the less space there was to move. Finally we were totally stuck and it began to feel dangerous. The lack of space was the pickpocket's nirvana. Three times someone tried to rob me and each time I fought back. When I felt an unfamiliar hand in my pocket I grabbed the hand and hit it as hard as I could. At each occasion like this – no matter how crowded it was – the crowd managed to leave room for our little fight. One reason that I was so resistant, other than the fact that I was so angry, was that I thought that the thief, wanting to avoid the attention from police, wouldn't fight back. The Carnival was patrolled by both the police and the military in groups of eight. It was an experience – but I think it is enough to see it once.

THE NORTHERN COAST

After the carnival we sailed in Salvador's little archipelago and visited several villages on the islands. We then continued 450nm to the port of Cabedelo, situated by a small river just north of Recife. For many years an Englishman has been running a small shipyard business in Cabedelo and many long-distance sailors stop here. After 330nm our next stop was the city of Fortaleza. We were accompanied by *Moonlight* and, one evening, we went out on the town together. All the male crew on our boat was getting a lot of attention from young girls. When I quickly explained that the girls were prostitutes, they didn't believe me; the next morning they wondered how I knew. From Fortaleza we continued north 700nm along the coast of Brazil in a friendly south-east Trade wind to Belém on the Amazon River.

THE AMAZON RIVER

Everything in the Amazon area is gigantic. It covers almost 6,000,000km^2, an area much bigger than the whole of Western Europe. Its rainforest is the largest in the world. It has 30% of the remaining forest on the Earth, 10% of the animal and plant species (many not yet classified) and produces 20% of the world's oxygen. In terms of volume the Amazon is the largest river in the world and second longest at 6,275km (the Nile is 6,741km). The Amazon River contains 20% of the world's fresh water; its flow is 12 times bigger than the Mississippi River and it transports 12 billion litres of fresh water per minute, enough to supply New York for 60 years.

During the 1890s the exploitation of the Amazon area started in the Manaus area, which is in the middle of the rainforest. Rubber was the first product to be extracted and the British established an extremely lucrative worldwide monopoly. The rubber workers who collected the sap from the rubber trees were held as slaves and lived in poverty while the plantation owner lived luxuriously. However, the British monopoly ended when an Englishman smuggled out a rubber tree seed and planted it in one of the British colonies in Asia. The new plantations quickly became more effective than those in Manaus, the price on rubber decreased and the rubber market collapsed by the 1920s. Once again Manaus became a provisional city.

The rubber workers are still exploited. In the 1970s, the Brazilian activist Chico Mendes organized farm workers into a revolt against the oppressive garimperiros, the ore seekers, who damaged the forest by reckless cutting down of trees, destroying the farm workers' means of sustenance. In 1988 a local rancher and his son assassinated Mendes. Initially the police did not take action, but after strong international demands the guilty landowner was finally sent to prison for 19 years. Four years later a court of appeal set him free.

THE TRANS-AMAZON HIGHWAY

THE EXPLOITATION OF BRAZIL

In the 1970s Brazil decided to open up the Amazon area for the exploitation of its resources and built the Trans-Amazon Highway. The highway transformed the Amazon, and businessmen, gold diggers, cattle-breeders, explorers and poor workers without land went to the Amazon area to try their luck. The highway also made it easier to smuggle drugs from Bolivia to Brazil and further on to the USA and Europe; the road got the nickname 'The Trans-Coco Highway'.

The American multi-millionaire Daniel Ludwig's big forestry and pulp mill project in the 1980s is an example of the new developments; huge areas of forest were put aside for this purpose, but the project was not lucrative and almost put Ludwig into bankruptcy. The 'Projeto Grande Carajás' (1979–86) promised the biggest iron-ore finds. An industrial zone of 400,000km^2 – an area almost as big as California – was the area of exploration for ores. Gold is found in the Amazon area and many thousands of hungry gold diggers dig with their bare hands in a huge human anthill, hoping to become rich.

These developments require energy and the construction of 70 giant hydroelectric power plants have been planned in the Amazon area during the next 15 years. The power plants will put huge areas of rainforest underwater, killing animals and plants and making the locals homeless. The breeding of cattle is another threat against the rainforest, as the ranch owners burn down big areas to clear land for their animals. The fires are so big that they can be seen from space and the airports in the Amazon area have to shut down for several

months because of the smoke. But breeding cattle is not the main purpose of this reckless cutting of the rainforest, despite being subsidized by the government. It is the ore deposits that might lie underground that are the real prize. To get entry to the land that is owned or used by the Indians, the Brazilian government requires that at least one third of the land is cultivated. Therefore, the exploiters set the rainforest alight and breed cattle to secure real or expected finds of ore. The soil that seems to be so rich when it is a rainforest is not deep enough to sustain cattle breeding and will have to be abandoned after a couple of years. And the procedure is repeated. Only bushes grow in the abandoned areas. It is not only the rainforest that is impoverished. The existence of the remaining 200,000 Amazon-Indians is threatened. Many of them have been shot from helicopters by the exploiters who want to stop the Indians from disturbing the building of roads and illegal airports.

THE YANOMAMI

The Yanomami are a tribe of hunter-gatherers who were discovered in 1973 and have received a great deal of international attention. When the government proclaimed that 70 per cent of the Yanomami tribe's land could be exploited, thousands of garimpeiros, or independent miners, invaded their land, ignoring the borders, and became guilty of genocide against the Yanomami people. International criticism made the government relent, but the garimpeiros kept on stealing the Yanomami's land and killing their people. In the early 1990s Venezuela and Brazil created a special Yanomami reserve on both sides of the border. Despite this, the tribe is not protected against trespassing and brutal violence, and sadly, in a couple of decades, they may still be wiped out along with the rainforests they live in.

WHY IS THIS ALLOWED TO HAPPEN?

Why is this development and exploitation allowed? One reason is to develop the country's biggest resources without interference from other countries. As a state governor in the Amazon once explained: 'Humans are the centre of the environment and I will be the leader of the humans – not animals and forests'. Another reason is the greedy local rulers and the big landowners who live in Rio and Sao Paulo; they gain enormous short-term profits by cutting down the rainforest. However, the biggest pressure comes from two of the most influential institutions in the west: the International Monetary Found (IMF) and the World Bank. Until the beginning of the 1990s almost all projects that could help the countries to develop their export potential and make it possible to pay off their debts to the western banks were encouraged, without looking at the environmental aspects or social after-effects. Another factor is that we, the western world's consumers, get access to the resources that we want: wood and minerals. I am a typical consumer as *Jennifer* is built with teak, aluminium and stainless steel – some of these products might well come from the Amazon.

WHAT IS THE SOLUTION?

If the world is interested in keeping the Amazon rainforest as the main producer of oxygen and the source of new medicines, perhaps it should pay for it. Such an arrangement is a debt-for-nature-trade, where some of a nation's foreign debts are written off in exchange for keeping the rainforest. Another solution is to finance a renewable reserve for harvesting nuts, rubber and medicine plants and other products apart from wood. Such reserves can produce materials forever, and feasibility studies have shown that they are more lucrative than cutting down the rainforest for a one-time profit. These solutions have not been followed, however, for the simple reason that the big forest companies cannot make enough profit from a sustainable export business.

THE AMAZON TRIBUTARIES

In Belém I almost disappeared one night, with the strong current on the river. Visiting sailboats anchor in the middle of the river outside Belém's yacht club. To get to the club landing you use your dinghy, preferably one with an outboard motor because the current can be strong. Normally I always have oars in the dinghy just in case, but considering the short distance across to the landing I decided oars were not necessary. When I was going to pick up Johanna and Sue the motor stopped and I drifted at a speed of 4 knots down the river into the black night. On the way I passed another Swedish sailboat and managed to get their attention. I was soon rescued and towed to the club dock. The Swede who helped me was Göran Cederström, an ex-teacher and the first Swede to sail solo around the world; he later wrote the book, *From Sea to Sea*. Göran was visiting the Amazon with his new boat. On his way into the river he had been hit by a river-boat that didn't care about visiting sailboats. The whole rig had broken and the hull was damaged on one side.

We motored for ten days along the river and its many tributaries, from the city of Belém on the river's south beach, to the city of Macapá on the north beach. The trip went partly around the island of Marajó, the biggest river island in the world and the same size as Switzerland. We had mostly

good weather with daily cloudbursts of rain. Sailing in the main part of the Amazon River can be compared to sailing in Stockholm's archipelago, with its many islands and big bays. The main difference is that the colour of the water in the Amazon is brown and there is a strong tide, with up to 4m difference between high and low tide. Although the water looked dirty, it was fresh, and the people drank from it. We ran the water through the water machine so the brown colour was filtered away.

Most of the time we sailed on the small tributaries, sometimes until we went aground or got the mast stuck in the rainforests' surrounding branches. One afternoon the mast got really stuck in a huge tree. The tide had just started to go out and I was worried that we were going to get stuck on the flood bank, hanging on to the tree. After two hours of frantic work with saws and axes, we managed to get free. The whole deck looked like a forest with fallen branches and twigs. We saw plenty of birds – including parrots that talked a lot while they were flying above us – but no other animals. Sometimes we took the dinghy and rowed into the rainforest along small rivers, with the hope of seeing more river animals – fortunately we did not see any jacarés (alligators). However, we did see several white-pink fresh water dolphins that look totally different from their saltwater cousins. We could not find any hardwood such as teak or mahogany, as it had probably been cut down long ago. But we did pass many sawmills – simple wood shacks with a saw that seemed to be from the last century.

When we sailed up the tributaries we passed many cottages whose owners quickly ran to hide inside and shyly looked out through the doors. Occasionally a brave child would dare to come out and look at us. Every night we anchored by a little village and the inhabitants would curiously paddle out to us with their canoes. Just as in Micronesia we had bought pens, writing books and toys with us, which we distributed to everybody's enjoyment. On many of the tributaries no one had seen a sailboat before. One man told us that there had been a sailboat there 25 years ago, with white people with long hair. The people were very friendly and curious – and happily showed us around their small villages. We also traded some things with them: two musical cassettes for two paddles. The paddles are now named Michael (Jackson) and Bon (Jovi). The people we met had an Indian look; however, they were not Indians, but of mixed race. They lived very simply, grew manioc (a root fruit), fished and cut down trees. They were barely producing anything, except children – there were children everywhere. But they were happy and explained that they had everything they needed. To be able to sail in the Amazon along the biggest river and rainforest in the world was an amazing experience. One can only hope that some of it will still be there in the years to come.

THE INTERNATIONAL DATELINE AND THE EQUATOR

During February and March 1997 we sailed along South America's east coast: 1,500nm from Salvador to Belém, 300nm through the Amazon River, 450nm to Devil's Island, 175nm to Suriname and finally, 500nm to Trinidad, passing another big river, the Orinoco River. This was a total of 2,900nm.

From Salvador to Recife we had a headwind and counter currents, but north of Recife we got help from the equatorial stream at 2 knots and a tailwind: the south-east Trade wind helped us up to the Equator and the north-east Trade wind helped us from the Equator to the West Indies. When we came out of the Amazon River we crossed the Equator again, for the sixth and last time. The first time was in 1993 in the Galápagos Islands, the second in 1994 between Fiji and Kiribati, the third in 1995 between Palau and New Guinea, the fourth also in 1995 between Indonesia and Singapore, the fifth in 1996 between the Maldives and the Chagos Islands and the sixth in 1997 in Brazil. We crossed the International Dateline between Tonga and Fiji in 1993, and we crossed its counterpart, the Greenwich (or Prime) meridian, in the Mediterranean in 1992, between Cape Town and St Helena in 1997, and between the Azores and Stockholm in 1998. This time, the Equator and its Doldrums gave us no problems as the Trade winds were blowing continuously. However, we were worried about the pororoca – the collision between the Atlantic tide and the Amazon River water at the mouth of the river. Between January and April and mostly at full moon, huge waves are created when these powers meet each other. When we left the Amazon River it was March and full moon, but fortunately I had figured out the tide correctly and we didn't see a single wave.

DEVIL'S ISLAND

Just outside the French rocket base Kourou in French Guiana is a small group of three islands. The islands are a convenient stop for long-distance sailors sailing from Cape Town to the Caribbean because they do not have to clear in. Up until the early 1950s, this was the notorious penal colony, Devil's Island. Here the French used to send both criminal and political prisoners, where they died slowly under horrible circumstances. The most well known criminal prisoner was Papillon (Henri Charrière), who, in reality, did not escape from Devil's Island but from the mainland. Nevertheless, his book *Papillon* describes the hard life in the penal colony and the prisoners that managed to escape. The best-known political prisoner was Alfred Dreyfus, a Jewish captain in the French army. In 1894 Dreyfus was falsely accused of high treason and sentenced to life in prison on Devil's Island by the arrogant anti-Semitic French Army. The Dreyfus affair polarized opinion in France, and the influential writer Émile Zola – with his open letter, *J'accuse!* (I accuse!) – helped in getting another trial. Dreyfus was judged again in 1899, but the French army could not admit that they had falsely accused him. Embittered and innocent, he asked the French president for mercy, which he was granted. However, he was not exonerated until 1906. The Dreyfus affair was one of the biggest scandals in French political history.

In 1953 the Devil's Island penal colony was finally shut down. We walked around among the ruins, where the rainforest had already grown through many of the buildings. Many of the cells were relatively intact, with iron bars in the ceiling so that the guards could constantly supervise the poor prisoners. We left with Papillon's description of the unpleasant conditions in the solitary confinement cells fresh in our minds.

SURINAME

The three Guianas were areas that the first colonists – the Spanish and Portuguese – did not want. France, England and Holland then fought over them and got one apiece. Today Guiana (formerly British) and Suriname (formerly Dutch) are independent, while French Guiana is the only remaining colony in South America (if you do not count the British Falkland Islands).

With nearly 500,000 inhabitants Suriname is five times bigger than its former colonial power, Holland (many of its inhabitants actually live in Holland). We anchored outside the biggest luxury hotel in the capital city of Paramaribo, which we reached by two hours of sailing along the Suriname River. In the hotel we joined the elite of the country – there are many wealthy people in Suriname. As in most developing countries, the private sector is almost nonexistent and the people can only get rich in three ways: drug dealing, belonging to the political elite or stealing the country's natural resources, such as timber or bauxite. One can perhaps understand that local men want to make a fortune, but it is unbelievable that former colonial powers and naïve countries (such as Sweden) continue to give those countries foreign aid when they know that the money is stolen and ends up in a bank account in Switzerland or in tax havens in the Caribbean.

RETURN TO THE CARIBBEAN – THE BANANA WAR AND DRUGS

We sail through the West Indies, north with the Trade wind from Trinidad along the island chain of the Lesser Antilles and up to the Greater Antilles. From Cuba we go south, against the Trade wind and the current – often in gales – passing and stopping in the Cayman Islands, Jamaica, Curacao and Bonaire back to Trinidad. The Caribbean has expanded from producing bananas and sugar to tourism, finance and the corrupt business with drugs – a trend that only increased during the banana war.

GEOPOLITICS

During our round trip in the Caribbean we cleared in and out of 20 jurisdictions; independent states as well as colonies. The USA, England, France and Holland still have colonies. The relatively limited area of the Caribbean is still politically influential on a global platform and the Caribbean Islands have many votes in the UN. There is a battle in the UN for Caribbean diplomatic influence, ie between mainland China and Taiwan. The last country that 'changed sides' (from Taiwan to China) was the Bahamas. Foreign aid is used for bribery; Japan is generous with foreign aid money on the understanding that the small island nations vote with Japan on the sensitive question of whaling. During the Cold War the area played a great role in the issues with Cuba. The USA was anxious to prevent the spread of communism in the Caribbean and gave generous foreign aid to the other island nations. The Cuban Missile Crisis in 1962 and the USA's invasion of Grenada in 1983 to prevent a communist coup, show how sensitive the situation was and still is.

THE BANANA WAR

The islands of the West Indies have historically been dependent on the production of salt, sugar and bananas. Sugar, the white gold, was incomparably the most important product. But with the abolition of slavery (the sugar industry required a lot of manpower) and the American and European protection of their sugar producers, the sugar industry collapsed. Some of the sugar plantations were converted to banana plantations and the 'green gold' became an important export product for many of the small islands. For several years France and England gave preferential treatment to their former colonies' banana businesses in the European Union (EU). However, the huge banana plantations in Central America are much more effective than the ones in the West Indies, and those 'dollar bananas' could therefore beat the West Indies bananas in Europe, despite the preferential treatment. In 1996 the USA sued Europe for unfair trading practices in the new World Trade Organization (WTO) and won. The verdict put the whole banana industry on the small island nations in a state of motion, and their leaders are constantly lobbying in the EU and Washington for a change. The question is whether the Europeans will keep on funding an ineffective banana industry when it is highly overpriced. If the WTO's decision stands, EU consumers will be able to buy 'dollar bananas' from Central America and the Caribbean will have to become more effective banana farmers or find other ways to survive – which they partly do with tourism, financial services and drug smuggling.

TOURISM

The tourist industry is, for most Caribbean island nations, the biggest source of income and sometimes also the biggest employer. Before Fidel Castro (who resigned in 2008), Cuba was the biggest tourist destination. Now Puerto Rico and the Bahamas have taken over that role, followed by Jamaica. In the much tinier Lesser Antilles, Barbados is the most popular destination. The Caribbean used to be afraid that Cuba would export its revolution as it did to Grenada in the beginning of the 1980s; now they are afraid that the relationship between Cuba and the USA will become the norm. When this happens, the entire Caribbean will hear a 'big sucking sound' as most of the Americans travel to Cuba instead.

Another terrifying scenario that has already happened is the phenomenal increase of the cruise industry. More than ten million tourists per year go on a Caribbean cruise, similar to the number of people that reach the islands by plane. To attract the cruise ships, most of the states have built a tax-free harbour for the passengers. One of the biggest cruising destinations is the US Virgin Islands, where on some days up to seven big cruise ships can be anchored.

It means that 10,000 tourists invade the little capital city of Charlotte Amalie every day. The Cayman Islands for example, with a population of only 40,000, have one million tourists per year, 70 per cent of whom are cruising passengers. The local tourist industry is upset and accuses the cruising industry of pirate tourism; this means that the tourists don't spend any money on the islands, apart from buying T-shirts. They eat, shop and play the casino aboard the ship and leave mountains of rubbish behind for the islands to clear up. The government charges a landing fee of $5–15 for each passenger, which the cruising industry is critical about. They would rather not land them anywhere, and just sail around for a week and let the passengers spend their money aboard. Out of shame they have to let the passengers visit the 'paradise harbours'.

THE BOAT INDUSTRY

One of the most positive factors within the West Indies tourist industry is the large increase of the boat industry. Several world-class marinas and shipyards have been built to meet the demand. In the early 1990s, hundreds of boats were destroyed by hurricanes in the northern West Indies. Trinidad – which is outside the hurricane belt – has now prepared four shipyards and marinas that can accomodate up to 1,000 boats during the hurricane season. St Vincent has built a shipyard and marina for superyachts and St Lucia's Rodney Bay Marina is one of the best in the West Indies archipelago. There are now several big marinas in Antigua able to accommodate the biggest yachts in the world.

The islands in the Caribbean have different views on the boat industry. Some governments took a long time to see the potential of this part of tourism. Barbados is a good example. For many years, Jimmy Cornell organized the Atlantic Rally for Cruisers (ARC), with 150–200 boats that sail together from the Canaries to the Caribbean. For the first four years, Barbados was the finish. But the customs and immigration authorities were unpleasant and bureaucratic, and the government was not interested. When the promise to build a marina was broken in 1990, the ARC moved to St Lucia's Rodney Bay Marina. St Lucia's government had the customs and immigration clerks stay open day and night to clear in the sailing boats when they arrived to the recently finished marina. Only too late, Barbados realized that millions of tourism dollars disappeared – 200 boats with an average of five people each gives a total of one thousand people to provision, repair, rent cars, take a cab, do some shopping, go to restaurants and bars and change crews. All of this gives a lot of income to a small economy with approximately 100,000 poor inhabitants. The island nations provide differing facilities to visiting sailing boats. Several islands have welcomed yachtsmen by creating National Marine Parks, for example Saba, the

Virgin Islands, the Cayman Islands, Bonaire, St Lucia, and Turks and Caicos. In those parks there are mooring buoys for sailing and diving boats to use (sometimes for a small fee) to avoid anchoring and to protect the corals. Dominica, on the other hand, one of the poorest countries in the Caribbean, doesn't allow sailing boats to use the buoys or dive without going through a local diving shop at a cost of $60. This system gives the local diving industry a de-facto monopoly and decreases the tendency for visiting sailing boats to go to Dominica.

Of the three categories of sailing boats – long distance sailors, charter boats and rental boats – it is the latter that has increased spectacularly during the 1990s, and within the rental boats sector, it is the catamaran's popularity that has increased the most. Jokingly, the order of priority among sailors is that the Whitbread/Volvo Ocean/America's Cup sailors are at the top, then the circumnavigators and then those who have crossed an ocean. You'll find the rental boat sailors on the bottom of the scale (many are of course good sailors but have generated less fame) but rental boats are now the biggest group of sailboats in the Caribbean. During the 1998 Antigua Sailing Week races – which are the most fun, the biggest and have the most participants of all races in the West Indies, 45 per cent of the 250 participants were rental boats. Soon will they be a majority.

THE OFFSHORE FINANCIAL INDUSTRY

To diversify their economies, several island nations have set themselves as tax havens, dealing with banks, insurance, stock companies and ship registration. Financial activity increases when traditional farming products have a harder time competing on the world market. Even tourism is an uncertain industry; hurricanes, volcanic eruptions and poor economic periods in rich countries have a direct negative effect on the economy in the Caribbean – and the number of tourists decreases. The offshore financial industry, on the other hand, generates income despite a small infrastructure and small investments. The leading offshore nations are the British Colonies – partly due to the fact that British law is applicable. The Cayman Islands is the biggest offshore centre in the world (after London, Hong Kong, Tokyo and New York) with more than 500 banks including 46 of the world's 50 highest ranked banks. Turks and Caicos, Panama, Bahamas, Aruba and Curacao are well known tax havens while the British Virgin Islands and St Vincent are the latest additions. An offshore company, for example a bank, is a company that doesn't make deals in the host country – it is only situated there. Sometimes it does not even have a physical presence except a mailbox at a lawyer or accountant's office in the host country. Offshore companies can do any businesses they want without any interference from the authorities in the host country (eg Curacao) or the home country (eg England or Sweden): no currency regulation and no (or very low) income, company, or capital taxes. The host country has registration fees and low taxes, but the home country gets nothing. Some 25,000 registered companies can generate an income of a few million dollars per year, a big source of income for a small country. The offshore financial industry also creates jobs for secretaries, assistants, lawyers and accountants, although the last two categories are usually foreign-trained experts.

Panama, Bahamas and Liberia are notorious for letting the western world's commercial fleets use their country's flags as a convenience flag. Those countries have very low expectations when it comes to security, crew, inspections and so on, and many ships that sail under a flag of convenience are floating wrecks likely to cause big environmental accidents. Without an authority that controls the offshore industry, money laundering and enormous fraud can occur. One example is the Bank of Credit and Commerce International (BCCI) scandal, the world's biggest financial fraud in the early 1990s (this was before Enron and WorldCom frauds). Furthermore, the homeland governments lose tax income. The western world is already worried about a future where more and more transactions take place offshore and over the internet. When the tax income from companies decreases, ordinary employees will have to pay higher taxes – because they cannot flee offshore.

THE DRUGS INDUSTRY

The Caribbean, positioned between Central America and the USA, is a natural reloading area for drugs coming from South America to North America. It is estimated that 40 per cent of all the cocaine and heroin that goes to the USA comes through the Caribbean first. The trafficking takes place in almost every independent island nation and colony and several leading politicians – even state leaders – have been involved. The amount of drug money that circulates is enormous, as is the corruption that goes with it. The USA takes the view that the drug business – and illegal immigration – is a threat to their national security and has moved its southern military command from Panama to Florida to gain control over the drug traffic in the Caribbean. To stop drug trafficking, the USA has worked hard to get the small West Indies states to give them unlimited access to their airspace and territorial waters to enable them to chase smugglers. The agreement – the 'ship-rider agreement' – is looked at by the small neighbours of the USA as a re-colonization but they have still signed it. Barbados and Jamaica initially refused, but eventually agreed to it. One night I was stopped outside St Lucia by patrol boats from both the USA and St Lucia. They shone a bright searchlight at us and asked where we were heading, but they didn't board us.

CUBA – CHE GUEVARA'S MEMORY LIVES ON

Cuba is the highlight of our Caribbean sailing tour. We visit the old revolutionary museum in Havana and learn about the legacy of Che Guevara, Castro and Hemingway. We find the Cuban people friendly but living under harsh economic circumstances. Cuba has a difficult future ahead of it; an American trade embargo, loss of significant foreign aid from the former Soviet Union and a political system that is finding it hard to move into the 21st century.

BATISTA AND THE MAFIA

One surprising fact about Cuba is that 65 per cent of the total population (of nearly 11.5 million) are descended from the Spanish and consider themselves to be white. The rest of the islands in the Caribbean are made up of mainly black inhabitants who are the descendants of African slaves and a smaller group of the aboriginal Caribbean Indians. Cuba is the giant among the nations of the West Indies and is almost as big as England. It is situated 90nm, or one day's sail, from Florida (where about one million Cubans live), which explains the USA's sensitivity towards Cuba. The country was colonized by Spaniards and used as a reloading harbour for stolen gold and silver from the conquered Inca and Aztecs during the 17th and 18th centuries. The Creole descendants of the Spaniards and Cubans eventually showed their dissatisfaction with the political situation and demanded independence from Spain. Bloody revolts came one after another and in 1897 Spain finally gave in.

The USA, who had big investments in the Cuban sugar and tobacco industry, then decided to intervene. In 1898 the American battleship USS *Maine* exploded in Havana's harbour. It is suspected that the USA sank the ship to instigate a war against Spain, who was blamed for the incident. The officers happened to be ashore during the attempt, but not the crew (this can be compared to the attempted attack against American destroyers in the Gulf of Tonkin during the Vietnam war, which was later shown to have been staged by the Americans to justify the bombings of North Vietnam). The Spanish-American war was easily won by the USA and in 1892 the Cuban Republic was formed, with the stipulation that the USA had the right to intervene in Cuba's internal affairs. The Cubans feel that the USA stole their revolution. The Cuban general was not allowed to take part in the peace negotiations even though they already had won the independence revolution against Spain. The USA also took over Guantanamo Bay, where they built their naval base. The USA still maintains this foreign colony in hostile territory, which has been infamous as the prison of terrorists after the 9/11 World Trade Center disaster (until a change in policy by President Obama in 2009 started the closure of the prison).

After the revolution American investments kept on coming into Cuba, and the island practically became an economic colony of the USA. A number of brutal and corrupt dictators, supported by the USA, took power after the independence of Cuba. The last dictator before Castro's revolution in 1959 was Fulgencio Batista, a former sergeant in the Cuban army. He had strong bonds with the American Mafia, who planned to turn Cuba into an enormous gambling den and brothel, and had a huge aircraft carrier to ship drugs into the USA.

After Castro's revolution the Mafia moved their plans to Las Vegas instead. Batista's years in power resulted in unbelievable corruption, a brutal police force, overuse of the country's resources and an absolute resistance to social reforms.

CASTRO AND CHE GUEVARA

In 1956 the lawyer Fidel Castro and the Argentinean doctor Ernesto 'Che' Guevara started a guerilla war, and after three years they forced Batista out of Cuba. Castro and his revolutionary organization (called the July 26th Movement) were nationalistic – the goals were land reforms and freedom from foreign (American) influences. Castro was not a member of the Communist party, which did not take part in Castro and Che's revolt against Batista until it was clear that Castro had a chance of winning. It was not until the 1960s that Castro's July 26th Movement and the Communist party started to work together. Castro executed many of his political rivals and imprisoned several of those who had initially supported him in the fight but then changed political sides. Castro and Che's intention was to reform Cuba from scratch. They did not follow the constitution and held the opinion that public voting was meaningless. Large properties were confiscated and given to the farmers' cooperatives, and buildings, schools and healthcare in the countryside were improved. The upper class and the intelligentsia fled to the USA where they settled down in Miami and started a loud resistance

group against Castro's Cuba. Many of the confiscated properties belonged to American companies. This increased the pressure on the US government, which resulted in an American boycott. The tourists didn't come to Cuba anymore, the debt increased and the lack of imported raw material was acute.

Cuba turned to the Soviet Union, which made a deal to buy the entire Cuban sugar production at an outrageous price. The Soviet Union was happy to get a foot into Latin America. To keep the revolution going, Cuba needed an outside enemy and the USA's action played into their hands. In 1961, 1,400 CIA-educated and equipped exiled Cubans invaded the Bay of Pigs on the south coast of Cuba. Regardless of whether or not they were against Castro, the Cuban people were united against the return of Batista. The CIA had told the exiled Cubans that the USA would support the invasion, but President Kennedy refused to send in American support troops. The invasion was a fiasco.

In 1962, after the Cuban crisis, Castro and Che reluctantly realized that Cuba played an unimportant role in Moscow's interests (Churchill said once that states do not have friends, only interests). Instead of being an American colony, Cuba was now a Soviet colony, totally dependent on the so-called Eastern Bloc for its sugar exports, and fuel, food and engine imports. The letdown of the Soviet Union and the direction that the revolution had taken was a huge disappointment for Castro and the charismatic Che (his portrait can be seen in more places in Cuba than Castro's). As chief of the national bank, the romantic Marxist Che expected that the Cuban people would be just as idealistic and altruistic as himself, and that they would be willing to work for free to keep the revolution going. But the farmers did not like the co-operatives that forced them to farm certain agricultural products at set low prices by the state, and the middle class became antagonistic when nationalism increased to include the small companies too. Economic crises, the farmers' general refusal to work, food rationing and more and more disapproval was the end result.

Che and Castro developed in different directions, and Che left Cuba, taking his revolution to South America. In 1967 he was captured by the Bolivian Army and executed in front of American military advisers. We arrived in Cuba the same year that Che's grave was found in Bolivia and his remains were moved to Cuba. While we were staying on Cuba, Che Guevara was given a national funeral that was broadcast on television all around the world. Castro was probably happy that his former armour-bearer got to do one last duty for the revolution that had served its time.

THE ALMIGHTY DOLLAR

What is the outlook for Cuba today? What is the result of the revolution? When the Soviet Union collapsed at the beginning of the 1990s, foreign aid to Cuba also disappeared. The situation was very difficult and was called the 'Special Period'. Fuel and food were rationed, and even though no one was actually starving, the rations were barely enough. Almost all the manufacturers of products were owned by the state, with the exception of the tourism industry, where foreign companies (mostly Canadian and Southern European) could now own 100 per cent of hotel businesses. Small private farmer's markets and restaurants were allowed in homes (this has happened already in China in 1981).

One could say that Cuba has a stricter application of communism than China and Vietnam, but is less strict than North Korea. Cuba's literacy is higher than in the USA (an embarrassing fact for the USA) and its free healthcare covers almost the entire population, and is probably the best on the whole American continent, including the USA. Despite the economic crisis and the effect of the American Helms-Burton Act of 1996 against Cuba (which had the purpose of isolating Cuba economically) the people of Cuba did not hold the government responsible. By the end of the 1990s the 'Special Period' had declined in severity, before moving towards a more sustainable economy in the 2000s.

One reason that the Cuban economy didn't collapse during this time was the acceptance of the American dollar as a parallel currency between 1993 and 2004. Such an acceptance of reality must have been hard to swallow for the government; a sort of ideological somersault. There was a double economy; a 'pesos economy' and a 'dollar economy', where one dollar equalled around 24 pesos. There were plenty of dollar stores where you could find almost everything. By contrast you could find almost nothing in the pesos stores, not even food, because all the pesos food was sold by the rations system. The one million tourists that mostly came from southern Europe, Canada and South America to visit Cuba had to pay in dollars. We exchanged 20 dollars to pesos and could hardly use them all up; a bus ticket cost only one peso, and a visit to the private farmer's market cost us 70 pesos (three dollars) for two backpacks full of fruit and vegetables.

The biggest problem with such a double system is that only a few Cubans had access to dollars through the tourism industry, black markets or relatives abroad. A teacher earned 300 pesos per month, which was $13. The rent for a three-room apartment was only 30 pesos, or $1.50. The food rations cost about the same, 30 pesos. Healthcare and education was free and income taxes did not yet exist. Yet for ordinary Cubans it was hard to obtain dollars. The few pesos that Cubans had left could be exchanged for $5–10 per month. The dollars didn't last long when the prices in the dollar stores were the same as in the USA. In Havana we hired an electrician to repair our SSB-radio. He arrived at 11am on a Sunday morning and worked until 3am the next day. He asked for $50 for 16 hours of work, which is a normal pay for two months. When we asked what he was going to do with the money, he replied: 'Buy food'. The same response came from the woman who did our laundry: 'Buy food' she said.

The effect of the dollar economy was strange. Highly educated people such as teachers, dentists and engineers were working as porters at hotels and driving (often illegally) taxis – anything that was paid in dollars. Just imagine – one single dollar in tips was equivalent to two days of work. Prostitution, also based on the dollar, flourished: 'the biggest brothel this side of Bangkok' as one happy American put it. The dollar ceased to be legal tender in Cuba in 2004: although the dollar stores remained open they now only accepted the convertible peso, perhaps moving in the future to the Cuban peso.

THE AFTERMATH

Fidel Castro's two presidencies (1959–2008) created a society where everybody had food, a roof over their head, education and free healthcare. Can any other Third World country say that? The new society made the Cubans proud of what they have accomplished, but the revolution also caused the people to be poor. No one could climb the society ladder unless they were members of the system. The system also produced a raw power: power for the Communist party to imprison people (approximately 1,000) who had differing political opinions, and power to control the citizens in a controlled environment.

We spoke with many people during our six weeks in Cuba and met no one that did not feel free. They did not seem worried or afraid to speak their mind even if it was criticizing the system. The result of the dollar economy was the emergence of a new rich upper class with typical western consumer values.

It is not clear how the current regime under Raúl Castro (the brother of Fidel) will handle the trend towards a consumer society. The new regime is still communist but at the same time economic recovery is occurring slowly and the new administration has made hints of changes to come concerning the ownership of personal goods such as computers, DVDs and microwaves. In 2007 the Cuban economy grew by 7.5 per cent, which is higher than the average rate of growth for a Latin American country.

HEMINGWAY'S HAVANA

Cuba is one of the least exploited sailing areas in the Caribbean. We arrived in Cuba from the Bahamas and cleared in at Nuevitas, a harbour on Cuba's north-east coast that exports sugar. It was here that the Russians shipped their rockets in 1962.

The clearing in procedure reminded me of the one in Vietnam – eight uniformed men representing customs, immigration, border police, coast protection, agriculture and health authority plus a harbourmaster that came on board. They hardly spoke any English but were polite and friendly, despite all the paperwork. Every time we arrived or left a harbour, we had to do almost exactly the same procedure again. The cost was $23 per person for a visitor visa, and $50 for a sailing permit (compared to $1,200 in Vietnam).

We sailed along the north coast to Cuba's biggest tourist resort town, Varadero, from where there are direct flights to Canada and Europe. We continued to the Hemingway Marina, just outside Havana. The marina consists of a little shipyard, a yacht club and four canals where the boats are moored. We met several long-distance sailors, some from the USA. The USA does not ban its citizens from visiting Cuba, but according to the Trading with the Enemy Act (TWEA), it is forbidden to spend money there. The American sailors solved this problem by explaining, upon return to the USA, that they had European crew on board who had paid for everything during their stay in Cuba. They told us the best sailing was on the south coast among the cays of the islands. The water is crystal clear, the diving is fabulous and there are as many lobsters as you could wish for in the coral reefs – and almost no other boats.

With Hemingway Marina as our base, we explored Havana for ten days. The city is made up of many old monumental colonial buildings and is one of UNESCO's World Heritage sites. On the edges of Havana's main harbour you can see several Spanish-built forts, which kept the city well defended.

Havana is a living car museum. Many old cars from the 1940s and 1950s are still out on the streets and some are very well kept. The fact that the cars are in such perfect condition without a supply of spare parts says a lot about Cubans' ingenuity.

We visited a tobacco factory where hundreds of people, mostly women, sorted, rolled and packed the famous Cuban cigars. One of the nights we watched the famous shows at the nightclub Tropicana that have been playing ever since the days of Batista.

Ernest Hemingway spent a lot of time in Havana and every place that he patronized is a tourist attraction today. One of his cocktail bars, Bodeguita del Medio, still has a warm atmosphere: small and cosy with plenty of old photos and scribbles on the walls. The most popular drink is the mojito: rum with crushed ice and a lot of fresh mint. We drank mojitos and liked them – and we liked Cuba too.

JENNIFER IN TRINIDAD

We had a paying crew aboard *Jennifer* throughout our five months sailing around the Caribbean. During the Antigua Sailing Week *Jennifer* was the mother ship for a Swedish crew that took part with a charter boat with the Swedish boat journalist Curt Gelin as the skipper (they finished in second place in the charter boat category). Sue from England sailed with us for five months, from Cape Town to Turks and Caicos. Johanna's mother and sister sailed with us from Puerto Rico to Turks and Caicos. Clark, the avocado farmer from California who sailed with us in New Guinea in 1995 signed on from the Cayman Islands to Trinidad. When we sailed from Trinidad to Grenada in April 1997, *Jennifer* crossed her outward-bound course from 1992 (when we sailed from Grenada to Panama) and I officially became a circumnavigator. However, we were not back home in Sweden yet – we would stay another year in the Caribbean to sail charters and then sail back home during the spring of 1998. After sailing around the Caribbean we returned to Trinidad, stayed there during the hurricane season, and gave *Jennifer* a thorough overhaul.

After nine years and 95,000nm, *Jennifer* was worn out and perhaps more suitable as a long-distance cruising boat rather than a charter boat. For three months I worked on her in high humidity and temperatures of 30–35°C. Johanna took the chance to fly home to Canada, visit her parents and take a Cordon Bleu cooking course. Again there was a lot to do: the diesel engine and the sails needed checking, as did the electrical wiring, water maker (desalinator), diving compressor, generator, dinghy, stove and the rigging. The batteries, battery charger and alternator had to be replaced. Some of the mattresses, all the sails, curtains and deck cushions and the material on the sofas in the saloon had to be changed. The diving tanks had to be tested, the hull painted and polished, and everything on deck varnished. The hull osmosis was not that bad, and still only in the gel-coat. So I decided to postpone that cost for the future. The floor in the saloon wasn't fresh any more, so I had a carpenter put in a new teak floor on top of the old one, with very good results. The teak deck, which was 12mm thick originally, was worn out and the screw heads had begun to show. First I took out all the seams and approximately 800 screws and dropped epoxy glue in each screw hole. Then a boatbuilder planed the deck so it was level to walk on, and I plugged all the holes without putting back the screws. After that I sanded the deck smooth and oiled it. The deck regained its old glow and looked relatively fresh and new. Marketing took some time to get going: producing new brochures for the winter season, updating the homepage on the internet and contacting the agents. The whole renovation cost $30,000 and again I was in the red.

Trinidad is a big island considering it is in the West Indies. Fortunately it is close to South America and Venezuela, which means that it has plenty of oil and is not as dependent on bananas and tourism as many of its neighbours, although the big profits from oil and the closeness to drug producing countries in South America have started a big corruption problem. Like Fiji, Trinidad has a population that is half Indian and half aboriginal; none of the Carib Indians that Columbus met exist any more. Because Trinidad is safely outside the hurricane belt, there is a big demand for skilled workers in all the marinas. Many Europeans, including Swedes, have therefore started businesses in Trinidad. For example, Kent runs the Atlantic Yacht Service, which is one of the four boatyards where I lifted out *Jennifer*; Jonas runs a rig workshop and Ove is a boatbuilder. These men had all married West Indian women and consider Trinidad to be their home.

Many long-distance sailors spend the hurricane season in Trinidad during their Caribbean stay and few miss taking part in the festival at the end of February. As many as 25 Swedish boats stayed in Trinidad in 1997, many of them members of the Ocean Sailing Club in Stockholm. For example, *Peter Pan*, a small sailing canoe only 5m long with Nisse, a solo sailor; *Sylvia*, a Havsfidra with Hasse as a solo sailor; *7-UP* with the Toss family with two children – their boat was nearly destroyed during a hurricane in St Martin in 1992 and they spent three years repairing all the damage; and *Good Run* with Bengt and Margot, who run the Swedish SSB-radio network every day. Others were *Aprilia, Smile, Time Out, Charlotta, Odyssey, Sandra, Lady Swan* and *Stardust*. The oldest sailor in the Swedish colony was Karl-Erik who sailed his 45ft (14m) boat and also stayed in Trinidad. Kjell and Kattis were on their way around the world on *Stormfågel*, a nicely kept and equipped R40. Most of the Swedes had the West Indies as their goal and they stayed there for a year or two, and then returned to Sweden. Others headed to Panama and the looming South Pacific.

At the end of November *Jennifer's* repairs were done – newly painted, varnished, and polished, with a new floor and cushions in the saloon, she was ready for her last charter season in the West Indies.

SAILING HOME – THE LAST ATLANTIC CROSSING

We meet a new crew for the ninth and last Atlantic crossing to Sweden, having covered 4,500nm in total. We visit the Azores and break the rudder in the middle of the Atlantic. After rigging the spare rudder and getting moving again we reach England and finally, around midsummer, arrive back in Stockholm in 1998 – after 100,000nm and 10 years at sea.

THE LAST CREW

In the winter of 1998 we sailed charters in the West Indies and were booked for nine weeks, which felt good. Over Christmas and New Year my brother and sister and their families came to sail with us for three weeks. We were eleven people in total and had a great time. The season finished with the Antigua Sailing Week in April and May. Again we were the mother ship for a racing Swedish boat, *Servisen*. Directly after the race the new crew signed in and two days later we left for the Azores. On board, apart from Johanna and myself, were: Mikael, a salesman from Norrköping who owned a boat and was an experienced sailor; Jan, a dentist from Stockholm who also had a lot of sailing experience and had been crewed in the race; Erik, who had a doctorate degree in maths and who also worked part-time as a farmer; Ted, from Gothenburg, who owned a business and also sailed; Joakim, a shipping agent from Stockholm and Di Paulo, an Italian-American pizza baker and restaurateur from New York. Joakim had to sign off at the Azores because he ran out of time and Di Paulo signed off in England. In the Kiel Canal, Anders, a former long-distance sailor, charter skipper and carpenter from Stockholm, signed on for the last sailing to Stockholm.

THE RUDDER BREAKDOWN

The distance from Antigua to the Azores is 2,200nm and should take 18 days. The first day we spent practising sea safety and the reefing routines that we had started to go through on Antigua. To reef in good weather is easy, but when it is stormy the heavy sails get hard to handle and everybody has to know how to handle the ropes. The first ten days passed without incident: good weather in the south-east Trade winds, swimming with dolphins and whales while holding onto the rope behind the boat. Our fishing luck was good and gave us some dorado and tuna dinners. The wind was changeable – sometimes no wind at all. Sometimes we could put up the gennaker or even the spinnaker, which made the sailing more fun and much faster.

On the tenth day we heard a strange noise from the stern; a clinking sound from the rudder. We could hear it most clearly when a big wave heaved the boat. Immediately I realized that an old skeleton had come out of the closet – a rudder breakdown that we had had the year before in Cuba.

It was 1997 when we first left Cuba's south coast to sail to the Cayman Islands, with winds close to 25 knots. Suddenly I heard a noise and shortly after that a crack. The next second we saw the rudder floating in the water – it had broken at the waterline. A sailboat without a rudder is not much of a sailboat, and *Jennifer* immediately started to go around in circles. We took the sails down and called the Cuban coastguard via the VHF-radio. While we were waiting, Johanna and I tried steering the boat using the sail. I tried to remember the theory of how the sails functioned. By pulling in and letting out the sails it should be possible to steer, but it was not that easy. Two hours later the coastguard arrived and started the tow back to the small island of Cayo Largo. *Jennifer* turned strongly back and forth in the high sea and the towrope broke four times. To get the rope over to *Jennifer* at all was quite a challenge. Because of the heavy sea, the boats could not get close to each other and a diver had to swim over with the rope. Back on the Cuban mainland we realized that a new rudder had to be made with the remains of the rudder stock.

It was 18 days before we could sail again. The rudder breakdown was caused by our entry to Nuevitas on the north coast of Cuba when the wind had started to blow strongly. While mooring the boat I reversed at the highest speed and the engine locked itself in this position. Before I had turned off the engine we had run aground in the harbour and we were stuck for 20 minutes before we could get a rope to the pier and be pulled loose. When I later dived down to inspect the rudder I saw cracks on one side but not on the other, and thought that the rudder would make it to Trinidad, where we

would bring *Jennifer* up into the shipyard. I was wrong. Despite everything we were lucky; if the rudder had broken further out at sea, it would have been serious. As it turned out it cost $2,500 and three weeks of waiting.

Later when *Jennifer* was at the boatyard in Trinidad, Kent, the owner drilled a little hole on the bottom of the rudder, just in case. Immediately the water started to pour out. When it showed no sign of stopping, we opened up the rudder and it was full of water. Kent was not satisfied with the construction and partly rebuilt it. After that I figured the rudder would not give me any more problems. But, now on the Atlantic, we had a problem again, exactly halfway between Antigua and the Azores. I dived and saw the same crack that I had seen in Cuba. Now the question was whether the rudder would last all the way to the Azores. For the remaining seven days we sailed and worried that something would happen, but fortunately the weather was fine and so was the rudder. After clearing in on the island of Faial in the Azores, we immediately took off the rudder by pressing it down through the rudder stock hole and then catching it in the water. Through the harbour captain we learned that a Canadian lived on the island and worked with fibreglass. Joe took care of the rudder and promised to repair it in three days.

THE AZORES

While we were waiting for the rudder to be fixed, we explored Faial. The island is beautifully green and the town of Horta, where we moored the boat, is small and sheltered. During May and June the boats that sail between the Caribbean and Europe stop here on their way either to the Mediterranean or to northern Europe. A new marina was built in the 1980s to host this sailing invasion of around 1,000 sailing boats per year. Many of the boats paint their logo, with the boat's name, date and the names of the crew on the dock. Some boats create fantastic artworks. We improved *Jennifer*'s symbol from 1992 by filling in the colours and adding the names of our current crew. The other Swedish boats, including the Swan boats *Concept* and *Peak*, that had both been charter sailing in the West Indies, also painted their symbols on the dock. The meeting point for the sailors is Café Sport (Peter's Café) a robust, wooden, smoky bar with flags and bills from all over the world on the walls.

All the islands that make up the Azores are volcanic and there is a huge crater, about 3km in diameter, in the middle of Faial Island. From the edge of the crater there is a beautiful view over the sea and down into the crater. On the western side of Faial is a new area created by a volcanic eruption in the 1950s. Nothing grows here and it looks like a moon landscape, silent and mysterious.

Meanwhile, Joe had put fibreglass on the rudder and reinforced it. He guaranteed that it would last the boat's lifetime, which made us feel secure. After provisioning we started to sail 1,250nm north towards England.

EMERGENCY RUDDER

The first days were fine, although it was cloudy with rain and wind at 23 knots, but it came from the side and the speed was good, at 7 knots. It seemed to be a fast sail. On the fifth day we heard a familiar noise again, and shortly after that a loud crack. Johanna, who was steering, was totally perplexed: 'I can't steer', she said at the same time as *Jennifer* started to go in circles. I hurried to the stern and saw that the rudder had bent at the water line and was lying on the surface but was still in one piece. We quickly took down the sails and were soon rocking gently in the middle of the Atlantic. It soon became clear what we had to do. If the rudder started to hit the hull it would make a hole in it. I had to put on the wetsuit and get into the cold water. The waves were maybe 2–3m, but not catastrophically high. It didn't take long before I hit my face on the platform and got a nosebleed – I'm sure it looked worse than it was. We had to get a rope around the rudder so it would not sink when we pushed it through the rudder stock hole. After an hour we had tied a rope around the rudder and pulled it into the cockpit.

Now we had to try to sail. I had faxed the rescue service in Falmouth via the satellite unit, described our situation, and got the latest forecast. A storm was on its way to the Bay of Biscay. The best plan for us was to get to Portugal, which was the closest destination (except for the Azores, where I didn't want to return) or to Falmouth. To be sailing with only sails might be possible in theory with a long-keeled boat, but with our modern sailing boat with a divided keel and no fin in front of the rudder, it seemed impossible and we quickly gave up. Then we tried to use one of the two spinnaker booms as a steering oar. After trying different mounting arrangements and blocks, we thought that it might just work. The underwater surface area was very small and the steering minimal, so we could only have a small sail surface; we kept the mainsail down and put just a little bit of the genoa up. Just like the old Vikings, we sailed at sea steering with an oar. But our speed was low, only 1–2 knots, with 700nm left. At this speed it would take almost three weeks. When no one was listening, I asked Johanna how long our food supply would last, and she reassured me that we had enough food for a month.

The crew took it well but Di Paulo thought that we should send a

MAYDAY signal and ask for a tow. I explained that MAYDAY calls could only be used when people were really in danger, not when a boat just had problem with the steering. Also, we had been in contact with the rescue centre for the North Atlantic, and a tow in the middle of the Atlantic would cost more than *Jennifer* was worth. But the thought of sailing for three weeks without steering was not appealing. After some thinking I started to saw the rudder apart to try and rebuild it. After an hour the whole crew was engaged, and after a lot of sawing, bending and hammering we saw what had gone wrong. Because of all the water that leaked into the rudder, the welding seam on the storm skeleton in the rudder had rusted. The material was not stainless steel but ordinary iron, which in a way was lucky. Instead of breaking apart – which is what would have happened with stainless steel – the iron had just bent 90° and the rudder was still in one piece.

By the end of the day, with everybody's effort, especially Di Paulo's, we had a smaller rudder (maybe 20 per cent of the original size) that we had hammered, drilled and screwed together. Again, I had to get into the water to try to put the rudder into the hole. When it was done, we got it into place without me hitting anything. We didn't dare use the steering wheels; instead we attached the tiller to the rudder stock extension to get the best feeling in the rudder. This was our only chance and we were careful because the rudder could not be pressed too much. It worked, and soon we were doing 4–5 knots but zig zagging. It took several minutes to get back on course after a wave or gust of wind had pushed the stem, but our sailed distance increased significantly. If you looked at the wake behind the boat you might think that whoever was steering was drunk. We were now pretty sure that the rudder worked during normal circumstances, but would it be strong enough under gale and storm? We got the forecast continuously from the rescue centre and we soon saw that we had good luck; there were storms going on around us and if the rudder had not broken we would have sailed straight into them. However, because of our low speed, we avoided them. A Force 11 storm came up from the south and then turned ahead of us and disappeared to the north. There was another storm inside of the Bay of Biscay and a third one out on the Atlantic to the west of us. Thanks to the weather gods we made it to Falmouth in eight days. At Falmouth we were met by a patrol boat that took us into the marina.

A NEW RUDDER

Again we took off the rudder, and when the shipyard saw the damage they refused to repair it: 'we can't guarantee the work', they said, and suggested a new rudder. An order was sent to the Beneteau shipyard in France and a brand new rudder, now in stainless steel, was mounted on the boat. The rudder lift and various other jobs cost $9,000.

During the entire sail from England to Stockholm we had gales, rain and bad weather. Johanna must have wondered why I was talking so warmly about Stockholm's archipelago, because it was so cold, grey and unfriendly now. I remembered my own thoughts – why did people ever settle down to live in this harsh environment instead of staying where it was warmer down south? It took several months before I got used to the Swedish climate again.

How did the crew take this eventful journey? I would not have been surprised if they had left the boat when we reached Falmouth. We were also delayed and would not make it home before midsummer, as we had hoped. Di Paulo did sign off, but that was planned. In fact, the crew did not complain about the rudder breakdown, the difficulty in steering or about the delay. In fact, it was just the opposite – the breakdown had added a little more excitement to the sailing, and it was an Atlantic adventure that few people experience. Because of the delay I suggested the crew sign off in Kiel in north Germany or Kalmar in south-east Sweden to have time to make it home to celebrate midsummer with family and friends. No one was interested, and all of them preferred to spend midsummer on a small island in Gryt's Archipelago or Stockholm's Archipelago. Everybody made calls on their mobile phones to disappointed family and explained the situation. But the weather had other plans; with a stern wind and a hard gale the whole way – and a fast passage through the Kiel Canal – we reached Stockholm the day before midsummer. The mobile phones were used frequently and a small welcoming committee was waiting for us in the Wasa Harbour in Stockholm when we arrived.

PART III
WHAT NEXT?

HOW DID IT TURN OUT?

Here I sum up some of the highlights of the circumnavigation; what it was like having paying crews on board, and my relationships with Ylva and Johanna. I also offer some advice to sailors who are planning to have paying crews aboard their own yachts.

THE HIGHLIGHTS

How can I best describe my circumnavigation? Well, it was absolutely fantastic. I have visited places few people have the opportunity to go to and seen things that you can normally only read about. The time spent in Micronesia has left me with the strongest memories, partly because Johanna and I were alone for long periods, and partly because it was the most genuine, remote and beautiful area we visited.

I will never forget the trip down the Sepik River in New Guinea, or our arrival in Saigon as the first sailing boat after the Vietnam War. Also the Indian Ocean – 'the other South Sea' as I call it – with unforgettable visits to the Andaman Islands, the Maldives and the Chagos Islands. The latter, especially, was a fabulous experience: no inhabitants, only long-distance sailors who spent several months there. The feeling of being anchored in your little boat in a small lagoon and just 'existing' is hard for others to understand. When we entered the atoll both Johanna and I felt that this was as close to paradise as we could get.

GUESTS ABOARD

Sailing with people that I did not know was generally a good experience. Sometimes it was hard to always have people around, but *Jennifer* is big enough to give you a private life. I slept in the biggest cabin and occasionally, especially before dinner, spent half an hour on my own reading or listening to the radio.

The atmosphere on board has nearly always been good. There were occasional irritations. Sometimes the crew found me annoying or too particular; it is difficult when people live in your home and are not careful with your things. When you are naturally careful and tidy you have to learn to be more relaxed and accept a certain level of untidiness on board.

I have also been told I should say thank you more often to the crew. Perhaps I thought that certain tasks were to be expected and I haven't always shown my appreciation with thanks. Now I hope that I am more appreciative of others.

RELATIONSHIPS

It has been good to be part of a couple and experience different parts of the world both with Ylva and Johanna. Ylva and I broke up when she wanted a family, while the relationship with Johanna turned into a friendship. After coming home to Stockholm both of us lived on the boat during the autumn. We went from having only a couple of T-shirts and boat shoes in our wardrobe to having ten pairs of jeans, ten sweaters and ten different shoes, and the boat seemed to get smaller. But the biggest problem was that whilst I had returned home, Johanna was still away from home: she had no friends, didn't know the language, had no job and no money. If the relationship is not strong enough, you eventually wear each other down.

When we were sailing we were on neutral ground; we lived our dream and had clearly defined roles aboard. We both did what we wanted to do. Four months after coming home we broke up and Johanna went back to Holland. When we said goodbye I felt empty and lonely – four and a half years leaves some tracks. Hopefully I have learned something from this too.

ADVICE TO FUTURE CIRCUMNAVIGATORS

Would I recommend paying crews to other circumnavigators? Yes, but you have to be goal oriented, focused, service minded and have the capacity for planning. You also have to find it fun and interesting to meet new people.

Taking the day as it comes does not work when you are working professionally with agents; timeframes and travel routes have to be set and followed. If you want to be alone or together with your partner, the paying crew concept is not recommended. Otherwise, it is a fantastic way to finance your lifestyle and/or dream to sail around the world.

IS THERE A LIFE AFTER A CIRCUMNAVIGATION?

Here I think about what it is like to be back home. After ten years at sea, you have a different perspective on life. Having lived very simply it takes time to adjust to the modern world, where man is a consumer. I have seen the relationships between the Western world and the developing countries, the divide between parts of the north and south of the globe and realize the vital importance of protecting the environment for the future.

FULFILLING THE DREAM

How does it feel to be back home after ten years at sea? First, it feels very satisfying to have fulfilled a dream to sail around the world and to have managed to accomplish this daring feat. But it also feels strange, like you are somewhere in the middle, not home and not away either; and some things at home have changed. You live very simply on a boat – few clothes, almost no traditional leisure activities, more healthy food – and it takes time to change, to get used to life in civilization.

MAN AS A CONSUMER

After ten years at sea you see the world and people with different eyes. You prioritize differently. During those ten years I thought about modern civilization, especially the relationship between the highly productive people in the northern hemisphere and the relaxed people in the South Pacific. As northern Europeans perhaps we even get irritated with our southern European neighbours and their '*mañana*' culture. Even in 1937, Thor Heyerdahl had tired of modern civilization. But in the chapter about Micronesia I mentioned that I would never be able to live in the Southern Pacific culture – it is too late to change your lifestyle when you have been programmed to 'achieve' ever since you were a child.

The modern person's role seems to have changed over the last decades. During a stroll in a shopping centre in Johannesburg, I suddenly realized that the most important role for a human being today is to be a consumer. Without consumption of gadgets and services – some necessary and useful, but most of them fabricated – society would break down.

We have a lack of time in our society – it cannot be purchased and we cannot ask for more. When I got back to Stockholm and contacted my friends, I found they were booked several weeks in advance; one of them even had a six-week plan. I compared this with my own empty agenda that had only a couple of taxi shifts and meetings with my editor and publisher.

THE GLOBAL ENVIRONMENT

To return home is both exciting and scary. Where am I going to live and – most importantly – how am I going to support myself? To go back to work as a lawyer was unthinkable; it had been 20 years since I sat in a district court. The trading business was not possible either; to work as a trader you have to be ambitious – hungry to earn millions and work 12 hours a day. When you have already earned your money and lived your dream, this sort of job is not appealing any more.

After years at sea you have another perspective – a bird's eye view. You realize that the Earth is one, that everything is connected. In the global village everything is woven together. If there is an economic crisis in the USA, it affects us in Europe and Asia too. The same goes for the environment; pollution is partly local, but mostly it is global. Chernobyl, the ozone layer, and the greenhouse effect are good examples. Overfishing of the world's seas and clearing of the rainforests are others.

Over the years I have become increasingly interested in the global environment and our duty to manage the inevitable threat against the Earth. With unrestrained consumption in the western world and the goal to increase consumption in developing countries, the equations are unlikely to balance. The Earth can hardly grant the six billion people of today – not to mention the ten billion of tomorrow – all the living standards of the western world.

I do think there is a chance to stop this development, but the political intention – or courage – is lacking. It feels like the people of the world are sitting on a big bus going at high speed down a steep hill, towards the abyss. Everybody in the bus knows where we are headed, but no one can stop it. The worst are the politicians who are sitting in the driver's seat, going at full speed – and enjoying it.

A return to the agrarian farming society is unrealistic. We need a change

in global economic structures. This means a change in how we calculate the GDP and the national economy so that the politicians get the right information and tools to steer the development. The companies' external costs must be internalized – they must be accounted for instead of being paid for by the environment, ie by us all. I think a change in the tax system is needed so that harmful activities incur more taxes and ones that are more desirable pay less. With financial incentives, our society can lead the development towards a more lasting economy. The 20th century's political axis – the horizontal left/right axis – has in principle been about *who* owns and controls the means of production and, by extension, *who* will be allowed to consume. The politicians of the 21st century might have to use another axis – a vertical north/south axis – in principle this will be about *how* we produce articles and services and *how* we consume them. In terms of the environment, it does not matter who produces or consumes – it is how we do it that matters.

If nothing is done (and the few items that are discussed on international environmental conferences are not enough) we might see the results in a few decades: rising sea levels and flooding, storms, climate change, big city collapses, a lack of water both in the towns and for farming, polluted atmosphere and mass starvation as a result. This sounds pessimistic, despite the fact that I am normally a positive person. The more I read about the problem the more engaged I become.

THE CHALLENGE

'Is there a life after a circumnavigation?' is the name of this chapter. In a wider sense I wonder if in the future we will have a habitable Earth to live on. To amend Kennedy's well-known phrase: 'Do not ask the Earth what it can do for you – ask what you can do for the Earth.' My hope is that in time we may be to find some answers to this question.

A POST-CIRCUMNAVIGATION PLAN

In 1999, I finished the Swedish edition of this book with the question: 'Is there life after a circumnavigation?' Of course there is life after you have lived your dream. Life goes on, and you have to set new goals. I realize that everything is relative and others have certainly suffered worse fates, but coming home was quite a difficult time for me. I had no job, no place to live, no money and almost no contacts. After ten years of being away, I felt alone and needed to rebuild my life back home.

FINDING A PLACE TO LIVE – WITH ONE FOOT ON LAND

The first thing I had to decide when I got home was where I should live. I took the easiest way out and stayed on the boat for two years. The first year I lived on the boat at the Navigation Society's dock in Stockholm. There was already a little colony of people who lived there on various types of boats. The problem with living on this dock was that there was strong opposition among some of the members of the Society. The majority of members who did not live on board – and in many cases did not own a boat at all – were against members living at the boat club. After a year of these sorts of conflicts, I moved to the Pampas Marina in Solna, just outside Stockholm. An entrepreneur had built a first-class marina where it was permissible to live on the boat. Solna was the first city in the Stockholm area that allowed people to be registered on their boats and gain access to water and to waste disposal services – by arranging a proper draining system for the septic tanks on boats. Pampas Marina had also started to build its own house-boats in the harbour and offered them as a unique way of living. When the marina started to collect rent at market value for the house-boats many of the older residents who had lived for years at the marina without this charge left Pampas.

A SEASONAL HOME

When I tell people that I lived on a boat, many think that it sounds like a carefree existence. To live on a boat during the warm months of the year is a real treat, but during the winter, at –20°C, it is not quite as pleasant. The boat has to be kept shut, which means that the living space is all below deck, which makes it smaller. You need a lot more clothing – jackets, shoes, boots, and sweaters – which you have to store somewhere when you don't need them during the summer.

The problems living on board in winter included trying to heat the interior and getting rid of the condensation. I had hot water heating that was generated by either electrical cartridge or a diesel burner. Unfortunately, I got air in the system several times, the diesel burner leaked and condensation constantly dripped from the bulkheads and the hatchways. My clothing smelled of diesel and became damp if it was kept close to a bulkhead.

As you can see, the feeling of freedom and charm of living on a boat is not so obvious during the winter. During my third year in Stockholm, I caught up financially and bought an apartment in the city centre, unfortunately when the market was at its highest.

DEALING WITH THE BUREAUCRATS

When I arrived home in the summer of 1998, I had very little money. During ten years of sailing I had earned $650,000 and used up every bit of it. But I was in good health and had a boat that was paid for. But of course I still had living expenses. As soon as I got home, I registered for census purposes (domicile) in Sweden to become a part of the Swedish welfare state, mostly for protection in case of illness. During my years as a trader in Switzerland during the 1980s, I was domiciled there (rather than Sweden) for census. When I started my sailing, my Swiss registration expired when my work permit expired.

During the ten years at sea I was not domiciled anywhere, even if I was still a Swedish citizen. This gave me a problem every time I tried to renew my passport. Because of all the stamps and visas in my passport, I ran out of pages every couple of years. At all the Swedish consulates I visited they told me to go back 'home', to the country where I was domiciled in for census purposes. They could not handle the fact that I was not registered anywhere. After some failed attempts, I learned to tell the clerks, in as much detail as possible, about my circumnavigation. They eventually overlooked my lack of registration and I succeeded in getting new passports at various places around the world.

WORKING AND STUDYING AGAIN

TAXI DRIVER

After registering in Sweden, I decided to get a taxi licence. I had driven a taxi before and I saw it as the fastest way to support myself after coming home. There was a big demand for taxi drivers at the end of the 1990s, especially on nights at the weekend, and I got as much work as I wanted. But first I had to have a taxi licence, so I revised my knowledge and sat the exam. When I had passed all the appropriate tests I began work with Taxi Stockholm during the autumn. I mostly drove during the evenings, especially at weekends and over Christmas and New Year, which was better paid. A shift of 12 hours could put $200 directly in your hands, which is a lot of money if you do not have any to start with.

COMPUTER COURSE

While I was applying for the taxi licence, I registered myself at the employment office. I told them I wanted to study first then get a job. I had seen some computer courses that I wanted to take: WebMaster, Photoshop and PowerPoint. After a few weeks, I was accepted onto a ten-week full-time computer course. When I had finished the course I could produce my own home web page, edit my photos in Photoshop and work in PowerPoint. I used the course to prepare my own lecture notes. Nowadays I update my own home page on the web, and am also the webmaster for several other pages on the internet.

LECTURING

During the daytimes I wrote this book. It felt good to write and systematically go through my sailing log alongside all my photos and memories.

At the same time I started to give talks at boat clubs, and eventually for companies as a motivational speaker. The focus of the presentations was economics, marketing and daring to live your dream.

I have built up a number of PowerPoint presentations during the years: the Circumnavigation, the Canals of Europe, the Mediterranean and the Red and Black Seas. In addition, I have the lectures in different formats. For example, I have a 30-minute presentation prepared for the Rotary's breakfast meetings, a one hour presentation for some companies and a two-hour presentation for yacht clubs. I have ten different presentations on my laptop; all I have to do is press a key and I am ready to start.

CHARTERING IN THE STOCKHOLM ARCHIPELAGO AND THE BALTIC SEA

My plan was always to sail *Jennifer* during the summer months. Sailing was also going to partly earn me a living and also finance the boat. At the end of the 1990s computer and tele companies had plenty of money, and sailing charters with customers, contractors and staff were popular. The companies often ordered up to ten boats for charter with food, champagne, sleeping on board and entertainment all included. The price was relatively unimportant. These were happy days for everyone, including charter boat owners. It went on for two years; after that the market dipped, and I started thinking about longer trips on board *Jennifer*.

I had done one paying crew trip to the Baltic States in July 1999, when charter business with companies was slow. We sailed to Finland, and from there to several harbours in Estonia and Latvia, including Tallinn and Riga. In some of the smaller harbours, it was like returning to the 1950s. Some of the sailing, mostly in Estonia, took us through pretty narrow marked routes. This was partly because of shallow water outside the marked routes, and partly because of mines left over from the war.

THE PILOT BOOK FOR THE STOCKHOLM ARCHIPELAGO

During the summer of 1999 I had American charter guests on board, and realized that there were no good descriptions of the Stockholm archipelago in English, or even in Swedish. During my circumnavigation, I had been using many good pilot books, including ones for the South Pacific and the Caribbean, and had a vision of how a pilot book about the Stockholm archipelago could look. I talked to my publisher in Stockholm who, as it turned out, had a similar idea. After some discussion about how to go about it, we started the project that was to be called *Arholma-Landsort*.

The book was released at the Stockholm Boat Show in March 2001. The feedback and reviews were overwhelming. One Swedish paper wrote that it was the best book within its genre, and another wrote that it was going to be a new classic. After a few months all 7,000 copies were sold out, and we had to reprint the book twice. In the 2004 edition we added around 20 natural harbours and the island of Gotland. In 2007 we published the third edition, this time also in English. *Arholma-Landsort* is now the bible for the area and can be found on many boats in Stockholm's archipelago. With this book as the model, the publishing house produced pilots for the rest of the east coast and west coast.

THE CRUISING SEMINARS

During the autumn of 1998 an old friend of mine contacted me. He had been a charter captain in the Caribbean for several years and had during the 1990s arranged a number of cruising seminars during the Stockholm Boat Show, where he asked me to give a lecture about my circumnavigation. Of course I did and I was involved in boat show seminars for a number of years after that, including a symposium interviewing long-distance Swedish sailing veterans in 2001. In 2004, my friend sailed the world again, now as a charter skipper, and I continued with the symposia in 2004, 2005 and 2006. In 2002, the American, Tania Aebi took part as the first woman to sail solo around the world (and also the author of the book *Maiden Voyage*).

In 2004 the Englishman Tim Severin took part. Like Thor Heyerdahl, Tim has done several expeditions to prove that our ancestors could do long voyages. Tim told us about the Irish monk, St Brendan the Navigator, and his voyage across the Atlantic to North America during the 6th century, 200 years before the Vikings colonized Europe. He has written a number of books about voyages and expeditions, starting with *The Brendan Voyage* in 1982.

In 2006 I finally succeeded in getting the American Steven Callahan to come to Stockholm and talk to the symposium about his foundering in the Atlantic during the 1980s. A whale sank his boat, but he survived for 76 days, alone in his tiny liferaft that slowly moved with the current towards the Caribbean, where he was rescued. He wrote about this in his book *Adrift – Seventy-Six Days Lost at Sea*.

THE CANALS OF EUROPE AND THE MEDITERRANEAN

The charter market went down in Stockholm in 2000, but I had already started to think about sailing south to the Mediterranean. One weekend a friend, the chairman of the Swedish Ocean Sailing Club, sailed with *Jennifer*. He told me that he had helped a friend to sail through the canals in Europe. The idea was born. Instead of sailing the traditional way via the English Channel and Gibraltar, I was going to go through Europe's canals and rivers to the Mediterranean. But I did not want to go the straightforward route; I wanted to take the opportunity to see and explore as much as possible.

In the summer of 2001 we started from Stockholm, sailed to Poland and

then up the River Oder to Berlin, where, among other landmarks, we passed the Parliament building that Hitler had set on fire in 1933. Then we took the Mittelland Canal through Germany to the River Rhine, went up the Rhine with 4 knots counter-current to Koblenz, and further on into the beautiful River Mosel in France. Here we went through the picturesque Canal de l'Est to the rivers Saône and Rhône down to Port St Louise in the Mediterranean. I had had the mast transported by truck from Poland to Port St Louise to avoid storing it on the deck. In addition to not having the mast sticking out from both ends of the boat (and also making it difficult to get in and out of the locks), it was good to have the whole deck available during the canal trip. It took almost two months to go through the European canals and rivers from the Baltic to the Mediterranean.

When we reached the Mediterranean we sailed for two and a half months in the western part of the sea. The route was the French Riviera, Corsica and Sardinia, crossing the Tyrrhenian Sea to the beautiful small islands of Ponza and Ventotene and further on to Naples and Capri. From Capri we went to the Lipari (Aeolian) Islands, with the volcanic island of Stromboli and on to Palermo. From there we went to Tunis and Carthage, of the Punic war fame (a war between Rome and Carthage about 200 BC).

The last leg was the three-day sail to the island of Mallorca, the largest island in the Balearic group, and part of Spain. After cruising in the Balearics for a couple of weeks, I hauled *Jennifer* out of the water for the winter. This was in the middle of October 2001. I had had paying crew the whole summer, a total of approximately 60 people. Two of them, who hadn't known each other before, got married the next year. This was the fifth couple who had tied the knot after meeting on *Jennifer*.

THE MIDDLE EAST

The following summer, in 2002, we had a full program. Again I had paying crew; almost 60 people sailed on *Jennifer* in total. We started to sail from Mallorca back to Tunis and further on to Malta, Crete and to Rhodes, where we cleared out of Greece and then over to Marmaris, where we cleared into Turkey. We sailed along Turkey's south coast and out across the sea via Cyprus to Syria and Lebanon, which was our goal for the season. Those two countries were the highlight of the summer. In Syria we cleared in and stayed in the little seaport of Lattakia. We visited the old city of Palmyra, far into the desert, close to Iraq. We also visited the well-known crusader castle Krac des Chevaliers. In Lebanon we stayed at a first-class marina in Beirut's affluent suburb, Jonieh. From here we visited the ancient town of Baalbeck and the

Bekaa Valley, where we got to see Hezbollah's military camp. Syria, then in control of Lebanon, had always denied their presence. When we had lunch in the Bekaa Valley, I read in the *Herald Tribune* that a United States senator had wanted to bomb it.

After our visit to the Middle East we turned back and sailed west to Port St Louis in France via Cyprus, Turkey, Greece and Italy. Here we took down the mast, put it on a truck to Travemünde in Germany, and started on the canal trip back home to the Baltic Sea. I had chosen an unusual route; the Rhône-Rhine canal that links those two giant rivers together. We turned into the Rhine just north of Basel and went with the current the entire time. On our way to Duisburg we passed the notorious Lorelei cliff, its many rocks infamous for causing numerous shipwrecks. From here, the route continued on the northern German canals toward Lübeck and Travemünde, where we put the mast back in place. I took on a new crew in Travemünde and they got to experience a storm on the Swedish east coast. The wind strength was 43 knots. It was a stretch that we would not forget because it was really cold and tough. Finally we arrived in Stockholm, tired and exhausted, on 10 October 2002. The crew really bonded during this trip and we still keep in touch. The two years in the Mediterranean and the canals resulted in a new book.

CRUISING SWEDEN

The summers of 2003 and 2004 were spent on the coasts around Sweden – 2003 on the east coast, to prepare the new material on the island of Gotland for my pilot book, and 2004 on the west coast, to prepare a completely new pilot book, including researching the harbour information and selling space for advertising. When visiting the shipyards on the island of Orust for research, I renewed my contact with a friend whom I had met in the Caribbean during the 1990s. He was now the owner of a 64ft (19m) yacht, *Merengue*. She had just got a new teak deck, which inspired me. I decided that we should put a new teak deck on *Jennifer* as her old deck was now definitely worn out. This is how *Jennifer* came to stay on Orust on the Swedish west coast over the winter 2004–5 for a major renovation. Once I had access to good and relatively cheap boat carpenters, I took the chance to add other jobs that had been on the list. Besides the teak deck, I put in a new autopilot, a new electrical winch, new electrical system, rebuilt the forepeak, sanded all the floors, put in new cushions and much else besides. The final bill came to $75,000. I could afford all these improvements because I had decided to sail to Croatia via Amsterdam and Paris the following summer and was already fully booked nine months in advance. Many people wanted to sail in Croatia and on the French canals.

PARIS AND CROATIA

During the summer we crossed the Baltic and via the Kiel Canal entered the North Sea to Amsterdam, where we took down the mast and shipped it by truck to the Mediterranean. We continued on a canal route through Holland, Belgium and France, to Paris. It was a great moment when we glided in under the famous bridges in Paris and stayed at the centrally situated Arsenal Marina. From Paris, we continued along the small central canals and sailed over the Loire River on a huge aqueduct, visited the wine region of Sancerre and eventually arrived in Port St Louis, where we stepped the mast. The canal trip took five weeks, and we changed crews several times.

The cruise to Croatia followed almost the same route as in 2001: Corsica, Sardinia, the Lipari Islands, Sicily and then around the Italian boot to Croatia. Over the next two months we sailed around the archipelago of Croatia, from Venice in the north to Dubrovnik in the south. It was wonderful to sail into the Venice lagoon and stay at a marina across from the famous Doge's Palace and St Mark's Square.

Croatia is a fine place for sailing, with islands such as Hvar and Korcula and medieval cities such as Split to visit. The most popular area is the Kornati National Park, a small archipelago with many bays, natural harbours and good restaurants at reasonable prices. During the winter of 2005–6 *Jennifer* stayed in the new Kastela Marina, close to the city of Split. My pilot book on the Mediterranean sold out in 2005, and in 2007 the publisher released a new edition, including our sailing through Amsterdam/Paris/Port St Louis and Croatia in 2005.

THE BLACK SEA AND THE RED SEA

Over the summer of 2006, I sailed to warmer waters, this time into the Black Sea. We went from Croatia, to Albania, to Athens, through the archipelago of the Aegean Sea to the Dardanelles and ancient Troy, to Istanbul. This is a very exciting city, where we spent a week over midsummer and then continued on through the Bosporus into and around the Black Sea to Georgia, Ukraine, the Crimea peninsula and the cities of Jalta, Sebastopol and Odessa. We went to Romania near the Danube delta, Bulgaria and then back to Istanbul. From there we returned to the Aegean Sea along the Turkish coast with stops in ancient Pergamon and Ephesus with their famous and relatively well kept ruins, down to Marmaris where I kept *Jennifer* during the winter of 2006–7.

For the summer of 2007 we set sail to the Red Sea. The itinerary went via Cyprus and Israel, through the Suez Canal, down to the Sinai Peninsula and up the Akaba Bay. From there we sailed down the Red Sea all the way to Suakin in Sudan, about 30nm south of Port Sudan.

We spent the summer in the Red Sea and experienced some of the best diving in the world. From Sudan we returned via the Suez Canal to Alexandria and its huge new library and then across the Mediterranean to the Aegean Sea, continued through the Greek archipelago and lay *Jennifer* to rest in Athens for the winter of 2007–8. The highlights this summer were visits to Jerusalem, Masada in Palestine, the Pyramids, ancient Petra in Jordan, St Catherine's Monastery on the Sinai Peninsula and hiking up to Mount Sinai. The adventures in the Mediterranean, the Black Sea and the Red Sea became a book in 2008.

LIBYA AND NORTH AFRICA

We set sail for Libya and Tunisia in North Africa in the summer of 2008. We had arranged for our visas well in advance through a Libyan agent. However, on arrival we were refused entry and our passports were not translated. We had to sail to Malta and back (a total of 360nm) to have our passports translated. Once in Tripoli all went well and lots of documents were signed. We visited many places outside of Tripoli, including the old and beautiful Punic/Roman ruined cities of Leptis Magna and Sabratha, both on the UNESCO World Heritage List. We were one of the first sailing yachts to come to this area in many years (none of the agents could remember any yacht ever visiting Tripoli) and it was interesting and exiting albeit very expensive. For the rest of the summer we sailed to Malta, Greece, Albania, Montenegro, Croatia and then on to France via Sicily, Capri, Rome, Elba, Marseille and to Port St Louis, where I laid *Jennifer* to rest for the winter 2008–9.

SQUADRON SAILING

After returning to Sweden I worked as a squadron leader in different parts of the world for a Swedish charter operator, mostly during the winter months. These places included Croatia, the Caribbean, and Tonga and Tahiti in the South Pacific. In squadron sailing the charter company advertises a sailing flotilla and people with an interest in sailing in that region sign up for the flotilla. You don't have to know how to sail, and you don't even have to go with a big group; singles, couples or families work well too. Normally the squadron has three to six boats and a total of around 15–40 people. On each boat, one of the guests registers as a skipper and is responsible for 'his' or 'her' boat. The squadron leader, who has often been in the area before and knows it, leads the group and is the skipper on the main boat. There is usually a skipper's meeting every morning, where the route for the day and lunch breaks are decided. Not all of the boats have to follow this routine; the ones who want to sail on their own can do so, as long as they inform the squadron leader. Sailing in the Mediterranean is usually for a week, while further away locations such as the Caribbean, the South Pacific or the Indian Ocean normally last for 10–14 days, exclusive of travel there. The squadron job is a fun activity, especially during the winter. The guests have often dreamed of sailing in exotic and tropical waters and are always inspired and positive.

THE FUTURE – TO THE FAR EAST

In 2006 I turned 60. Nothing had really changed, at least not in my mind. But my body is no longer as flexible and it says no from time to time. When you are young, life seems everlasting, but when you are older you realize that it will end one day. During 2006 some of my friends died of cancer, an illness that until recently had only happened to my parents' generation.

I often get asked about doing another circumnavigation and I sometimes ask myself the same question. When I am giving a lecture, I sometimes wonder why I am standing there and not out cruising the world.

To make a long sailing trip covering a number of years to exciting and/or tropical waters is a big project. I would probably be able to fill the boat with paying crew and finance the sailing, but factors out of my control could easily make such a calculation unsure. A new epidemic, war in the Middle East, terrorism, world economic depression and other factors could make people cut down the time they spend on holiday. One of the down sides of having paying crew is that you have to stick to a set schedule. You cannot stay longer at a place just because you really like it.

Since coming home in 1998, I have succeeded in standing with one leg on land and one at sea. If I stay healthy, I count on being able to keep on living this way until I am at least 70 years old. I am happy and grateful that I can make a living by sailing and sailing-related activities and that my hobby is also my job. Of course is it rough sometimes. As in all small-scale businesses, there are problems of different kinds. For me it can be storms and running aground, serious and expensive problems with the boat as a result of these incidents, concerns about how many bookings there will be the next summer, worries of not being able to maintain the schedule or that the books would not sell. The paying crew have booked their tickets and count on *Jennifer* to be there on time, both at the start and the finish of the leg. The winters have to be filled with meaningful activities that will bring in money to pay the rent; there is no salary from an employer that comes in at the end of every month. During the winters I have so far been writing books, arranging sailing seminars and squadron sailing.

During the summer of 2009 I will sail through a historical Europe – on the River Danube to the Black Sea through Vienna, Bratislava, Budapest and Belgrade. The mast will have to be shipped by truck to Romania. From there I will sail via Istanbul into the Mediterranean again where *Jennifer* will rest in Marmaris during the winter 2009–10. Hopefully I will be able to write a book about the Danube River trip.

In 2010 however, I will again make a long cruise, probably lasting four to five years in length. From the Mediterranean we will sail via the Red Sea to India, Thailand, China, Japan, Alaska, Canada and California. From there we will sail further to Hawaii and Micronesia and to the South Seas. I have always wanted to sail to the Far East and Alaska, and this time I will do it. To revisit Micronesia, which was the highlight during my ten years circumnavigation, will be exiting. Paying crew is welcome to join us in the future! Keep an eye on: www.yacht-jennifer.nu

EXCERPTS FROM *JENNIFER'S* GUEST BOOK

RED SEA–SUEZ CANAL–ALEXANDRIA–TURKEY

Thank you Lars and *Jennifer* for a fantastic 31 days in the summer of 2007. The memories will remain with me forever – dolphins swimming in the Red Sea, the 'ghost' giant container ships waiting to be spotted on night watch when sailing to Suez. The heavy sea and boiling surf as we tried to find the entrance to the Nile and the port of Rosetta, the fleet of Egyptian fishing vessels trawling all around us on night watch. The passage from Egypt to Turkey – my longest passage at 340nm – a fantastic voyage around all those beautiful bays in Turkey. I was also extremely proud of my promotion to chief log watcher and septic tank instructor. Thanks again Lars. It has been great and so has the crew. I feel that I have made some new friends and hope we will all sail together again on *Jennifer* in the future.
Malcolm Sanford

THE DARDANELLES–ISTANBUL

We are moving through the pulsating, tanker-trafficked Dardanelles pushed forward by an open wind from the Black Sea to the western Mediterranean. Dark green olive trees, crops, fields and mysterious harbours straight out of the *Iliad* can be seen on both sides. In the opening of the Sea of Marmara, a group of dolphins meet us, staying under the boat and tumbling with each other. They are brownish pink with white bellies, with happy eyes and smiling mouths. They are talking and suddenly dive down into the cobalt depth, and soon after, to our surprise, come up again as projectiles to land on their bellies. Some are swimming in a galloping formation where the crocked fins look like a cogwheel that rolls through the waves. They are swimming as fast as an arrow without moving a fin. It is very relaxing and the teenagers onboard are enjoying the first lazy week of the summer break and are not moving a fin either!

Jennifer is not only a ship to live on but also a lifestyle and a mental state, where we recharge our batteries and are living for the moment. The summer of 2006 was our 'Turkish Delight'.
Thomas Munkhammar

ATHENS–ISTANBUL

Jennifer holds a special place in my heart. I will miss the grumble of the engine starting up for an early sail, the co-ordinated rhythm of the boat gently rocking back and forth, the crisp refreshing burst when we first swam the clear waters of the Aegean Sea. It will be odd not to wake up to the usual Swedish chitchat in the galley or the sound of Marie humming a soothing tune while preparing for 'coffee time'! The early morning sails were my favourite part of the day. It felt like it was *Jennifer* against the ocean while we were sitting on top of the wave and discovering it. It also left time for more sailing instructions in 'Swinglish', which provided for much entertainment at my end. Thank you so much for this experience – it was truly a blessing and so much more than I could have ever asked for. It was a pleasure to be in your company. I was always trying to soak up and ask as much as possible. I admire the way you live your life and that you have brought a dream to life.

Thank you.

Michelle Scott, Georgia, USA

THE CANALS OF EUROPE

I went with Lasse and *Jennifer* as a paying crew for a couple of months on the European canals through France and Germany in 2002. We passed familiar places by the canal route, which made it exciting and different. To join in Lasse's enthusiasm for visiting all tourist attractions along the way was extra rewarding. My concern about the huge barges in the streaming water, canals and big locks was eased by Lasse's calmness. I had dreamed about a trip on the canals in Europe for many years and so now my ambition had come true. After going on the canals we faced a very tough sail to Stockholm, in autumn storms, rain and temperatures of 7°C. The positive group dynamic and lasting friendships show the quality of *Jennifer* and her skipper. Another memory I have of sailing on *Jennifer* is the great summer we spent sailing from the island of Gotland. Thanks Lasse!

Björn Söderlind

THE WEST INDIES

We sailed on Jennifer in the early 1990s. We arrived at the Caribbean island of Martinique, where *Jennifer* was waiting for us. After that we sailed for ten days around the beautiful islands of St Lucia, St Vincent and further south towards Granada. We did wonderful diving, terrific sailing and ate fish and seafood we had caught ourselves. Our captain, Lars, guided us with great skill and patience through the crystal clear water. We learned about the history of the islands, met local people and provisioned with fruits that we had never

seen before. A warm and a fantastic friendship developed among the crew on board and today we still keep in touch with each other. During long winter evenings, we take out our photo albums and films and remember our trips on *Jennifer*. With such a fantastic 'generous' boat with a nice crew it is impossible to not succeed. Take the chance and go sailing!
Åke Fagelberg, Kalmar

CROSSING THE ATLANTIC AND NEW GUINEA

I have had the privilege to sail with Lars and *Jennifer* three times. I got in contact with Lars through a mutual friend and became one of the crewmembers on *Jennifer*'s maiden voyage in 1988, from the Isle of Wight to the Canary Islands and out to the West Indies. That voyage had everything, including a storm in Biscay, a constant headwind and heavy rain to Las Palmas. We also had 17 sunny days with following wind crossing the Atlantic and almost a month sailing in the Lesser Antilles of the Caribbean. We had many adventures and our memories are full of exciting experiences, especially during the final month when we 'helped' Lars to explore the islands, on land and in the water, where he was going to take his future charter guests. The most memorable experience was the visit to the island of Dominica and reaching the peak of Le Petit Piton on St Lucia.

I had a second chance to sail with *Jennifer* from Antigua to the Mediterranean in 1992. I took Lars's advice to arrive a week before he cast off to experience Antigua Sailing Week. It is a week that ends the charter season, with partying and feasts, in which most of the charter boats with crew participated. Someone said that there were races going on between the boats during these days but I never noticed that. After the last day the main part of the fleet sailed towards the Azores, where we stayed for a couple of days to socialize again. We also experienced a strong wind but the sailing was also made up of periods of calm when it was exciting to catch fish. We caught a lot mackerel and tuna – and had wonderful fish dishes for supper every night.

In 1995 a friend and I signed on *Jennifer* on Madang on Papau New Guinea. This was when Lars was sailing around the world. On the second day we left the boat and went on a five-day trip down the Sepik River in a hollow tree trunk, stayed with aboriginals in their villages along the river and got to see parts of the world that few have seen before. To me it is the most beautiful adventure I have experienced. The diving in the archipelago around New Guinea was amazing. Because few people/boats come to Papau New Guinea the reefs were quiet and untouched and we could see sharks, rays and turtles during every dive. I will always remember the time aboard *Jennifer* and am so grateful that I took the chance to go.

A big thanks to Lars!

Håkan Olsson

APPENDIX

JENNIFER'S DISTANCES OVER 10 YEARS

Year	Month	Destination	Nm	Nm/year	Total
1988	Sept	England	0		
	Dec	The West Indies	4,100	4,100	4,100
1989	Jan–Apr	The West Indies	1,000		
	May	Atlantic crossing	5,000		
	June–Sept	Sweden		1,000	
	Oct–Nov	Atlantic crossing	5,100		
	Dec	The West Indies	200	12,300	16,400
1990	Jan–Dec	The West Indies	1,500	1,500	17,900
1991	Jan–April	The West Indies	1,000		
	May	Atlantic crossing	5,000		
	June–Sept	Sweden	1,000		
	Oct–Nov	Atlantic crossing	5,100		
	Dec	The West Indies	200	12,300	30,200
1992	Jan–April	The West Indies	1,000		
	May	Atlantic crossing	3,800		
	June–Sept	The Mediterranean	5,000		
	Oct	Gibraltar	450		
		The Canaries	750		
	Nov	Atlantic crossing	2,700		
	Dec	The West Indies	100	13,800	44,000
1993	Jan	Venezuela	200		
	Feb	Panama	920		
		Coco Island	550		
		Galápagos	450		
	March	Pacific crossing	3,030		
	April	Marquesas Islands	100		
		Tuamuto Islands	500		
	May	Tahiti	200		
	June	Bora-Bora	100		

	July	Cook Islands	550		
		Nuie	585		
	Aug	Tonga	250		
	Sept	Tonga	200		
	Oct	Fiji	450		
		Fiji	200		
	Nov	New Caledonia	720		
	Dec	New Zealand	875	1,080	54,080
1994	Jan	New Zealand	400		
	April	Tasmanian Sea	1,300		
	May	Great Barrier Reef	600		
	June	Tonga crossing	2,700		
	July	Tonga	400		
	Aug	Fiji crossing	450		
	Sept	Fiji	200		
	Oct	Fiji	200		
	Nov	Tuvalu	200		
		Kiribati	700		
	Dec	Marshall Islands	360	7,885	61,865
1995	Jan	Bikini	420		
		Majuro	420		
		Kosrahe			
	Feb	Ponape	320		
		Turk Lagoon	380		
	March	Guam	700		
		Yap	450		
		Palau	250		
	April	New Guinea	1,000		
	May	New Guinea	1,200		
	June	Cairns	550		
	July	Darwin	1,200		
	Aug	Indonesia/Ambon	600		
		Indonesia/Bali	900		
	Sept	Singapore	750		
	Oct	Vietnam	600		
	Nov	Thailand	600		
		Singapore	720		
	Dec	Malaysia/Thailand	550	12,110	73,975

1996	Jan	Thailand	200		
	Feb	Andaman Islands	400		
	March	Sri Lanka	800		
		Maldives	420		
	April	Maldives	500		
	May	Chagos	600		
	June	Seychelles	1,200		
	July	Seychelles	1,400		
	Aug	Madagascar	700		
	Sept	Zanzibar	400		
	Oct	Kenya	250		
	Nov	Durban	1,700		
	Dec	Cape Town	850	9,420	83,395
1997	Jan	St Helena	1,680		
	Feb	Salvador	1,900		
	March	Brazil	1,470		
	April	Trinidad	1,450		
	May	Antigua	300		
	June	Puerto Rico	200		
	July	Cuba	1,000		
	Aug	Curacao	1,500		
	Sept	Trinidad	500		
	Oct	Trinidad	0		
	Nov	Antigua	300		
	Dec	Grenadines	300	10,600	93,995
1998	Jan-April	The West Indies	1,000		
	May	Atlantic crossing	4,500		
	June	Stockholm	505	6,005	**100,000**

COST OF YACHT AND EQUIPMENT

Jennifer's cost as new with extra equipment converted to US dollars. (Exchange rate $1 = 7 Swedish krona)

Cost of Beneteau 500 in September 1988, 15 x 4.75 x 1.8m: **$267,142**

EQUIPMENT

From the boatyard after the completion of *Jennifer* in September 1988.

		$US (to nearest dollar)
Deck	teak deck	9,000
	bathing ladder	428
Interior	fore peak	3,000
Freezer	compressor freezer	3,000
Battery	4th battery	285
	battery charger	1,143
Tanks	extra diesel tanks	1,143
	sewage tank	714
	foot pump/fan etc	857
Rig	1 spinnaker equipment	1,286
	extra spinnaker fall	714
	extra spinnaker boom	1,143
	extra up haul/down haul	857
	extra jib fall	714
		$24,284

EXTRA EQUIPMENT

In England, directly after delivery of *Jennifer* in October 1988.

		$US (to nearest dollar)
Sail	jib 44+7=51m^2	1,000
	storm jib, 16m^2	714
	main sail, 140m^2	1428
	spinnaker, 180m^2	714
Sailmaker	sun tent	1,000
	spray-hood	714

	sea beds	286
	cushions	429
	sail cover/boatswain's chair	429
	sofa cover	286
Security	8-man liferaft Avon	1,714
	fire extinguishers x 3	143
	emergency flares	143
	life buoys and bars x 2	143
	lifejackets x 10	429
	life harnesses x 10	429
	jack stays x 2	143
	EPIRB	143
Anchor	CQR anchor x 30kg	286
	chain x 60m	286
	anchor rope x 50m	143
Tools	Heyco tools	286
	drill and various	714
Navigation	charts	714
	pilot books	286
	sextant	286
	binoculars x 2	286
	lights	143
Diving	Bauer compressor 1001	2,857
	bottles 4 x 10 litres	571
	buoyancy control x 4	857
	backpacks x 4	286
	regulators x 4	571
	fins x 10	143
	snorkel/mask x 10	428
	diving computer	143
	various	428
Interior	extra stowage shelves	2,857
	table in the cockpit	714
	wood	571

	material, 45m saloon sofa	2,571
	sheets x 26	1,286
	towels x 78	857
	duvets, pillows x 10	714
	curtains	286
	coat hangers x 60	286
Instruments	SatNav	857
	Decca Navigator	571
	VHF 8100	714
	VHF portable	286
	Brooks and Gat Hydra 330	3,000
	antennae	286
	SSB-ICOM	2,143
	back stay isolation	429
	battery meter	286
	installations	429
Pantry	plates/pots	1,000
	cutlery	286
	barbecue/various	429
	propane tanks	286
Electrical works	belt driven generator, 6kW	1,143
	special frame	571
	installation	1,143
Entertain-ment	CD-player	714
	type recorder	143
	speakers	571
	installation	1,143
Heating	Taylor diesel	571
Brass	lanterns/clocks	571
	mirrors/signs	429
Water machine	HRO 60, 1 hour4,428	
	installation	571

Dinghy	Avon, 4m Mariner, 9.9hp	2,000 1,000
Various	fenders/radar reflector ropes/hoses/cords various	429 571 1,428
		$58,571

NEW EQUIPMENT

Wind generator	Windbugger frame	1,143 571
Solar panel	panels x 3, 55w frame	1,429 286
Heating	electrical heat radiators installation	286 429 285
Rig	mast step and installation	714
Electrical	converter/battery charger	3,571
Anchor	anchor, 24kg, 70m chain	714
Satellite communica-tion	Inmarsat C/GPS	7,428
Laptop & printer	Tandy and Kodak	2,429
Radar	Furuno, 16nm	1,429
GPS 2	Garmin and Magellan	1,000
Entertain-ment	TV/video/camcorder	1,714

Storm equipment	sea anchor/drogue	1,000
Propane	aluminium tanks x 2	714
Mobile phone	Audiovox	1,000
Autopilot	CPT band driven	2,000
Sail sewing machine	used	1,143
Sun protection cockpit	Bimini top	1,143
Rain cover cockpit	plastic	714
Deck cushions	large x 2	1,429
5th diving set	tank/reg/BCD	571
Rifle	shotgun 12 ga	286
Anchor gear	Tiger	2,286
Fishing	rollers x 2	429
New teak floor	(Trinidad)	1,429
Sail, new	mainsail (Australia) genoa (Fiji)	2,286 2,286
Dinghy	AB-dinghy	2,429

Galley	new stove new counter	714 714
Fans	fans x 8	857
		$46,859

Total capital invested in *Jennifer* 1988–98: **$396,856** excluding taxes.

USEFUL BOOKS

Various other editions of most of these books are also available and some of the older books are out of print. Check the internet for the best sources and prices for secondhand books (h = hardback, p = paperback, where known).

GENERAL CRUISING BOOKS

World Cruising Routes: Companion to World Cruising Handbook: Jimmy Cornell: Adlard Coles Nautical
World Cruising Handbook: Covering all the Maritime Nations of the World: Jimmy Cornell: Adlard Coles Nautical
Sailing Alone Around the World: Joshua Slocum: Adlard Coles Nautical (p)

EUROPE

Sailing Directions for West Europe: William Hurst and the Cruising Association
Greek Waters Pilot: Rod Heikell: Imray
Turkish Waters Pilot: Rod Heikell: Imray

THE ATLANTIC

The Atlantic Crossing Guide: RCC Pilotage Association: Adlard Coles Nautical
Atlantic Islands: RCC Pilotage Association: Imray
South Atlantic and South America: RCC Pilotage Association

CARIBBEAN

Cruising Guide to the Leeward Islands: Chris Doyle: Cruising Guide Publications
Sailor's Guide to the Windward Islands: Chris Doyle: Cruising Guide Publications
Cruising Guide to the Virgin Islands: Nancy and Simon Scott: Cruising Guide Publications
Trinidad and Tobago: Chris Doyle: Cruising Guide Publications
Venezuela and Bonaire: Chris Doyle: Cruising Guide Publications
Cuba: A Cruising Guide: Nigel Calder: Imray
The Path Between the Seas: The Creation of the Panama Canal: David McCullough: Simon & Schuster (h/p)
Grenada: The Untold Story: Gregory Sandford and Richard Vigilante: Macmillan Caribbean (h)
Caribbean: James A Michener: Random House (h/p)

Green Gold – Bananas and Dependency in the Eastern Caribbean: Robert Thomson: Latin American Bureau (h), Monthly Review Press (p)

THE PACIFIC OCEAN

Landfalls of Paradise: Cruising Guide to the Pacific Islands: Earl Hinz: University of Hawaii Press
The Pacific Crossing Guide: RCC Pilotage Association: Adlard Coles Nautical
South Pacific Anchorages: Warwick Clay: Imray
A Yachtsmans's Fiji: Michael Calder: Western Marine Enterprises
Cruising Guide to the Vava'u Island Group in the Kingdom of Tonga: RCC Pilotage Association: Imray
Australian Cruising Guide: Alan Lucas: Imray
Operation Crossroads: The Atomic Tests at Bikini Atoll: Jonathan M Weisgall: Naval Institute Press (h)
The Edge of Paradise: America in Micronesia: P F Kluge: University of Hawaii Press
The Kon-Tiki Man: Thor Heyerdahl: Christopher Ralling: BBC Books (h/p)
Fatu-Hiva: Back to Nature: Thor Heyerdahl: HarperCollins (h), Signet (p)
Poisoned Reign: French Nuclear Colonialism in the Pacific: Bengt & Marie Therèse Danielsson: Penguin Books Ltd (p)
American Caesar – Douglas MacArthur 1880–1964: William Manchester: Back Bay Books (p)
Pacific Rising: The Emergence of a New World Culture: Simon Winchester: Diane Pub Co. (hb), Pocket Books (p)
Tuiavii's Way: A South Sea Chief's Comments on Western Society: Erich Scheurmann: Legacy Editions (p)
We, The Navigators: Ancient Art of Landfinding in the Pacific: David Lewis: University of Hawaii Press (p)
The Last Navigator: Stephen D Thomas: Henry Holt & Co (h), TAB Books (p)
Hawaii: James A Michener: Buccaneer Books (hb), Random House US (p)
Rascals in Paradise: James A Michener: Secker & Warburg (h), Mandarin (p)
Return to Paradise: James A Michener: Random House (h), Corgi (p)
Tales of the South Pacific: Jack London: Amereon (h), Corgi (p)
In the South Seas: Robert Louis Stevenson: Penguin Classics (p)
The Bounty Trilogy: C B Nordhoff and J N Hall: Little, Brown & Co (h/p)
Typee: A Peep at Polynesian Life: Herman Melville: HarperCollins (h), Penguin Classics (p)
Micronesia Handbook (Moon Handbooks): David Stanley: Avalon Travel (p)
South Pacific (Moon Handbooks): David Stanley: Avalon Travel (p)

SOUTH EAST ASIA

Cruising Guide to Southeast Asia: Stephen Davies and Elaine Morgan: Imray

Ring of Fire – Exploring the Last Remote Places of the World: Lawrence Blair: Bantam Books (h/p)

A Bright Shining Lie – John Paul Vann and America in Vietnam: Neil Sheehan: Random House (h), Vintage (p)

The Best and the Brightest: David Halberstam: Random House (h), Fawcett Books (p)

Mountbatten: Philip Ziegler: HarperCollins (h), Fontana Press (p)

Indonesia Handbook (Moon Handbooks): Bill Dalton: Avalon Travel (p)

THE INDIAN OCEAN/AFRICA

Indian Ocean Cruising Guide: Rod Heikell: Imray

East Africa Pilot: Delwyn McPhun: Imray

Red Sea Pilot: Elaine Morgan and Stephen Davies: Imray

Cecil Rhodes – The Race for Africa: Antony Thomas: BBC Books (h/p)

The Covenant: James Michener: Secker & Warburg (h), Corgi (p)

SOUTH AMERICA

South American Handbook: J Brooks, J Candy and P Hughes: Trade & Travel Publications (h/p)